Crime Profiles

The Anatomy of Dangerous Persons, Places, and Situations

Terance D. Miethe

Richard C. McCorkle

University of Nevada, Las Vegas

Roxbury Publishing Company
Los Angeles, California

Library of Congress Cataloging-in-Publication Data

Miethe, Terance, D.
McCorkle, Richard C.
    Crime profiles: the anatomy of dangerous persons, places, and
      situations/Terance D. Miethe, Richard C. McCorkle
    p. cm.
    includes bibliographical references and index.
    ISBN 935732-94-2
    1.Crime. 2. Criminals
    I. McCorkle, Richard C., 1954- II. Title
    HV6251.M54 1998
    364—dc21   97-23654
                                                   CIP

CRIME PROFILES:
The Anatomy of Dangerous Persons, Places, and Situations

Publisher and Editor: Claude Teweles
Copy Editor: Sacha Howells
Production Editors: Dawn VanDercreek and C. Max-Ryan
Assistant Editors: Joyce Rappaport and Colleen O'Brien
Production Assistants: Renee Burkhammer and David Massengill
Typography: Synergistic Data Systems
Cover Design: Marnie Deacon Kenney

Printed on acid-free paper in the United States of America.

This paper meets the standards for recycling of the Environmental Protection Agency.

ISBN: 0-935732-94-2

Roxbury Publishing Company
P.O. Box 491044
Los Angeles, California 90049-9044
Tel: (213) 653-1068 • Fax: (213) 653-4140
Email: roxbury@crl.com

Preface

The purpose of this book is to examine the offender, victim, and situational elements surrounding seven major forms of crime. National crime and victimization data are used to develop profiles of each crime type. After describing the "syndromes" associated with each crime, current crime prevention strategies are evaluated in light of these profiles. Through the process of contrast and comparing crime types, we hope the reader gains some appreciation for the diversity of criminal behavior and the commonalities underlying it.

Several people have played a major role in the completion of this book. Kriss Drass and Randy Shelden have provided various types of encouragement throughout the life of the project. Connor Cherer contributed endless hours of data coding and library research. Robert F. Meier has been a major intellectual force in the conception of the book and in the development of many of the ideas expressed here. We would also like to thank the following people who read and commented on earlier drafts of the manuscript and proposal: Robert S. Agnew (Emory University), Thomas J. Bernard (Pennsylvania State University), Mitchell B. Chamlin (University of Cincinnati), Dean J. Champion (Minot State University), Paul Cromwell (Wichita State University), Scott H. Decker (University of Missouri-St. Louis), Chris W. Eskridge (University of Nebraska-Omaha), Charles B. Fields (California State University-San Bernardino), Richard C. Hollinger (University of Florida), Steve F. Messner (State University of New York-Albany), Jon'a F. Meyer (Rutgers University), Frank R. Scarpitti, (University of Delaware), L. Thomas Winfree, Jr. (New Mexico State University), Richard A. Wright (Arkansas State University). Finally, we would like to offer thanks to Claude Teweles at Roxbury Publishing Company for his support and encouragement.

—*Terance D. Miethe*
—*Richard C. McCorkle*

Table of Contents

List of Tables and Figures

Chapter One

Introduction to the Study of Crime Types

Simplicity is highly regarded in almost all areas of life. When giving directions to lost motorists or showing novices how to perform new tasks, the phrase "keep it short and simple" is good practical advice. Simple solutions are preferred to complicated ones in public debates about tax reform or possible remedies to social problems. Like ordinary citizens, social scientists often seek the most parsimonious descriptions and explanations of human behavior. The allure of rural living and the use of such language as "the bottom line," "no nonsense," and "quick fixes" give further indication of the cultural value we place on simplicity.

Our pursuit of parsimony in science and everyday life, however, is constantly confronted by a competing reality of complexity. The details we forget to provide may result in motorists losing their way. Concerned citizens and informed public officials know that quick and simple solutions are rarely possible. Social scientists also recognize the value of parsimony and the inevitable complexity of human behavior. Impelled by a public desire for simple descriptions and explanations on the one hand, and the academic pursuit of accuracy on the other, social scientists often straddle the proverbial fence between parsimony and complexity. However, this happy median is rarely achieved.

The friction between simplicity and complexity is clearly revealed in the study of crime. From the perspective of ordinary citizens, crime and crime events are remarkably simple to describe and

1

explain. The following television and newspaper headlines capture the essential feature of crime:

- Student Found Slain Near Home

- Ex-NBA Player Pleads Guilty to Kidnapping

- Gang Attack Kills Two

- Little League Coach Arrested for Child Porn

- Pastor Charged with Child Abuse

- Police Videotaped Beating Illegal Aliens

- Three Given Life Sentences for Hate Killings

- Wedding Ceremony Turns Into Murder Spree

Media headlines about crime, like citizen accounts, outline particular criminal behaviors, offenders' profiles, characteristics of the victims, and the events' situational contexts. Criminal behavior is described with action verbs (such as beaten, stabbed, attacked) or with reference to legal definitions of crimes (such as murder, kidnapping, child pornography). Offenders are described by their relationship to the victims, and we often spend much time and emotional energy trying to uncover the apparent motivation for their actions. These motives may be revenge, jealousy, money, frustration, or an assortment of other factors. Victims' descriptions include age (especially when they are children or elderly persons) and status (such as student, employee, or non-resident). Situational contexts are described by the physical locations of the crimes, the time of day, and the primary activity taking place when the offenses occurred. Knowledge of these "simple" elements satisfies our basic curiosity about crime. Equipped with this knowledge, citizens can reach some closure on their pursuit of answers to the *who-, what-, when-, where-,* and *why*-type questions surrounding crime.

Crime Typologies in Criminological Research

Criminologists employ a variety of classification schemes to capture the basic components of crime. Crime typologies serve multiple purposes, but they are designed primarily to simplify social reality by identifying homogenous groups of crime behaviors that are different from other clusters of crime behaviors (see Clinard, Quinney, and Wildeman 1994; Meier 1989). These classification systems increase our understanding of the shared features of criminal events and the effectiveness of current crime prevention strategies.

Crime typologies are sometimes simple and sometimes complex, focusing on either one or several of the following elements: (a) the criminal behavior, (b) offender attributes, (c) victim characteristics, and (d) the situational context. Previous efforts at developing crime types based on these elements are summarized below.

Legal-Based Typologies

The most widely used crime typologies derive from legal definitions of criminal behavior. Three types of legal-based typologies have been used to classify crimes.

The crudest legal classification distinguishes between misdemeanor and felony offenses. The major distinguishing feature in this scheme is the seriousness of the criminal act, with prison sentences of more than one year being reserved to felony offenses. Under this typology, felonies as diverse as murder (punishable by up to a life sentence or death) and auto theft (punished usually by probation or less than one year of imprisonment) are treated equally even though they vary dramatically in offenders' motivation, situational contexts, and reactions from criminal justice officials. The wide disparity in the classification of particular offenses (such as the possession of marijuana) as either misdemeanors or felonies in different jurisdictions also limits the utility of this typology.

An alternative legal classification groups together offenses according to the source of victimization. Three general classes of crime are derived from this typology:

- *Crimes against the person,* including murder, sexual assault, robbery, and battery.

- *Crimes against property,* including burglary, larceny, forgery, embezzlement, and auto theft.

- *Crimes against public order,* including disturbing the peace, trespassing, drunkenness, drug use, and prostitution.

When compared with the simple felony-misdemeanor distinction, it should be easy to see that this three-group legal classification more successfully emphasizes the similarities and minimizes the differences between offenses within each group. For example, crimes against the person are more similar to each other than they are to crimes in the other two categories.

The most widely accepted legal typology is the crime classification used in the Federal Bureau of Investigation's *Uniform Crime Reports* (UCR). Under this typology, a general distinction based primarily on the perceived severity of the offenses is made between Index Crimes (also called Part I Offenses) and Non-Index Crimes (Part II Offenses). Index Crimes, the major focus of criminological research, include the following legally defined offenses:

- *Murder and Non-Negligent Manslaughter.* Causing the death of another person without legal justification or excuse.

- *Forcible Rape.* Sexual intercourse or attempted sexual intercourse with a female against her will, by force or threat of force.

- *Robbery.* Unlawful taking or attempted taking of property that is in the immediate possession of another, by force or threat of force. Locations of robbery include (a) highway (streets, alleys, etc.), (b) commercial house, (c) gas or service station, (d) convenience store, (e) residence, (f) bank, and (g) miscellaneous.

- *Aggravated Assault.* Unlawful and intentional causing of serious bodily injury with or without a deadly weapon, or unlawful intentional attempting or threatening of serious injury or death with a deadly weapon.

- *Burglary.* Unlawful entry of any fixed structure, vehicle, or vessel used for regular residence, industry, or business, with or without force, with the intent to commit a felony or larceny. Distinctions are made between the type of structure (residential versus nonresidential) and time of day.

- *Larceny/Theft.* Unlawful taking, carrying, leading, or riding away by stealth of property, other than a motor vehicle, from the possession of another. It includes (a) pocket picking, (b) purse snatching, (c) shoplifting, (d) theft from motor vehicles, (e) theft of motor vehicle parts and accessories, (f) theft of bicycles, (g) theft from buildings, (h) theft from coin-operated devices or machines, and (i) all other larceny.

- *Motor Vehicle Theft*. Unlawful taking, or attempted taking, of a self-propelled road vehicle owned by another, with the intent to deprive the owner of it permanently or temporarily. It includes (a) automobiles, (b) trucks and buses, and (c) other vehicles.

- *Arson*. Willful or malicious burning or attempted burning of property with or without intent to defraud. It includes the burning of (a) one's own property, (b) the property of others, and (c) public property.

There are clear differences in the UCR classification within and between crime types based on the nature of the physical act and the resulting harm. Murders, for instance, differ from other crime types in that the legally prohibited acts result in the death of others, whereas differences within the general category of burglary depend on whether the crimes occur in the day or at night and involve residential or nonresidential locations.

While the Part I classification does not give adequate attention to the so-called victimless crimes (such as gambling, drug offenses, and prostitution) and the many forms of organizational and occupational crime (such as embezzlement, stock and securities fraud, and collusion), the UCR typology provides an important basis for the further development of a crime classification scheme. If the goal of a crime typology is to reduce complexity without distorting differences within and between categories, the UCR classification is a clear improvement over the other legal typologies.

Clinard, Quinney, and Wildeman (1994: 4-5) provide a comprehensive listing of the major problems with legal typologies based exclusively on the definition of criminal behavior. The problems with legal typologies include (a) their failure to include aspects of the offender, the circumstances associated with the offense, and the social context of the criminal act, (b) the final legal status of the original criminal act may bear little resemblance to the actual behavior due to plea bargaining, (c) specific legal definitions vary by time and place, thereby presenting problems for comparative analysis, (d) they create the false impression that criminals specialize and confine themselves to the type of crime for which they happen to be caught or convicted, and (e) they assume that offenders with certain legal labels (such as burglars, robbers, and rapists) are all of the same type or are products of a similar process. The uncritical acceptance of state definitions of crime, when many noncriminal acts may be more injurious to society, is another major criticism of legal typologies.

Offender-Based Typologies

Typologies based on the characteristics of offenders have a long history in criminology. The three most distinguished early Italian criminologists—Cesare Lombroso, Raffaele Garofalo, and Enrique Ferri—developed various typologies according to the personal characteristics of offenders.

As presented in his book *The Criminal Man*, Lombroso (1889) argued that some criminals were of a different physical type from noncriminals. "Born criminals" were genetic throwbacks to an earlier stage of human evolutionary development. This criminal type exhibits a number of physical stigma—like eye defects and abnormalities, facial asymmetry, large ears, large jaws, and long arms—that distinguish them from other criminals and noncriminals. Lombroso estimated that less than half of the offenders were born criminals.

Lombroso identified other criminal types, including "insane criminals" and "criminaloids." Insane criminals exhibit low intelligence and psychological defects and commit impulsive, obscene, and cruel acts. Criminaloids, the most frequent criminal type, exhibit normal physical and psychological makeup, and commit crimes precipitated by unusually stressful life events. Among this general category of offenders, Lombroso's "criminals by passion" possess noble traits like affection, integrity, and altruism. The crime of passionate criminals is often murder; these offenders kill those who dishonored their families or have been unfaithful to them. Another criminal type, "occasional criminals" or "pseudo-criminals," involves largely opportunistic persons with little previous involvement with or commitment to crime.

The offender-based typologies developed by Garofalo and Ferri complement Lombroso's scheme. Focusing on the physical attributes of offenders, their criminal histories, and criminal motivations, Ferri (1917) identified five types of criminals: (a) the insane, (b) the born, (c) the habitual, (d) the occasional, and (e) the passionate. Garofalo (1914) placed greater importance on psychological degeneracy than physical abnormalities in his four categories of criminal types: (a) typical criminals, or murderers who kill for enjoyment, (b) violent criminals, (c) criminals deficient in pity and probity, and (d) lascivious criminals.

Other researchers have developed typologies and classification systems that derive from offenders' personal attributes. For example, Sheldon (1949) classified individuals according to their body physique—endomorphic, mesomorphic, or ectomorphic. The major assumption underlying this approach is that there is a strong association between physique and temperament, with mesomorphic body builds linked with a higher likelihood of aggressive and criminal behavior. Alternatively, Katz (1988) used the interplay between criminal motivations and rationalizations in the development of the following typology: (a) novice shoplifters, (b) youthful "bad asses," (c) gangbanging "street elites," (d) "hardman" robbers, (e) "righteous" killers, and (f) cold-blooded murderers.

Offender classifications based on mental disorders and personality traits have been the mainstay of clinical psychologists and psychiatrists. From this perspective, criminal typologies have been associated with the identification of single personality traits and groups of traits. Clinical labels like "impulsive," "anti-social," "neurotic," and "psychotic" are often used to distinguish differences within and between types of offenders.

While offender-based typologies have a long history, they often suffer from serious problems of oversimplification and minimize the characteristics of victims and the situational elements of crime. The labels used to describe these offenders are typically vague and not easily applied to specific instances of crime.

Victim-Based Typologies

Another form of individualistic typologies places primary importance on the diversity of victim attributes as the major classification dimension. Previous classifications of victims derive from the following singular characteristics: level of shared responsibility, behavioral patterns, structural position, and the extensiveness of the victimization career.

The most widely used basis for classifying victims is in terms of their level of shared responsibility for the criminal act. Mendelsohn (1956) used the following categories to identify victim groupings: (a) completely innocent victims, (b) having minor guilt, (c) as guilty as offenders, (d) more guilty than offenders, (e) most guilty/fully responsible, and (f) simulating or imagining. The particular actions of victims during victim-offender encounters guide the level of shared responsibility. Sheley (1979) highlighted the relative activity of victims and offenders in his typology: (a) active offender—passive victim, (b) active offender—semi-active victim, (c) active offender— active victim, (d) semi-passive offender—active victim, (e) passive offender—active victim. Under this scheme, victims' responsibility increases as they become more active, and offenders less active, in the commission of criminal offenses.

Victim typologies based on behavioral patterns are similarly concerned with shared responsibility. In this case, however, the primary distinction rests on the extent of victim consent, facilitation, or precipitation. Facilitation is reserved for those situations in which victims unknowingly, carelessly, negligently, foolishly, and unwillingly make it easier for criminals to commit and consummate a crime (Karmen 1990). Leaving front doors wide open for someone to "break" into homes or leaving keys in cars' ignitions are examples of victim facilitation. Precipitation, in contrast, implies greater victim responsibility. When applied to homicide, victim precipitation means that victims were the first in homicide dramas to resort to physical force which led to their subsequent deaths (Wolfgang 1958).

Typologies derived from the structural position of the victim involve the relative vulnerability of some groups to victimization compared to others. According to Karmen (1990:102), these vulnerable victims include the following: (a) the less powerful (such as women in patriarchal society, unorganized consumers), (b) the weak (such as the elderly or handicapped), (c) the helpless and/or the defenseless (such as very young children and institutionalized populations), (d) the have-nots, (e) the different (such as racial, ethnic, and religious minorities), and (f) the deviant (such as homosexuals, transsexuals, and drug addicts).

The final way of developing victim typologies focuses on the extensiveness of individuals' history of criminal victimization. Under this approach, four categories have been identified: (a) one-timers, (b) occasional, victims of two or three isolated and unrelated victimizations over a lifetime, (c) recidivists, who exhibit a frequent and persistent pattern of victimization within a short period of time, and (d) chronic, whose lives are continuing series of victimizations (Fattah 1991).

Although victim typologies have been widely used to identify groups of persons with similar experiences, they are limited like most offender-based typologies by their oversimplification and the use of categories that are neither mutually exclusive (individuals cannot be classified in one and only one category) nor exhaustive (not all individuals fall under the classification scheme). Victim typologies also largely ignore the situational context in which crime occurs and the characteristics of the offender.

Situational Context-Based Typologies

Over the last two decades, social scientists have become increasingly aware of the situational context of crime. From this perspective, some physical settings and situations are more dangerous than others, and the primary task of criminologists is to identify the key features of these "hot spots" and dangerous places. The presence of a lethal weapon, the ease of access to the victim and escape routes, the presence of drugs and alcohol, the group context of offending, the temporal and physical setting, and the level of protection provided to the victim are some of the many situational dynamics that influence the likelihood of criminal events. The designation of facilitating places, facilitating hardware, and facilitating others as necessary conditions for some criminal events also emphasize the importance of the situational context of crime (Lofland 1969).

One of the most basic typologies of situational context focuses on the issue of crime domains. These domains include (a) work, (b) school, (c) home, and (d) at leisure. As a domain for criminal activity, crimes that occur at work may be quite different than offenses in other settings in terms of victim-offender dynamics, the availability of guardians for protection, the accessibility and visibility of the potential crime target, and the ability to resist detection. School crimes may be more likely than other domains to be motivated by identity threats and status-enhancement concerns. Similar differences are thought to exist across the other domains.

Multi-Trait Typologies

Although single-trait typologies based on either legal categories, offender characteristics, victim attributes, or situational contexts have been widely employed in the study of crime, these approaches collectively suffer from the major problem of oversimplification. To overcome this deficiency, several multi-trait behavioral typologies have been developed.

The most popular multi-trait crime typology is the behavior systems approach developed by Clinard and Quinney (1973). Five dimensions are used in the development and classification of criminal behavioral systems: (a) legal aspects of selected offenses (including definitions of criminal conduct), (b) criminal career of the offender (involving the progression in crime and one's criminal self-concept), (c) group support of criminal behavior, (d) correspondence between criminal and legitimate behavior, and (e) societal reaction and legal processing. When these dimensions are considered simultaneously, Clinard and Quinney (1973) identified the following nine behavior systems:

- Violent Personal Criminal Behavior (including homicide, assault, and rape).

- Occasional Property Criminal Behavior (including forgery, shoplifting, vandalism, and automobile theft).

- Public-Order Criminal Behavior (including prostitution, homosexuality, drunkenness, and drug use).

- Conventional Criminal Behavior (including larceny, burglary, and robbery).

- Political Criminal Behavior (including conspiracy and political demonstrations).

- Occupational Criminal Behavior (including such offenses as embezzlement, expense account misuse, bribery of public officials, and selling fraudulent securities).

- Corporate Criminal Behavior (including the restraint of trade, false advertising, manufacturing unsafe food and drugs, and environmental pollution).

- Organized Criminal Behavior (including drug trafficking, loan sharking, off-track betting, money laundering, and racketeering).

- Professional Criminal Behavior (including confidence games, pocket picking, forgery, and counterfeiting).

The major strength of this typology is its use of multiple traits or dimensions for identifying crime types and its intuitive appeal to most criminologists. Similar to other typologies, however, this approach can be criticized for its exclusion of other dimensions (like victim attributes or criminal motivations) and its failure to account for differences within each crime type. To illustrate these within-crime differences, violent personal offenders are assumed to have little development of a criminal career (because their acts are largely spontaneous and impulsive), but the professional hit man and the chronic neighborhood thug often have a firmly entrenched criminal self-concept and career pattern. Major exceptions can be found within each behavior system.

An alternative multi-trait typology is provided by Gibbons (1992). Under his "role-careers" approach, social psychological characteristics of offenders—like their self-image and role-related attitudes—change over their developmental careers and varying contact with law enforcement agencies and correctional institutions. Gibbons identified 20 offender types based on patterns of illegal role behavior exhibited by criminals, their self-image patterns, and role-related attitudes. Some of these types include "professional thieves," "naive check forgers," "psychopathic assaultists," and "violent sex offenders" (Gibbons 1992). Unfortunately, the primary weakness of this typology is that the categories tend to overlap, their specific characteristics are not clearly delineated, and the resulting typology reflects a loosely mixed, and somewhat contradictory, combination of legal, sociological, and psychological orientations.

Major Dimensions Underlying Crime Types

Much of the controversy surrounding the utility of crime typologies centers on the particular dimensions selected to distinguish between categories. The Clinard and Quinney (1973) typology is based on legal definitions, the offender's criminal career, group support for this behavior, its link to legitimate behavior, and society's reactions. Victim typologies are often based on the level of shared responsibility between the victim and offender. Among the multitude of potential dimensions for distinguishing crime types, we think the following attributes are especially important: (a) the offender's criminal career, (b) the offender's versatility, (c) the level of crime planning, (d) motivations for offending, and (e) target-selection factors.

The Offenders' Criminal Careers

As used by Clinard et al. (1994), offenders' criminal careers involve their social roles, self-conception as criminals, identification with crime, and progression in criminal activity. Of these elements, most attention has focused on the differences between novice (first-time) and chronic (also called repeat or habitual) offenders.

Offenders' criminal careers are a major distinguishing factor in the development of crime typologies because they are associated with characteristics of offenses and the effectiveness of particular crime control efforts. Specifically, when compared to chronic offenders, novice criminals tend to exhibit far less sophistication in their criminal acts and may be more readily deterred by crime-prevention efforts and the threat of legal sanctions. Accurate estimation of the relative prevalence of novice and chronic offenders for particular types of crimes becomes important for establishing priorities in crime control activities.

Offender Versatility

Offender versatility is based on characterizations of offenders as "specialists" or "generalists." Specialists are criminals who focus on the same type of crime (like pocket picking) or use the same general *modus operandi* (method of operation) to conduct similar types of offenses (like credit card and bogus check frauds). Generalists, in contrast, may have preferences for particular crime targets, but exhibit greater flexibility in their choice of offense.

Contrary to common media portrayals of criminals as skilled specialists, offense specialization seems to be the exception rather than the rule (see Chaiken and Chaiken 1982). Typical offenders are thought to operate within clusters of crimes like violent or property offenses, but exhibit little specialization. The importance of the relative frequency of specialists and generalists is that specialists may be more easily deterred from their chosen crimes by either threat of legal sanction or target-hardening activities (such as added security alarms to thwart home invasion). The versatility of generalists, in contrast, enables them to continue criminal activity by simply changing their offense behavior in response to specific crime-control efforts. An example of this process is the home burglar who switches to a convenience store robber when alarms and property identification programs make household goods more difficult to steal and sell, and later reverts to street mugging when greater security and surveillance equipment is added to convenience stores. Similar to the criminal careers of offenders, the effectiveness of crime-control practices depends on the relative prevalence of specialists and generalists among types of offenses.

The Level of Crime Planning

Another major dimension of crime typology involves differences between premeditated or planned actions and impulsive or spontaneous ones. Unless the offender is an extremely poor strategist, planned criminal activities are more likely to be successful than spontaneous acts committed with little forethought. Spontaneous acts done "in the heat of passion" are more difficult to deter through the threat of legal sanction because, by definition, spontaneous action means that offenders are not thinking about the consequences of their behavior. In contrast, premeditation and planning imply the ability to weigh alternative courses of action. If viable legitimate alternatives are provided to these potential offenders, the desire to commit specific forms of criminal activity may be abated. Again, the effectiveness of current crime control efforts depends on the relative frequency of planning and spontaneity in criminal events.

Offender Motivation

Uncovering offenders' motives is a major preoccupation of both criminal lawyers and citizens. When hearing about a criminal act and its participants, we immediately wonder why it happened. Motives for crimes are diverse and difficult to prove, but criminologists tend to differentiate between "instrumental" and "expressive" motives. Instrumental motives reflect some future goal or ends. Money, revenge, status enhancement, control, and domination are often considered instrumental goals of crime. Expressive motives are aligned with spontaneous and impulsive acts that are done in rage, anger, and with little thought of consequences.

From the perspective of crime control practices, this distinction by offender motivation is important. Expressive acts, for example, may not be easily deterred by formal sanctions, but social programs designed to enhance self-monitoring and anger control may yield some reductions in the prevalence and likelihood of particular types of crime. For instrumentally motivated crimes, the task is to identify the relative frequency of each type of motivation and to develop noncriminal alternatives to achieve the particular goal. Depending upon the specific instrumental motivation, these noncriminal alternatives may involve activities as diverse as job programs, educational enhancements, recreational programs, and sensitivity training.

Target-Selection Factors

A dominant image of criminals is that they make a series of rational decisions about crime commission and target selection by weighing the relative costs and benefits of alternative courses of action (Cornish and Clarke 1986). However, criminals differ not only according to whether they exhibit rational planning and calculation, but also in the importance they place on particular factors in selecting their targets. Interviews with offenders revealed three general types of target-selection factors: (a) convenience and familiarity, (b) the level of protection or guardianship, and (c) expected yield and target attractiveness (Miethe and Meier 1994). For any given crime and subsequent efforts to control it, the importance of each target-selection factor depends on the offenders' criminal careers, offense versatility, level of crime planning, and motivation for offending. For example, property alarms and guard dogs may deter novice offenders, but these protective actions may have no impact on the criminal choices of professional offenders.

The Current Approach

The inevitable conclusion from our review of single-trait and multi-trait approaches is that a definitive typology of crimes or criminals is not possible (see also Clinard et al. 1994; Meier 1984). Criminologists disagree on the major dimensions of crime, the purposes to be served by the classification system, and the comprehensiveness or inclusiveness of the scheme. The problem with developing a perfect typology is compounded by the fact that the very definitions of crime and criminals are volatile social constructs that vary according to the prevailing social, economic, and political conditions in a society. When the behavior under question has competing definitions and there is enormous variation within each category, the pursuit of the definitive and defensible typology may be an exercise in futility.

Rather than abandon entirely the typology approach, we acknowledge the importance of crime classification for simplifying social reality. However, the usefulness of any crime typology rests ultimately on whether there are uniform behavioral patterns within and between the major categories. The primary goal of this book is to investigate these similarities and differences in the offender, victim, and situational elements for major forms of crime.

Using various sources of data, this book examines seven general classes of crime: (a) homicide and aggravated assault, (b) sexual assault, (c) personal and institutional robbery, (d) residential and nonresidential burglary, (e) motor-vehicle theft, (f) occupational and organizational crime, and (g) public-order crime. Within each of these general crime types, we identify the most common "syndromes," defined as combinations of offenders, victims, and situational characteristics. These syndromes provide an indication of both the amount and nature of the diversity in behavioral patterns within each crime category. Although other crimes such as arson and larceny could be examined, the general crime types included here correspond to the legal and behavioral classifications most commonly presented in criminological textbooks.

Sources of Crime Data

Several data sources are used in this book to describe crime trends over time, offender characteristics, victim attributes, and the situational elements of crime events. These sources include national and local police data on reported crimes, national victimization surveys, and interviews with offenders.

Uniform Crime Reports and Local Police Data

The primary source of information on crime trends over time and the characteristics of offenders is the FBI's Uniform Crime Reports (UCR). Derived from monthly voluntary reports from local law enforcement agencies, annual UCR data provide the most comprehensive picture of crimes known to the police, covering more than 90 percent of the total national population (UCR 1995). These police reports include information on various aspects of crime, including (a) the number of particular offenses known to the police, (b) crime and arrest trends from the early 1930s to the present, (c) offense-specific arrest rates by age, gender, race, state and cities, region of the country, and size of the community, and (d) specific elements of the offense such as the type of weapon used, temporal patterns, the physical locations of crimes, and the amount of injury and loss to the victim. Supplemental data about the nature of all known homicide incidents (like the victim-offender relationship, motive, and victim characteristics) are also included in this data source.

Although UCR data have no rival in terms of their comprehensive coverage and longitudinal nature, these data nonetheless have several well-known limitations that may distort crime trends and characteristics of offenders (see Gove, Hughes, and Geerken 1985). First, the vast majority of crimes that occur in this country are not known to the police. Victimization surveys indicate that less than half of the violent personal crimes like rape, robbery, and assault are reported to the police, and only about one-third of property offenses like burglary and car theft are reported (Bastian 1995). Second, only about one-fifth of the known index crimes are cleared by an arrest (UCR 1995). If there is some bias in the characteristics of known crimes (such as crimes involving intimates being less frequently reported than those involving strangers), our conclusions about high-crime areas and high-risk situations based on UCR data would be inaccurate. Similarly, if crimes committed by particular social groups are more likely to be known to the police and result in an arrest, trends based on UCR data about the social profile of offenders would be distorted. Third, UCR data undercount the prevalence of crime because only the most serious offense in a behavioral incident is counted. The full adoption of an incident-based reporting system like NIBRS, however, will rectify this problem. While some researchers conclude that UCR data provide an accurate estimate of the extent of serious crime (Gove et al. 1985), the potential bias in reporting and arrest practices necessitates some caution when interpreting official crime data.

Crime data from the Las Vegas Metropolitan Police Department are used in this book to augment UCR trends and to examine in greater detail characteristics of victims and offenders in subcategories of crime. For example, these local police data will be used to confirm whether gender differences in national arrests for robbery hold across different types of robberies and to illustrate the types of weapon used in different robbery situations. Although data for any particular city may not accurately reflect national patterns, police reports in Las Vegas and other cities help fill voids in the available national crime data.

National Crime Victimization Surveys

The most comprehensive data source on crime victims is the annual series of the *National Crime Victimization Survey* (NCVS), sponsored by the Bureau of Justice Statistics and conducted by the U.S. Bureau of the Census. The annual NCVS series started in 1973 and involves a sample of about 60,000 American households. The survey asks an assortment of questions about personal and household victimization, including the type of crime, weapon use, injury and economic losses, the location of the crime, whether it was reported, and the perceived characteristics of the offender(s). Sociodemographic characteristics of the survey respondents (such as their age, race, gender, family structure, household size, home ownership, and the size of the city where they live) are also available to derive estimates of national victimization rates across individuals and households. Numerous secondary analyses of NCVS data (especially those published by staff of the Bureau of Justice Statistics) are used in this book to highlight trends in victimization and its social and physical characteristics.

Interviews with Offenders

One of the most important but often neglected sources of data about crime involve offenders' own accounts. Perpetrators of crimes are in the unique position of being able to describe, in their own words, the motivations and causes of crime, the level and nature of crime calculus, and the perceived effectiveness of crime control activities in deterring their criminal desires. Narrative accounts by offenders also provide rich details about the situational dynamics of crime and target-selection processes.

Criminals have a vested interest in distorting the reality of their offending (because they are admitting to crime commission), but most researchers have found them to be quite insightful about their criminal motivations, crime histories, and target-selection factors (see Bennett and Wright 1984; Feeney 1986; Gabor et al. 1987; Wright, Logie, and Decker 1995). Accordingly, interview data from convicted offenders are employed in this book to examine the topics of criminal motivation, the level of planning and spontaneity in crime, and the factors involved in their selection of particular crime targets. These topics cannot be addressed adequately without eliciting the opinions of crime offenders.

Outline of Remaining Chapters

The remaining chapters describe particular crime types and are organized in the same manner. After defining the crime type, we summarize (a) trends over time and the social correlates of the crime rate, (b) the offenders' sociodemographic profiles, (c) victims' characteristics, and (d) situational elements and circumstances (including the motivation for offending, the victim-offender relationship, temporal elements, the physical location of the crime, weapon use, co-offending patterns, alcohol and drug use, and target-selection factors). Information about offenders, victims, and situational characteristics are then used to develop the most common "syndromes" that underlie each crime type. Each chapter concludes with a discussion of the criminal justice response to this crime and possible interventions aimed at reducing particular criminal motivations and opportunities. The final chapter draws upon the previous chapters to describe the anatomy of dangerous persons, places, and situations.

Chapter Two

Homicide and Aggravated Assault

V iolence has been a common theme in the United States and other countries. Acts of civil unrest such as worker strikes, political protests, and civil rights demonstrations often erupt into violence, causing death and physical injury. Longstanding terrorist campaigns and isolated instances of terrorism against state and civilian targets are a daily occurrence on the international scene. The Oklahoma City bombing that killed 168 people and the letter bomb attacks by the Unabomber have made it clear that the U.S. is not immune to these violent acts. Although collective acts of violence and terrorist attacks are more visible and receive greater media attention, most violence in this country lacks an ideological motivation and involves a dispute between a single victim and offender.

This chapter reviews current knowledge about two of the most serious acts of interpersonal violence: homicide and aggravated assault. After defining these violent crimes, data is presented on (a) trends in homicide and aggravated assault over time, (b) the social correlates of these crime rates, (c) the offender profile in violent crime, (d) victim characteristics, and (e) situational elements and circumstances of the crime. Several homicide and assault syndromes are then described that combine offender, victim, and situational elements. The chapter concludes with a discussion of the criminal justice response to violent crime and current crime-prevention strategies.

Definitions of Crime Types

Homicide and aggravated assaults are similar in that they both involve the application of force and the physical injury of one by another. The similarity of these offenses is further revealed by empirical research that shows that many murders and assaults involve "similar participants, interacting in similar ways, for similar reasons, in similar settings" (Luckenbill 1984:25; Block 1977; Pittman and Hardy 1964). The primary difference lies in whether the criminal act results in death or injury. However, situational elements in many cases—poor aim, the type of weapon, the availability of immediate medical care—may be the only practical difference between homicides and aggravated assaults.

From a legal perspective, homicide is defined as the killing of one human being by another. There are two general types. Noncriminal homicides are killings under a lawful justification or excuse, such as self-defense slayings, accidental deaths, and the execution of a death sentence by authorized state agents. Criminal homicide is comprised of murder and manslaughter. Most jurisdictions recognize several degrees of both murder and manslaughter. First-degree murders are those acts committed with deliberation, premeditation, and malice aforethought, or murders that occur in conjunction with another felony. In second-degree murders, the act is deliberate but not premeditated and the intent is only to do physical injury to the victim (Samaha 1987). Killings "in the heat of passion" and under physical provocation by the victim are often classified as voluntary manslaughters. Negligent or involuntary manslaughters are unintentional killings while acting in a wanton, reckless, or careless manner or during the commission of another unlawful act other than a felony.

Assaults are often distinguished according to whether they are simple or aggravated attacks. Aggravated assaults involve deliberate and serious physical injuries to another or cases in which a weapon is used regardless of injury. Simple assaults, in contrast, typically involve minimal or minor physical injury and no weapon.

Trends over Time and Social Correlates

Rates of homicide and aggravated assault in the U.S. have vacillated over time. Starting in the 1930s (when systematic data was first collected by the FBI), homicide rates decreased prior to and during World War II, increased in the post-war period, steadily rose throughout the 1960s and 1970s, declined briefly in the early 1980s, generally increased until 1993, and have decreased over the last two years (see Figure 2.1). Assault rates followed a more dramatic and uniform increase from the mid 1950s to 1995. An estimated 21,597 homicides and 1,099,179 aggravated assaults were known to the police in 1995 (UCR 1995). These numbers represent a 5 percent increase in homicide and a 32 percent increase in aggravated assaults over the last 10 years.

Figure 2.1

Homicide and Aggravated Assault Rates in the U.S. over Time

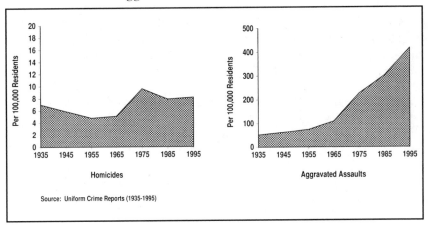

Source: Uniform Crime Reports (1935-1995)

Changes in homicide and assault rates over time have been attributed to several factors. First, the "legitimation of violence" hypothesis (Archer and Gartner 1984) argues that during wartime pro-violent values are reinforced and these values are carried over to post-war periods. Increases in homicide rates after World War II, the Korean War, and during and after the Vietnam War are consistent with the idea of a legitimation of violence. Second, both homicide and suicide rates have been associated with business cycles (Henry and Short 1954). Higher homicide rates occur in periods of growing economic prosperity characterized by relative deprivation for some groups. Third, rising homicide rates in the 1960s and 1970s have been linked to increased gang activity and drug trafficking in central cities. Patterns of violence in large cities strongly influence national trends. For example, about one-fourth of all murders and assaults in the U.S. in 1991 occurred in the large central cities—New York,

Los Angeles, Chicago, Detroit, Houston, Philadelphia, and Washington, D.C. (UCR 1991). Fourth, increases in homicide and assault rates since World War II have been attributed to changes in people's routine activities and lifestyles that make them more visible, accessible, and exposed to risky and dangerous situations (Cohen and Felson 1979). Fifth, the unprecedented increase in the number of persons in the 15-to-24 age group has contributed to the rise in rates of murder and assault in the 1960s and 1970s. This age group has the highest risks of offending for violent crimes.

It is important to note that UCR data on homicide and assault underestimate the actual prevalence of violence in the U.S. because many individual acts of violence go unreported to the authorities, and multiple occurrences of violence in a criminal episode are often only counted once in crime reports. Nonetheless, the following estimates from UCR data and victimization surveys provide a chilling picture of the magnitude of interpersonal violence in American society over the last two decades:

- More than 450,000 Americans have been victims of homicide in the last twenty years. Between 18,000 and 25,000 homicides occurred every year since 1972 (UCR 1995; UCR Supplemental Homicide Reports 1995).

- One out of every 154 Americans will be a victim of homicide. The lifetime risks of homicide victimization are 1 out of 503 for white women, 1 in 170 for white men, 1 in 125 for African American women, and 1 in 26 for African American men (Dobrin, Wiersema, Loftin, and McDowall 1996).

- More than one million assaults each year involving serious injury are known to the police for every year since 1990 (UCR 1995).

- About 5 percent of American households experience a violent crime each year (Rand 1993).

Social Correlates of Homicide and Assault Rates

Homicide and assault rates vary widely by geographical areas and degree of urbanization. In recent UCR data, homicide rates were highest in southern states with a rate of 9.8 murders per 100,000 inhabitants, followed closely by western states at 9.0 per 100,000

(UCR 1995). Murder rates were substantially lower in the Midwest (6.9) and the Northeast (6.2). Southern and western states also had the highest rates of aggravated assault, and the lowest rates were again in the Northeast. Both homicide and assault rates were about twice as high in large urban areas as in rural counties (UCR 1995).

There was enormous variation in homicide and assault rates across U.S. cities. Many large Southern cities like New Orleans, Atlanta, and Birmingham, Alabama far exceeded the national rate of 8.2 per 100,000 population (see Figure 2.2). Some Midwestern cities such as St. Louis, Detroit, and Chicago also had high homicide rates, but other cities in the region did not. Among select cities in Western states, Los Angeles had the highest rate and Seattle was below the national average. Cities with the highest rate of aggravated assault from 1992 to 1994 were (a) Little Rock, Arkansas, (b) Atlanta, (c) Tampa, (d) St. Louis, and (e) San Bernardino, California. Even the city with the twenty-fourth highest rate (Boston) had an assault rate more than twice the national average of 438 per 100,000.

Rates of homicides and aggravated assaults in the U.S. can be explained by the presence or absence of several other social corre-

Figure 2.2
Murders per 100,000 Residents in Selected Cities, 1995

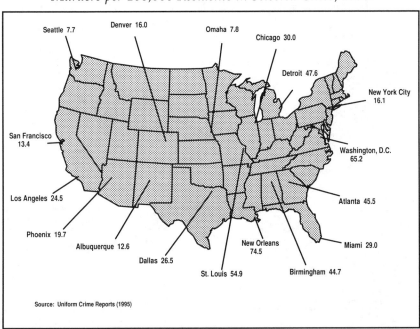

Source: Uniform Crime Reports (1995)

lates. Cities and neighborhoods with high unemployment, rapid population turnover, overcrowding and housing decay, high ethnic diversity, substandard schools, high rates of single parent households, and high income inequality have the highest rates of homicide and assault. High murder and assault rates in some cities, and in the "bad side of town" within them, are often attributed to elements of social disorganization including low economic opportunity, the diversity of language and values, and the low supervision of youth (Miethe, Hughes, and McDowall 1991; Sampson and Groves 1989).

Although media reports of political terrorism and deadly civil unrest give the impression that violence is more prevalent in foreign lands, the U.S. is by far the most violent industrial nation in terms of its homicide rate (see Figure 2.3). The U.S. homicide rate of 9.4 per 100,000 in 1990 was more than twice as high as India's rate, more than four times higher than Canada's and China's rate, and almost nineteen times higher than Japan's homicide rate. Explanations for the higher homicide rate in the U.S. include the wider availability of handguns, the greater social acceptance of violence as a method of conflict resolution, and the fact that violence is deeply woven into the fabric of American culture, including our street talk, prime-time

Figure 2.3
International Comparisons of Homicide Rates for Selected Countries
in 1990 (Per 100,000 Residents)

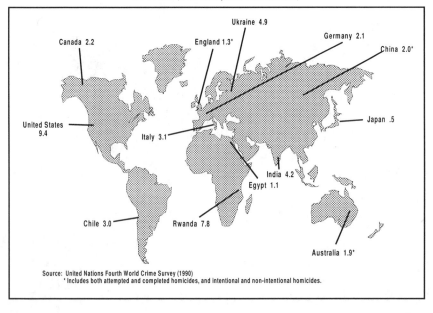

Source: United Nations Fourth World Crime Survey (1990)
* Includes both attempted and completed homicides, and intentional and non-intentional homicides.

television programming, "gangsta rap" and other music lyrics, and sports and leisure activities.

Offender Profile

When compared to their distribution in the U.S. population, murder and assault offenders are disproportionately male, young (under 25), African American, and urban residents (see Figure 2.4). According to UCR data, more than nine out of 10 homicide offenders are male, three-fourths are between the ages of 15 and 34, more than half are African American, and more than half of all murders occur in cities with more than 100,000 residents (UCR 1995). Police data rarely provide reliable information on offenders' employment history or social class, but the high concentration of violence in low-income areas within urban areas (see Miethe and Meier 1994; Reiss and Roth 1993) suggests that low socioeconomic status is another element in the typical offender profile. Combining these attributes reveals that poor, young, African American, urban males are the most prone to violent offending.

Figure 2.4
The Offender Profile in Homicide and Aggravated Assault

Homicide Offenders	Aggravated Assault Offenders
Male (90%)	Male (82%)
African American (58%)	African American (42%)
Young (15-34 yrs. old) (78%)	Young (15-34 yrs. old) (67%)
City Resident over 100,000 (57%)	City Resident over 100,000 (43%)
Poor, low-income	Poor, Low Income
Prior Arrest Record (68%)	Prior Arrest Record (66%)
Family History of Abuse or Neglect	Family History of Abuse and Neglect
No Offense Specialization or Escalation	No Offense Specialization or Escalation
Spontaneous, Heat of Passion Offender	Spontaneous, Heat of Passion Offender

Source: Castillo and Jenkins (1994); Messner and Tardiff (1985); Perkins and Klaus (1996); Supplemental Homicide Reports (1995); UCR (1995); Wolfgang (1958)

The demographic profile of violent offenders has changed over time in some cases but not in others. Racial and gender differences in homicide and assault offending, for example, have changed little over time. The proportion of homicide offenders under the age of 25, however, has shown a marked increase. This age group accounted for 30 percent of homicide offenders in 1970 and rose to 57 percent by 1995. Murderers under 18 years old increased from 6 percent in 1960 to about 15 percent in 1995 (UCR 1960, 1995). As described shortly, these young killers differ from other murderers in their personal characteristics, victim attributes, and situational elements of their crimes.

Court data on felony defendants provide some additional details about the typical violent offender. For example, more than half of the murder and assault suspects in the 75 largest U.S. counties have a prior felony arrest (Smith 1993). About two-thirds of these violent defendants have arrest records when misdemeanor arrests are included. Background checks during presentence investigations and clinic interviews of violent offenders often reveal a family history of abuse and neglect and the onset of antisocial behavioral patterns at an early age.

Offense Specialization and Escalation

Given that most homicide and assault offenders have prior arrest histories, one question involves whether these criminals specialize in violence and whether there is a pattern of escalation from nonviolent to violent crime. Large-scale cohort studies of the same offenders over time reveal two general trends. First, only about one out of every five persons ever arrested had an arrest for violent crime. Most arrestees for violence had long criminal careers dominated by arrests for nonviolent crime (Reiss and Roth 1993). Studies of recidivism provide limited support for specialization in that only about 7 percent of murderers released from prison are rearrested for murder within three years (BJS 1989). Second, the small number of chronic adult criminals who do specialize tend to commit either violent crime or property crime, rarely switching between the two (Blumstein et al. 1986, 1988; Farrington et al. 1988). Prediction of future violent behavior from arrest records, however, has proven to be highly inaccurate (Reiss and Roth 1993).

Planning and Spontaneity

Another aspect of the offender profile is the extent of planning and premeditation in the commission of murder and assaults. Within this context, a distinction is made between planned or premeditated acts (that is, those involving rational planning and the relative weighing of costs and benefits) and impulsive or spontaneous acts (that is, those in which the offender is guided by the "heat of passion").

Television crime dramas and the recent proliferation of stalking laws across the country give the impression that most murders and assaults are meticulously planned. They are not. Research findings indicate that most violent crimes are spontaneous, triggered by a trivial altercation or argument that quickly escalates in the heat of passion (Luckenbill 1977; Oliver 1994; Polk 1994; UCR 1995). More than half of murders in which the motive is specified involve actions that are largely spontaneous, such as mutual brawls and arguments (UCR 1995). Even for the one-third of murders that occur during the commission of other felonies (UCR 1995), it is likely that most murders happen in the heat of the moment and are not planned in advance. As situationally induced acts of violence, they exhibit little premeditation or planning.

Victim Profile

Social scientists have long recognized the similarity between the sociodemographic characteristics of violent offenders and their victims (see Miethe and Meier 1994; Singer 1981). Victims and offenders of both homicide and physical assault are generally similar in gender, race, and age, and live as neighbors, or at least in residential propinquity. Data from the UCR Supplemental Homicide Reports (1995) indicate that, like their offenders, homicide victims are disproportionately male, African American, and between 20 and 34 years old (see Figure 2.5). About nine out of every 10 homicides involving one victim and one offender are intraracial. Studies of homicides in particular cities reveal that typical victims have never been married and are employed (Messner and Tardiff 1985). The most dangerous occupations for homicide victimization at work are: (a) taxicab drivers and chauffeurs, (b) police and other law enforcement officials, (c) hotel clerks, (d) garage and service-station employees, and (e) stock handlers and baggers (Castillo and Jenkins 1994).

The typical victim profile of assault is similar to that of homicide. Persons with the greatest risks of assault victimization are male, young (16–24), African American, never married, make less than $7500 per year, and live in central cities (Perkins and Klaus 1996).

The contributory role of victims in violent situations has been studied under the topic of "victim-precipitated" crime. According to Wolfgang (1958), victim-precipitated homicides are cases in

Figure 2.5
The Victim Profile in Homicide and Aggravated Assault

Homicide Victims	Aggravated Assault Victims
Male (77%)	Male (15 per 1,000)
African American (49%)	African American (17 per 1,000)
Young (20-34 yrs. old) (47%)	Hispanic (16 per 1,000)
Same Race Victim and Offender (90%)	Young (12-24 yrs. old) (26 per 1,000)
Single and Never Married (50%)	Family Income <$7,500 (21 per 1,000)
Urban Resident	Urban Resident (15 per 1,000)
Employed (50%)	
High-Risk Occupations:	
1. Taxicab Drivers & Chauffeurs	
2. Police/Law Enforcement Officials	
3. Hotel Clerks	
4. Garage & Service Station Employees	
5. Stock Handlers & Baggers	

Source: Castillo and Jenkins (1994); Messner and Tardiff (1985); Perkins and Klaus (1996); Supplemental Homicide Reports (1995)

which the victims are the first to resort to physical force, which then leads to their subsequent slaying. Victim-precipitated assaults occur when victims initiate physical force or insinuating language against subsequent attackers (Curtis 1974). Up to one-half of all criminal homicides may be provoked by victims who initiate physical violence (Miethe 1985). A smaller but still substantial proportion of assaults are provoked by the victims. The prevalence of victim precipitation in murder and assault cases is clearly contrary to the popular image of victims as totally innocent bystanders to predatory attacks.

Various explanations have been offered to account for the sociodemographic profile of homicide and assault victims (see Fattah 1991; Karmen 1990). According to a "routine activity" and "lifestyle" approach (Cohen and Felson 1979; Hindelang, Gottfredson, and Garofalo 1978), persons with social attributes that indicate high contact with motivated offenders (such as living in high-crime neighborhoods), potential attractiveness as crime targets (such as accessibility and visibility), and low protection or guardianship have the greatest risks of victimization. Given that those who are male, young, single, unemployed, and live in urban areas engage in a variety of public and private activities that increase their proximity and exposure to dangerous people and places, it makes sense that differences in routine activities and lifestyles may account for their differential risk of victimization. Tests of the validity of this theoretical framework for explaining violent victimization, however, have been largely inconclusive (see Miethe and Meier 1994).

Situational Elements and Circumstances

Three necessary elements for homicide and assault are the presence of (a) an offender, (b) a victim, and (c) a situational context for the crime. The situational context defines the micro-environment for crime and includes the motivation for offending, the victim-offender relationship, the physical setting, and particular situational dynamics. Each of these elements is described below.

The Motivation and Circumstances for Murder and Assault

One of the most perplexing questions in understanding crime is that of motivation. Motive is at the heart of criminal trials, television crime dramas, and our personal infatuation with crime. Inquisitive minds want to know why—not only why friends or family members are picked as crime targets, but also why offenders commit their crimes. As in law, the search for the true motive for crime is elusive. Consider the diversity of possible motivations alleged for the following high-profile violent offenses over the last decade:

- Theodore John Kaczynski, the alleged Unabomber, has been tied to letter bombs that have killed 3 people and injured 23 others over the last two decades. His anti-technology ideology is a possible motive for his actions.

- Eric and Lyle Menendez were convicted of first degree murder for the brutal shotgun slaying of their parents in Beverly Hills. Their defense was based on the "abuse excuse." The apparent motives for the murders ranged from the brothers' fear of their father's continual abuse to their desire to collect $11 million in insurance.

- Susan Smith claimed that her two young boys were abducted by a stranger in a carjacking. After a massive search, she later confessed to killing her children by driving her car into a lake with the two boys in the back seat. She may have been motivated by her belief that her lover did not like children.

- Ruth Cole, the wife of the owner of a large newspaper in Washington state, was convicted of attempted murder when she tried to hire a hitman to kill the judge who convicted her son of being the Southside (Spokane) rapist and sentenced him to multiple life terms. One possible motive was retaliation.

- Four young black males approached a white male, Bernard Goetz, on a subway at night in New York City. Goetz pulled a gun from under his jacket, fired, and shot them. Convicted in criminal court for a firearm violation, he was also ordered to pay $43 million in damages in a civil case filed by one of his attackers. Self-protection, retaliatory street justice, and "hate crimes" were some of the motives suggested in the case.

- Lorena Bobbitt cut off her husband's penis with a kitchen knife while he was sleeping and later threw the severed member out her car window. She was found not guilty of malicious wounding by reason of insanity. Alleged motives include her husband's unsatisfactory sexual performance and her desire to pay him back for a history of spousal abuse.

- Timothy McVeigh and Terry Nichols are accused of the bombing of the Federal Building in Oklahoma City that resulted in 169 deaths (including one rescue worker). Speculation is that both defendants are part of an anti-government militia and that the bombing was a warning message. McVeigh was convicted of multiple murders in Federal Court and was sentenced to death in August 1997. Nichols was not yet gone to trial.

Although the accurate determination of motive in any crime is highly subjective, social scientists have used several approaches to categorize motives. One strategy is to distinguish between instrumental and expressive motivations. Under this framework, violent acts with instrumental motivations are directed at some valued goal beyond the act itself. The Menendez brothers may have killed their parents for the instrumental goal of protecting themselves or collecting the insurance payment. Ruth Cole attempted to hire a hitman for the instrumental goal of revenge. In contract, expressive actions are those motivated exclusively by rage, anger, frustration or, more generally, the heat of passion. Many violent acts are best considered spontaneous and unplanned outbursts of violence rather than goal-directed actions (Oliver 1994; Polk 1994). When the motivation for violence is to resolve conflict or to settle a festering argument, however, the classification of the offense as either an instrumental or expressive act becomes more difficult. Likewise, shootings by rival gang members may be driven by both instrumental and expressive motives—enhancing their own or their groups' standing, retaliating for stealing a girlfriend, defending turf, or just "kickin' around, raisin' hell."

The predominance of expressive motivations for homicides and assaults is supported by two general observations. First, convictions for voluntary manslaughter (an expressive act in the heat of passion) are far more common in criminal courts than convictions for first-degree murder (an act often judged to be instrumentally motivated). Second, although differences in convictions for murder and manslaughter may be due in large part to plea bargaining practices, independent examination of "murder rap sheets" and case narratives offers some support for the greater prevalence of expressive, nonutilitarian motivations for homicide (Luckenbill 1977; Polk 1994).

A variety of categories is used in the UCR Supplemental Homicide Reports (1995) to classify the motives or circumstances surrounding homicide. Among incidents in which a particular murder circumstance is specified, the most common motives, in decreasing order of prevalence, are arguments (49 percent), participation in other felony crimes, especially robbery and drug offenses (33 percent), youth gang activity (10 percent), brawls under the influence of drugs or alcohol (4 percent), romantic triangles (2 percent), and miscellaneous situations such as killings by babysitters, gangland slayings, and sniper attacks (2 percent). If arguments and brawls are considered spontaneous events, the majority of homicides are motivated by expressive rather than instrumental concerns. Studies of homicide in Chicago provide additional support for this conclusion. Among those killings with a clear motive, more than half of Chicago homicides are classified as expressive crimes (Block 1995).

It is widely assumed that the motives for aggravated assault are similar to those for homicide, but national data on assault are less widely available and analyzed. Evaluations of the proportion of assaults that are instrumentally motivated is somewhat problematic because assaults spurred by monetary gain are defined in police records as robberies. Nonetheless, several studies indicate that most assaults and murders result from emotional outbursts that are precipitated by trivial disputes and arguments (Curtis 1974; Luckenbill 1977; Wolfgang 1958). The variety of these disputes is clearly illustrated by the following brief police descriptions of homicides and aggravated assaults in Las Vegas:

- The victim and suspect were fighting over a drug debt and money when the suspect pulled a gun and fired four or five rounds. One round struck the victim in the chest.

- The suspect said that she had stabbed the victim during a fight over $20 he owed her.

- Two people were in a verbal argument concerning the whereabouts of a firearm. After telling the suspect he gave the gun to someone else, the suspect became irate and punched the victim. This person then ran upstairs, retrieved a firearm, and shot the other man several times.

- The victim was confronted by an ex-boyfriend at work. The suspect said, "I can't believe you've been talking about me to all your friends," as he began removing a five-inch hunting knife from its sheath. A struggle ensued with the victim suffering multiple stab wounds.

- The suspect tried to pass the victim's car and "flipped him off." Another suspect in the back seat then started shooting at the victim.

- A verbal altercation between the victim and suspect started during a pick-up basketball game. Suspect went to a gym bag and brought out two handguns. Suspect shot once in the direction of the victim but missed. Victim rushed the suspect and was then shot several times in the abdomen and upper chest. The victim was seriously injured.

- The victim was stabbed multiple times by a friend. The motive was apparently a $400 phone bill. The victim survived the attack.

- The victim was walking by a housing project when a large group of males started yelling profanities and asking him what he was doing there. The victim and suspect

exchanged words which eventually led to a fistfight between the victim and four suspects. One suspect pulled
out a handgun and shot the victim in the shoulder as he
ran from the area.

- The victim and several friends were at a party. Rival gang
members arrived and a fight broke out. Multiple shots
were fired. No one was seriously injured.

- The suspect and victim were attending a party. The suspect was belligerent and was asked to leave. The victim
approached and continued to argue with the suspect.
The suspect pulled out a semi-automatic handgun and
racked a round into the chamber. The victim said he "saw
the gun and I dared him to shoot." The suspect then fired
5–7 shots, hitting the victim and another person.

These descriptions emphasize the prevalence of disputes as the
underlying motivation for many homicides and assaults. They also
illustrate that violent crimes derive from expressive concerns "in
the heat of passion" and in situations of escalating conflict (see also
Luckenbill 1977; Oliver 1994; Polk 1994).

The Victim-Offender Relationship

One major distinction between types of homicide and aggravated assault involves the relationship between victims and offenders. Three types of relationships are often identified: (a) familial
(especially spouses and siblings), (b) acquaintances (including
friends, neighbors, and co-workers), and (c) strangers.

Based on the analysis of national homicide data (UCR 1995), the
vast majority of homicides known to the police involved acquaintances (57 percent), while fewer involve strangers (25 percent) and
relatives (18 percent). Most typical acquaintances are people who
are visually recognized by or had previous sporadic contact with
offenders. In decreasing order of frequency, friends, girlfriends, boy-
friends, neighbors, and co-workers make up the remaining "acquaintance" murders (UCR 1995). Spouse slayings are the most
prevalent family murders (8 percent of all homicides), with wives
nearly three times more likely to be victims than their husbands.
About 4 percent of homicides involve a parent killing their offspring,

2 percent involve children killing their parents, and 2 percent are murders between siblings.

Over the last two decades, several patterns have emerged in the nature of the victim-offender relationship. First, slayings among intimates (including relatives and romantic partners) have remained fairly stable over time, ranging from 28 percent of homicides in 1976 to 25 percent in 1995 (UCR 1976, 1995). Second, the number of lethal and nonlethal attacks by strangers has increased over time. This rise in stranger violence is especially troubling because it suggests a greater sense of randomness in the selection of crime targets and less individual control over the risk of victimization. The term "mushroom," derived from the Super Mario videogame, is sometimes used to describe innocent victims caught in gang crossfire (Sherman, Steele, Laufersweiler, Hoffer, and Julian 1989).

UCR data provide limited information on the victim-offender relationship in aggravated assaults. However, given the other similarities between homicide and assault, the vast majority of aggravated assaults should also involve acquaintances and family members. Using data from multiple U.S. cities, Mulvihill, Tumin, and Curtis (1969) found that about 40 percent of aggravated assaults involved acquaintances and nearly 20 percent involved family members. Somewhat lower rates of aggravated assault by acquaintances (33 percent) and relatives (7 percent) were found in national victimization data (Perkins and Klaus 1996), but these surveys tend to underestimate crimes among intimates. These findings provide some validation for the claim that assaults, like homicides, typically involve persons with prior relationships.

Situational Dynamics

Aside from motive and the victim-offender relationship, homicides and assaults involve other situational elements that define the nature of these crimes and their social, spatial, and temporal distribution. Major situational dynamics include temporal and spatial aspects, weapon use, co-offender patterns, and the use of alcohol and drugs.

Temporal and Spatial Patterns. Violent crimes do not occur in a vacuum. Rather, they vary dramatically across time and physical space. Dangerous times, places, and situations for homicide and assault are summarized in Figure 2.6.

Figure 2.6
Dangerous Times and Places for Homicide and Aggravated Assault

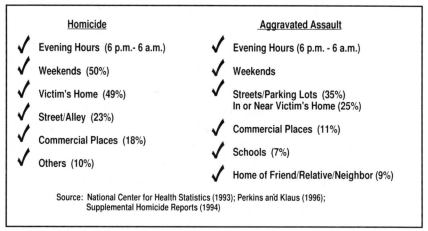

Source: National Center for Health Statistics (1993); Perkins and Klaus (1996); Supplemental Homicide Reports (1994)

Most homicides and assaults occur in the evening hours and disproportionately on weekends. Nearly two-thirds of aggravated assaults happen in the evening (Perkins and Klaus 1996), and about one-half of homicides take place on weekends (National Center for Health Statistics 1993). The dangerousness of weekend nights, especially Saturday nights, is due to several factors. First, there is more public activity over the weekend, increasing one's visibility to criminals and exposure to risky and dangerous situations. Second, our cultural heritage of unwinding on the weekend and the increased use of drugs and alcohol on weekend nights further increase the dangerousness of this time period.

The most dangerous physical locations for murder and assault are victims' homes and on the street. About one-third of aggravated assaults occur on the street or in parking lots, and one-quarter in or near the victims' homes (Perkins and Klaus 1996). Victims' homes are the most common place for assaults involving known parties, but about half of stranger assaults happen in open, public places like streets and parking lots (Miethe and Meier 1994). Nearly half of the homicides in Las Vegas take place within the home. Among Philadelphia murders within the home, Wolfgang (1958) found that men tended to kill their wives in the bedroom (where male masculinity may be most commonly challenged) and women killed their husbands in the kitchen (where knives and other cutting objects are more readily available). Given the large amount of time people spend in their homes, the high risk of violent crime in this location is understandable.

Over the last decade, violent crimes that occur in the workplace have received much national attention. Disgruntled employees who shoot multiple co-workers are often noted, but such attacks make up less than 10 percent of all work-related homicides (Dobrin, Wiersema, Loftin, and McDowall 1996). Instead, about three-fourths of the homicides at work occur during robberies and other miscellaneous crimes. Because they are common locations for robberies or involve greater contact with dangerous people, the following industries have the highest risks of work-related homicides per 100,000 workers: (a) taxicab services (26.9), (b) liquor stores (8.0), (c) gasoline stations (5.6), (d) detective and protective services (5.0), (e) justice, public order, and safety industries (3.4), (f) grocery stores (3.2), and (g) jewelry stores (3.2) (Castillo and Jenkins 1994). However, only a small proportion of all homicides and assaults take place in commercial establishments and other work settings.

Weapon Use in Murder and Assault. While gun control is a hotly debated and volatile public issue, police data clearly reveal that firearms are the most common weapons in homicides and a common weapon in aggravated assaults. A firearm (primarily a handgun) is used in about two-thirds of all homicides, followed, in decreasing order of prevalence, by knives or cutting instruments, personal weapons (such as hands, fists, and feet), blunt objects, and strangulation (UCR 1995). Contrary to media images, poison and explosives are rarely used as murder weapons. Homicides by firearms have generally increased over time, whereas those involving cutting instruments have decreased in frequency. Rather than indicating an increase in gun use in homicide, however, these changes over time may reflect the greater effectiveness of paramedic units and trauma teams in reducing the lethality of nongun injuries.

Weapon use in aggravated assault cases exhibits greater parity. The most common weapons involved in assaults are those such as clubs or other blunt objects, followed closely by personal weapons, firearms, and knives or cutting instruments. Aggravated assaults with firearms have increased over the last three decades, while assaults involving personal weapons have decreased (UCR 1970, 1995).

The type of weapon used in both homicide and assault cases, however, varies dramatically for different groups of people and violent situations. The UCR Supplemental Homicide Reports indicate that more men than women use firearms in homicides, more women use knives or sharp objects as deadly weapons. African Americans are more likely than other racial and ethnic groups to use firearms in homicides. Firearms are used in more than 90 percent of homicides involving youth gangs, but in only about two-thirds of all other murder situations (UCR Supplemental Homicide Reports 1988-1992). Similarly, a firearm is the weapon in about three-fourths of the murders committed by strangers compared to only about half of deadly attacks on family members.

Co-Offending Patterns. Although typical homicides and assaults involve single victims and single offenders, media attention tends to focus on violent acts with multiple offenders or multiple victims. Between 1988 and 1992, 63 percent of homicides involved one offender and victim, 29 percent involved multiple offenders and one victim, 5 percent were mass slayings by one offender, and only 3 percent involved multiple victims and multiple offenders.

The motivations and situational elements underlying homicides and assaults in a group context are quite different from those found in other offenses. Trivial altercations often motivate one-on-one attacks, but youth-gang attacks and hate crimes against particular groups of people are the primary circumstance surrounding violence committed against one victim by multiple offenders. When one offender commits multiple victimizations, the victims are usually family members or co-workers. Homicides and assaults involving multiple victims and multiple offenders typically occur in group melees and mass disturbances.

The presence of others may lead to either the escalation or cessation of violent situations. Given that many homicides and assaults are initiated by efforts to "save face" (Luckenbill 1977), the mere presence of others in potentially violent situations may have an audience effect that provides added pressure to resort to violence as a way of showing personal strength and enhancing status among peers. This type of group facilitation is most evident in violent offenses committed by juveniles. In contrast, others may intervene in conflict situations or be perceived as legal witnesses to the actions, thereby minimizing further violence. It is impossible to determine how many assaults or potential murders are diverted by the mere presence of or actions taken by bystanders. Nonetheless, it seems clear that the presence of others may either constrain or enhance the escalation of violent situations.

Alcohol and Drug Use. Social scientists have widely recognized the importance of drugs and alcohol as situational elements in many violent offenses (Luckenbill 1977; Parker and Rebhun 1995; Wolfgang 1958). The distribution, sale, and use of drugs has been implicated as a criminogenic factor in about 10 percent of all homicides and a substantial share of those in urban areas (Reiss and Roth 1993). Drug and alcohol use by offenders or victims is a common theme in violent crime, with about 60 percent of arrestees for violent offenses exhibiting positive drug tests (Reiss and Roth 1993). Between 20 and 40 percent of convicted murderers have been diagnosed as alcoholics (Greenberg 1981). Battles over the distribution of drugs in large metropolitan areas are a major contributory factor in increasing homicide rates in the last two decades.

Drugs and alcohol are associated with homicide and assault in three distinct ways. First, sellers of illicit drugs compete with other distributors, and violence may be an effective means of reducing this competition. Second, sellers may be violently attacked by buyers who are trying to steal their drug supplies or cash to support a habit. Third, drug and alcohol use in many cases occurs within a group context. When the presence of others similarly situated is coupled with the reduced inhibitions often associated with drug and alcohol use, a rather trivial comment or action may quickly escalate into a violent episode.

Target-Selection Strategies

From the perspective of the "reasoning criminal" (Cornish and Clarke 1986), offenders make a series of rational choices about crime commission and target-selection by weighing the relative costs and benefits of alternative courses of action. Once a decision is made to commit crime, three general characteristics are thought to underlie the selection of particular crime targets: (a) convenience and familiarity, (b) the level of protection or guardianship, and (c) the expected yield and target attractiveness.

Although most homicides and assaults involve disputes that occur in the heat of passion (suggesting that these crimes lack a rational calculus), target-selection factors are nonetheless important for explaining the nature and distribution of violent crimes. Convenience and familiarity, for example, may account for why family members and acquaintances are the most common targets for murder and assault. Nonstrangers are more convenient and familiar targets because most people spend more time with friends and family than strangers and we are more aware of the particular habits and routines of intimates, allowing for better timing of the crime event and greater anticipation of protective actions by the victim. Similarly, gender differences in the ability to protect oneself and physically resist an attack may explain why wives are far more likely than husbands to be victims of domestic violence. The expected yield and target attractiveness may account for the high concentration of felony homicides involving robbery and drug dealing, offenses that have the highest potential financial return. Under these conditions, target-selection factors are just as important in understanding homicide and aggravated assault as they are in accounting for more instrumentally motivated crimes like burglary, robbery, and motor vehicle theft.

Homicide and Aggravated Assault Syndromes

The simultaneous examination of offenders, victims, and situational elements of homicide and assault reveals several types of crime syndromes, which differentiate types of violent offenses (Block 1995). Five major syndromes are examined here: (a) interpersonal disputes, (b) instrumental felony offenses, (c) youth group offending, (d) chronic violent offending, and (e) politically motivated violence.

Interpersonal Disputes

A dominant characteristic of many homicides and assaults is that they involve an interpersonal dispute or conflict. Regardless of whether the victim and offender are family members, acquaintances, or strangers, the triggering event in most violent crimes is a disagreement, dispute, or conflict involving two parties that escalates in seriousness. Fights initiated by verbal conflict over money, infidelity, ownership of property, courage and masculinity, status or moral character, and entitlements are clear examples of interpersonal disputes. Within this context, several authors (Black 1984; Polk 1994) note that homicide is often a dispute or conflict resolution strategy.

There are several major features of interpersonal disputes. First, they often have a long history and may erupt into violence under the most innocuous situations. This longstanding conflict and its underlying basis may not be fully understood by individuals outside the dispute situation. Second, victims play active roles in the creation of interpersonal disputes, often initiating the confrontation by verbal challenges or physical contact with the subsequent offenders. Victim provocation by verbal threats or physical force is widely recognized as a causal factor in many homicides and assaults (Miethe 1985; Mulvihill et al. 1969; Wolfgang 1958). Attacks against family members and co-workers are often propelled by stressful dispute situations such as being fired from a job or being told that a spouse is unfaithful and wants to divorce.

The stages of development of interpersonal disputes are clearly illustrated in Luckenbill's (1977) study of homicide. According to the author, many homicides are interpersonal disputes involving "character contests" that follow particular stages of escalation. Five stages underlie the typical homicide transaction (Luckenbill 1977):

> 1. The victim makes a direct offensive verbal attack against the offender. About 40 percent of victims initiate the homicide drama with a verbal threat, and about one-third of the victims refuse to comply with a request from the offender.

> 2. The offender interprets the victim's words and deeds as offensive. About 60 percent of offenders learn the meaning of the victim's actions from inquiries made to the victim or bystanders.

> 3. The offender makes the opening move to "pay back" the victim in some manner for the previous insult or offense.

> 4. The eventual victim "stands up" to the offender's opening move, responding with increased hostility.

> 5. Commitment to battle ensues and the victim is left dead or dying. About 35 percent of offenders carry guns or knives and nearly 65 percent leave the crime scene to obtain weapons.

Although all types of people are susceptible to interpersonal disputes, confrontations involving victim provocation and "face saving" efforts are more common among some groups and situations than others. Wolfgang (1958), for example, found that victim-precipitated homicides were more common in mate slayings and killings involving female offenders and male victims, alcohol use, and victims with previous records.

A subculture of violence has been suggested by many researchers as an explanation for the social and spatial distribution of homicide and assault. From this perspective, within particular social groups—like young, urban, and minority males—there is a way of life, a value system, in which violence is an expected, tolerated, and even demanded way of resolving conflict (Wolfgang and Ferracuti 1967). Anger-provoking stimuli are differentially perceived within this subculture, with minor verbal comments and gestures being interpreted as "fighting" words. Learned in early childhood socialization practices and reinforced on the streets and in peer groups, violence in subcultural groups has become a way of life. Obviously, not all homicides and assaults in inner cities involve character attacks and interpersonal confrontations, but the frustration and anger that often typify urban poverty are conditions that enhance the frequency of these violent situations. Empirical support for the accuracy and validity of the subculture of violence thesis, however, has been limited (Erlanger 1974; Polk 1994).

Instrumental Felony Offenses

A large minority of homicides occur during the commission of another felony. These felonious killings account for about one-third of all homicides (UCR 1995). The particular circumstances surrounding these homicides vary widely. Felony-initiated homicides include, in decreasing order of frequency, robberies (54 percent), narcotic drug laws (32 percent), burglary (4 percent), arson (3 percent), rape (1 percent), and motor vehicle theft (1 percent). Robbery homicides have decreased in frequency over time, whereas fatal motor vehicle thefts (like carjackings) and drug-related homicides are relatively rare but have gained popularity over the last decade. Although the situations in which these offenses occur are quite different, they are similar in that the assault or murder is not the primary motivation for the crimes.

Assaults and homicides that occur in the context of other offenses are characterized by several diverse motivations. Regardless of the type of primary offense, the offender may kill the victim for instrumental reasons such as to eliminate an eyewitness or to facilitate escape. Physical assault may also be committed in these cases to further degrade and humiliate victims or intimidate them into silence. In contrast, physical injury and death may occur during the heat of passion or a fit of rage while committing the primary violation. Drug-related homicides and assaults may involve fights over turf, informing to police, or disputes over the quantity or price of an illegal substance.

Over the last decade, there has been an apparent rise in the prevalence of gratuitous violence. Surveillance cameras and videotapes often show crime suspects physically attacking and shooting victims for no obvious reasons. A suspect will sometimes come back to the crime scene and kill or inflict further injury even when the victim is already subdued and provides no threat to the offender. Terms such as predators and psychopaths are often used to describe these ruthless killers.

When compared to other types of murder circumstances, felony homicides are more likely to involve offenders who are African American, work with co-conspirators, and are strangers to their victims. Their willingness to use violence to complete other offenses also suggests that these offenders are more likely than other murderers to have extensive records of criminal involvement. Victims of these homicides are typically at the wrong place at the wrong time. A customer who is slain or seriously injured in a convenience-store robbery and a resident who comes home unexpectedly to interrupt a burglary are the clearest examples of these unlucky and unfortunate victims.

Youth Group Offending

A third syndrome involves situations of youth violence carried out within group contexts. Homicides and assaults in these situations include street-gang activity (like drive-by shootings and initiation rituals) and less structured gatherings of youth. Motivated by either instrumental or expressive concerns, the key aspect of these violent crimes is that they occur in the presence of multiple co-offenders who facilitate and may even encourage violent behavior. The group nature of adolescent offending is widely observed across a variety of settings.

As indicators of the seriousness of youth violence, a growing proportion of homicides now involve juvenile gang killings. Juvenile gang slayings comprised less than 1 percent of homicides in 1976 but increased to about 10 percent in 1995. The number of homicide offenders between the ages of 14 and 17 and the homicide rate for this age group have more than doubled in the last two decades (Fox 1996). These escalating trends in juvenile violent crime have become a major concern in law enforcement and public policy, sparking debates about issues such as decreasing the age requirement for certification of juveniles as adults and the imposition of the death penalty on juveniles.

Murders and assaults by youths that occur in a group context are different in several respects from violent acts by single offenders and other violence syndromes. First, youths often have greater bravado when accompanied by others, doing things they would not try alone. Second, the presence of friends and associates in dispute situations may serve to intensify and further escalate violent episodes because both offenders and victims may feel greater compulsion in a group setting to save face at almost any cost. Third, alcohol and drugs that reduce individual inhibitions are commonly consumed by juveniles in a group context. Under these conditions, it isn't surprising that much youth violence appears to be nonutilitarian, arbitrary, and not easily explained by the personal characteristics of individual offenders.

Especially when conducted in a group context, violence has become a status-granting activity for many contemporary youth. The "bad ass" is both feared and admired. Public displays of physical prowess and toughness are ways of maintaining and enhancing one's "rep." Unfortunately, one of the many seductions of gang-banging and group rumbles with rivals is that violent encounters often enhance the status and power of the victors in their peer group. Violent youth offenses committed against rival gangs in isolation or in a group context perpetuate the likelihood of further violence.

Chronic Violent Offenders

A fourth crime syndrome involves the chronic violent offender. These individuals often have a fairly distinct developmental history and are identified by a pattern of violent offending that takes place over an extended period of time. Although extremely rare in frequency, serial murderers—persons who kill three or more victims in separate instances over time—are the most widely known chronic offenders. More common offenders in this syndrome, however, are those with more extensive but less visible criminal histories.

Serial killings make up only about 1 or 2 percent of homicides in the U.S. each year (Reiss and Roth 1993); cohort studies reveal that a small group of offenders are responsible for a large proportion of violent crime. The Philadelphia birth cohort study (Wolfgang, Figlio, and Sellin 1972), for example, found that 18 percent of the delinquent boys accounted for 71 percent of the homicides and 69 percent of the aggravated assaults committed by the entire group. Most of the incarcerated murderers and assaulters in California have long histories of assaultive crimes (Peterson and Braiker 1980). Dispelling the myth that people specialize exclusively in violent crime, Reiss and Roth (1993) concluded that most violent crimes occur as part of a long, active criminal career dominated by property offenses. However, some of the most infamous serial murderers (like Jeffrey Dahmer, John Wayne Gacy, and Ted Bundy) have no prior history of property crime.

A dominant characteristic of chronic violent offenders is their tendency to react with violence in a variety of circumstances. Violence becomes for these offenders the solution to a wide array of problems, ranging from problems with family and girlfriends and job instability to poor school performance. According to Athens (1989), four stages characterize the development of the "dangerous violent offender":

> 1. *Brutalization:* These offenders are typically coerced by physical force to submit to authority as children and adolescents. They are accustomed to seeing the brutalization of others and they have been taught by others in their primary groups to resort to violence in order to accomplish their objectives.
>
> 2. *Belligerency:* As a consequence of the first stage, offenders have become deeply convinced that they must use violence in their future relations with others.
>
> 3. *Violent Performances:* These offenders set out performing a series of violent acts in which they intentionally and gravely injure other people.
>
> 4. *Violent Personality:* As a result of their violent performances, others come to define them as violent people instead of as just people who are capable of violence. Others in their peer group come to confer a sense of empowerment on them, and this in turn reinforces their use of violence.

From this developmental perspective, violence becomes modified and extended through the reactions it receives from others. Because violence may resolve conflicts (if only temporarily), empowers its user, and is a status-enhancing activity in some contexts, chronic violent offenders are resistant to change. These offenders tend to be young, less educated, poor males who lack the ability and effort to achieve in society's legitimate opportunity structure. Their impulsiveness and uncontrollable rage may also limit their effectiveness as criminals in illegal crime markets.

Serial murderers are somewhat similar to other chronic violent offenders in their developmental history, but they are fundamentally different in their motivations and in other specific ways. First, serial murderers often prey on strangers and drifters, teenage runaways, and others whose sudden disappearance is unlikely to provoke immediate suspicion (Hickey 1991). Second, serial murderers tend to kill people who fit a particular profile (such as females, people with a particular hair color, children), whereas other chronic violent offenders are less discriminatory in their selection of crime victims. Third, serial killers rarely use guns and seek to kill by stealth and deceit (Holmes and DeBurger 1988).

Holmes and DeBurger (1988:55-60) have identified four types of serial murders based on the motivations for offending. Their classification includes:

1. *Visionary Type*: kills in response to voices and visions that emanate from the forces of "good" or "evil." David Berkowitz ("Son of Sam") fits this profile.

2. *Mission-Oriented Type*: believes he or she must rid the community or society of certain groups of people—elderly persons, prostitutes, children, or particular ethnic or racial groups. The Green River slayer, who has killed more than a dozen prostitutes near Seattle, appears to be driven by such a particular mission.

3. *Hedonistic Type*: stereotyped as a "thrill seeker" and who derives some form of satisfaction from committing murder. Subcategories include those who kill for "pleasure of life" and "lust murderers" who become sexually involved with the victims and often perform postmortem mutilations. The Hillside Strangler (Kenneth Bianchi) and his accomplice (Angelo Buono) fall into this type of category.

4. *Power/Control-Oriented Type*: derives a fundamental source of pleasure by controlling and exerting power over a helpless victim. Some such offenders enjoy watching their victims cower, cringe, and beg for mercy.

Politically Motivated Violence

The final major violence syndrome involves acts with political motivations. The term "political" in this context means that the violence is used either to maintain prevailing conditions, to improve the position of one group at the expense of others, or to illustrate the inadequacies and lack of responsiveness of the prevailing regime.

Two general types of political violence are identified. First, political violence may involve individuals or groups who commit acts of terrorism and violence against the state and its agents. The Unabomber attacks on particular targets, the bombings of New York City's World Trade Center in 1993 and the Federal Building in Oklahoma City, hate crimes against particular groups, and assorted attacks by radical environmentalists (such as spiking trees to protect them from loggers) are examples of such political acts. A second type of political violence against civilian targets and rival groups may be conducted or supported by state agents. Police vigilante activities, death squads in South America, and civil strife in many foreign countries are examples of this type of political violence. Although the characteristics of the offenders are different, both types of political violence involve instrumental acts designed to maintain, enhance, or negate prevailing social conditions.

Bias-motivated hate crimes have received growing attention in the U.S. over the last two decades. Of the hate-motivated crimes known to the police (UCR 1992), the largest proportion involve acts of intimidation (37 percent), followed by the destruction of property and vandalism (23 percent), simple assaults (20 percent) and aggravated assault (16 percent). During the same time period, nearly three-fourths of hate crimes involved race and ethnic bigotry (primarily anti-African American) and a smaller proportion involved religious bias (primarily anti-Jewish) and sexual preference (primarily anti-homosexual). The growth of anti-government militia and hate groups is likely to increase the number of these crimes in the future.

Government data on terrorism in the U.S. reveals a total of 165 terrorist incidents between 1982 and 1992 (FBI 1993). Nearly 80 percent of the incidents involve bombing attacks, and the crime targets are most often commercial business establishments (36 percent), military personnel or establishments (20 percent), or state and federal government buildings or property (19 percent). International terrorism against U.S. citizens by noncitizens killed 12 and wounded 48 Americans in 1995 (U.S. Department of State 1995). Reliable estimates of police vigilante activities and state-sponsored violence in this country are not available.

Violence Prevention and Intervention Strategies

Efforts to reduce murder and assault have taken a variety of forms. Here we review crime prevention and intervention strategies as they relate to the major violence syndromes. These strategies include the criminal justice system response, social-welfare and personal-betterment programs, and opportunity-reduction approaches.

The Criminal Justice Response

The most widely adopted strategy to control violent crime involves direct intervention by the criminal justice system. By punishing and incarcerating offenders, four primary objectives are achieved. First, punishment is thought to be a *deterrent* for criminal activity for both the individual offender and society at large; violent crime is controlled by instilling the fear of punishment. Second, criminal inclinations are controlled by the criminal justice system through various types of treatment and *rehabilitation* programs for offenders. Third, criminal justice authorities can make repeat offending physically impossible by the *incapacitation* of offenders through incarceration. Fourth, the application of state-sponsored punishment serves as *retribution* when the gravity of punishment fits the seriousness of the crime. Whether or not the criminal justice system has achieved or can achieve any of these goals has been the subject of much debate among practitioners and criminologists (see Wright 1994).

For the threat of legal sanction to be a deterrent, punishment must be swift, certain, and severe, and the criminal act must be a planned, calculated, rational one. Deterrence is most likely to affect offenders who engage in instrumental rather than expressive crimes and who have low commitment to crime as a way of life (Chambliss 1967). But does punishment for cases of murder and assault meet each of the conditions necessary to be a successful deterrent?

Certainty of punishment is problematic in murder and assault cases. First, not all homicides and only about one-half of the aggravated assaults are known to the police (Perkins and Klaus 1996). Second, of those serious violent crimes known to the police, only about two-thirds of murders and one-half of aggravated assaults are cleared by the arrest of a suspect (UCR 1995). Third, only about two-thirds of those arrested for murder and less than one out of five of those arrested for aggravated assault are convicted of a felony (Langan and Dawson 1993). An even smaller proportion of those arrested for these crimes are both convicted of a felony and given a prison sentence. Although people may perceive the risk of punishment to be far higher than it is in reality (which is an important condition for deterrence), there is very little certainty of punishment for these violent crimes.

The severity of punishment varies dramatically for homicide and assault. More than 90 percent of convicted murderers receive a prison sentence compared to only 45 percent of those convicted of aggravated assault (Langan and Dawson 1993). Taking into account "good time" and other early release programs, it is estimated that the average murderer serves about nine years in prison, and the average person convicted of aggravated assault serves only about two years (Langan and Dawson 1993). Prison sentences for murderers are longer than they are for any other crime, but it is doubtful that the severity of this punishment is commensurate with public demands for retribution.

As primarily impulsive and spontaneous acts done in the heat of passion, the typical murder or assault does not fit the rational conception of crime that underlies the deterrence doctrine. In this case, the question becomes: how is the threat of legal action supposed to deter criminal intentions when by definition the typical homicide and assault offender is guided by emotionalism rather than rationalism?

Proponents of deterrence argue that most violent crimes are the result of spontaneous disputes because the threat of legal action, as intended, deters planned, calculated offenses. However, police descriptions of violent episodes clearly support the characterization of these offenses as impulsive and spontaneous acts that are situationally induced. The fact that many violent crimes occur when the perpetrator is under the influence of drugs or alcohol further questions the ability of the typical offender to consciously weigh the costs of a criminal act. Under these conditions, the nature of most murder and assault situations casts doubt on the deterrent value of criminal sanctions.

Legal sanctions have the most potential to deter instrumental felony offenses, youth group offending, chronic violent offenders, and politically motivated violence. Unfortunately, there are several cross currents in these violence syndromes that also question the effectiveness of deterrence. For example, both chronic violent offenders and those who commit murder and assault in the context of another felony offense would seem prime candidates for deterrence (because their acts are assumed to be planned and calculated), but these offenders may have such high commitment to crime as a way of life that getting caught and punished is just part of an acceptable risk of "doing business" (Chambliss 1967). Likewise, politically motivated offenders may be so committed to their mission that the threat of punishment by the state is of only secondary importance. The volatility of much juvenile group activity and the ease in which conventional behavior erupts into spontaneous frenzies of violence with little thought for consequences also questions the effectiveness of deterrence for these violent offenses. Ironically, being caught and punished may have little deterrent value for youthful offenders because "doing time" may actually amplify one's status or "rep" in the peer group, and incarceration may simply provide an opportunity to mingle with "homies" who have previously been busted.

Incarceration and the death penalty may serve the goals of retribution, incapacitation, and specific deterrence, but there is no substantial and unequivocal evidence that legal sanctions provide a general deterrent to potential murders and assaults. Although shock incarceration programs such as regimented boot camps have some intuitive appeal, these "rehabilitation" programs are not usually available for violent offenders, and evaluations of these programs in terms of reducing rates of repeat offending have not been encouraging (MacKenzie, Brame, McDowall, and Souryal 1995). Recidivism rates for murderers are often lower than for most offenders, but this probably has little to do with the ability of prisons to rehabilitate offenders. Rather, the lower recidivism rate is attributable to "maturational reform" (that is, murderers incarcerated for long periods of time simply grow out of their criminal inclinations) and the fact that their original criminal act involved a grievance with a particular person; killing that person ultimately eliminated the grievance.

Social Welfare and Personal Betterment Programs

A long-term, but potentially more effective, solution to murder and assault involves an assortment of social welfare and personal betterment programs that are directed at early intervention and changing pro-violent values in American society. These programs are diverse in their goals and scope, but all of them address one or more of the individual, situational, and cultural causes of violent behavior.

Social scientists have identified various risk factors that are associated with aggressive childhood behavior. Although our ability to predict future criminal behavior is woefully inadequate, the search for early risk factors becomes important because there is substantial stability in individuals' aggressive potential over the life cycle (Tracy and Kempf-Leonard 1996). According to Reiss and Roth (1993:105), some of the psycho-social risk factors at key stages in the developmental process include:

- in the preschool years: fearless behavior, hyperactivity-impulsivity-attention deficit, restless behavior, and poor concentration.

- in the early school years: daring and risk-taking behavior, poor ability to defer gratification, low IQ, low empathy, and abnormally frequent viewing of violence on television.

- early family experiences: harsh and erratic discipline, lack of parental nurturance, physical abuse and neglect, poor supervision, and early separation of children from parents.

- early school experiences: school failure and interactions involving bullying and peer rejection.

- factors associated with large low-income families, poor housing, criminal behavior by parents and siblings, and living in high-crime neighborhoods.

A number of programs and intervention strategies have been designed to alter these risk factors in violent offending. Drug interventions like the use of Ritalin for Attention Deficiency Disorder and Hyperactivity (ADDH) have been one option. School-based programs include the use of high-school students as tutors and mentors for younger students, "classroom on wheels" (a mobile school bus that provides preschool education to children in low-income areas), school retention programs for at-risk youth, and peer mediation and conflict resolution programs. These programs emphasize the undesirability of violent behavior, the learning and use of non-violent alternatives, and the development of academic and social skills to handle frustration, reduce peer rejection, and minimize poor school performance. Community-based programs like Head Start and organizations like the YMCA also provide early childhood intervention and educational courses on parenting, parent-child communication, and the development of basic social skills. These personal betterment approaches tend to be more successful when they are done early (in the preschool years) and involve combinations of parents, peers, teachers, and significant others in the community (Reiss and Roth 1993).

Other types of community-based programs include neighborhood beautification projects, youth recreational programs, and the development of parenting networks to supervise the activities of youth. These programs attempt to instill a greater sense of community pride and develop surrogate family structures that further embed individuals in mainstream culture. Job training and economic development in socially disorganized communities are some of the most basic ways to overcome years of frustration and despair for residents in low-income neighborhoods. New federal programs like "Weed and Seed" are designed to increase neighborhood restoration and revitalization by using law enforcement agencies to "weed" major drug dealers and the most violent offenders from the local community and then "seed" these neighborhoods with basic social services that improve the quality of life. Unfortunately, it is unclear whether these neighborhood restoration projects yield significant reductions in violent crime or simply displace violent crime to other neighborhoods.

Opportunity-Reduction Strategies

A final general strategy to control murder and assault involves efforts to reduce the opportunity for their occurrence. Often called "crime control through environmental design" or "situational crime prevention" (Clarke 1980), this approach emphasizes changing the physical structure of environments and individuals' routine activities and lifestyles. Collectively, these opportunity-reduction strategies attempt to make communities and their residents less exposed to risky and dangerous situations, less visible and accessible to potential offenders, and more protected against attacks. Gun ownership, physical security systems like locks and alarms, self-defense training, and temporary shelters for crime victims are examples of opportunity-reduction strategies for combating violent crime.

One of the most controversial issues in the field of crime prevention involves gun control. Opponents of restricting the availability of guns claim that gun ownership is a constitutionally protected right of Americans, whereas proponents of gun control point to the large number of homicides committed using handguns. Some social scientists argue that armed citizens deter potential offenders, and others find little evidence of guns deterring crime (Kleck 1991; McDowall, Lizotte, and Wiersema 1991). It is also debatable whether the elimination of guns in the U.S.—even if this were possible— would lead to a major reduction in murder and aggravated assaults or whether persons would simply substitute other weapons in crime situations.

Although the debate about gun control policy is virtually unresolvable, two observations suggest that restricting gun ownership may decrease rates of death and physical injury. First, between 3,000 and 6,000 people are killed and another 180,000 people are seriously injured each year by the accidental discharge of firearms (Wright, Rossi, and Daly 1983). Restricting gun ownership would decrease the number of these accidents. Second, firearms are more lethal and can kill from a farther distance than most other weapons. It is far more difficult to kill someone with hands, feet, or a blunt object, and these methods require direct contact with the victim. Because firearms empower individuals who may not have the physical strength or fortitude to directly confront others and because firearms pose a greater threat of death to victims and bystanders, the wide availability of firearms may increase the risks of serious violent victimization.

Increased physical security and self-defense training are other "target-hardening" strategies aimed at reducing the opportunity for violence. Convenience stores and banking institutions may decrease the likelihood of robbery homicides by hiring additional security officers or by installing more surveillance equipment. Likewise, basic self-defense training may enable a potential victim to overcome a perpetrator and thwart a serious assault. Self-protective actions in violent encounters typically lead to mixed results. Victimization data suggest that self-defense actions increase the likelihood that an assault will be only an attempted and not a completed attack, but unsuccessful attempts at self-defense often result in more serious injury to the victim. However, definitive conclusions about the effectiveness of these crime-reduction strategies are not possible because of methodological problems in trying to determine the precise point in the violent episode when the victim took protective measures.

Finally, individuals have some control over the risks of murder and assault by changing their routine activities and lifestyles. Going to bars or subway stations late at night and alone are risky activities in most cities. Excessive drinking and associating with delinquent peers is equally hazardous. Driving or walking the streets in a "bad" part of town at night is also unwise. Leaving a physically abusive relationship in favor of a domestic abuse shelter may provide temporary relief from the possibility of becoming a murder victim. Although it is impossible to design totally safe environments and eliminate entirely one's chances of victimization, small precautionary measures and minor changes in daily activities may dramatically reduce the risks of interpersonal violence.

Summary

The violent crimes of murder and aggravated assault are similar in terms of their spatial and temporal distribution, the social profile of offenders, victim characteristics, and situational aspects of the crime. Five violence syndromes are identified that have relatively unique aspects: (1) interpersonal disputes, (2) instrumental felony offenses, (3) youth group offending, (4) chronic violent offenders, and (5) politically motivated violence. The differences in these crime types lie in the motivations for offending, the situational elements of the crime event, and the background of the offender. Of the three general types of crime control strategies reviewed, social welfare and personal betterment strategies appear to be the most effective long-term solutions to violent crime, followed by opportunity-reduction approaches. The criminal justice response to murder and assault may serve the public demand for retribution, but the nature of these crimes makes legal sanctions largely ineffective in achieving the goals of deterrence and rehabilitation.

Chapter Three

Sexual Assault

F ew crimes elicit as much fear and disgust as sexual assault. Child molesters, rapists, and exhibitionists are widely viewed as sexual predators who pose a serious threat to society. Public surveys indicate that fear of rape victimization is the major crime concern of most American women and that the sexual abduction of children is a looming fear of parents. The stalkings of serial sexual predators are given wide media attention. Across the country, growing legislation has been enacted regarding the public notification and registration of convicted sex offenders. Throughout history and across cultures, offenses like mass rape, the sexual enslavement of women, the mutilation of sex organs, and systematic attempts to impregnate women for purposes of ethnic cleansing are common occurrences during civil and international wars.

Different types of sexual assault are described in this chapter. After defining the offenses, we examine the prevalence of sexual assault, its social correlates, offender characteristics, victim attributes, and situational elements of the crime. Four general syndromes of sex offending are identified based on offender, victim, and situational characteristics. The final section discusses the criminal justice response to sexual assault, treatment and rehabilitation programs, and opportunity-reduction strategies.

Definitions of Crime Types

The term "sexual assault" is used here to define a wide variety of conduct that has elements of both sexual activity and physical assault. These joint elements are most clearly revealed in what is called "forcible rape," defined as the "carnal knowledge of a female forcibly and against her will, also including assaults or attempts to commit rape by force or threat of force" (UCR 1995:23). For sexual contact involving persons under the age of consent (called statutory rape and child molestation), the victim's immaturity and the offender's relative position of power negates the requirement of physical force.

Over the last two decades, definitions of rape as forced vaginal penetration by a male offender have been expanded to include a variety of other types of sexual assault. Since *Rightout vs. Oregon* (1978), nearly all states have laws specifying that marital rape is a crime, nullifying the long historical legacy of a marital exemption from rape. Similarly, homosexual rape and any penetration by a foreign object are considered sexual assault in most states. The term "sexual assault" (rather than "rape") is now more commonly used to describe instances of forced sexual intercourse or contact. Legal categories of sexual assault—like first-degree or fourth-degree sexual assault—are often based on the degree of psychological and bodily injury to the victim, the number of offenders, the victim-offender relationship, and the age of the victim. Sexual offenses that involve family members (such as incest) are treated, depending on the jurisdiction, as either "intra-familial sexual assaults," or "lewd or lascivious conduct with a minor" (Samaha 1987).

Several additional sex offenses are common in American society, but they are not usually considered sexual assaults. These include: (1) exposing sexual organs in public (exhibitionism), (2) surreptitiously watching others engage in sexual activity (peeping and sexual voyeurism), (3) sexual fetishes (such as sex with animals or objects), and (4) the solicitation of sexual services for a monetary return (prostitution). These offenses are not treated as sexual assaults because they either do not involve physical contact with a victim, or they involve consensual sexual relations. However, non-contact sexual offenders (such as peepers and exhibitionists) are examined here because their behavior is often a developmental precursor to violent sexual assault (Davis and Leitenberg 1989).

Compared to other crimes, there is an extremely wide gap between the actual number of sexual assaults and those offenses known to the police. National victimization surveys indicate that less than one-third of sexual assaults are reported to the police (Perkins and Klaus 1996). Rates of reporting are far higher for (a) completed than attempted sexual assaults, (b) attacks by strangers than known parties, (c) cases with multiple offenders, (d) offenses involving the use of weapons, and (e) attacks resulting in additional physical injuries (Dobrin, Wiersema, Loftin, and McDowall 1996). Common reasons for not reporting sexual assault to the police include "it was a private or personal matter," "didn't think anything would be done," or "afraid of a reprisal from the offender" (Bachman 1994; Williams 1984).

Other studies, however, reveal that an even larger proportion of sexual assaults go unreported to the authorities. Russell (1984), for example, found that only about 10 percent of victims reported being raped. Rapes among acquaintances and college students may be reported in fewer than 10 percent of the cases (Koss 1992). Because data are not available for other types of sexual assault, it seems reasonable to assume that cases of incest and sexual misconduct within the family are widely underestimated.

The consequence of low reporting in sexual assault is that it places severe restrictions on the validity of inferences about the profile of offenders, victim attributes, and situational dynamics of the crime. Among types of sexual assault, official data on forcible rape seem to be more reliable than other types of sexual offenses. Regardless of the type of offense, however, we really don't know whether sex offenders known to the police are similar to those who remain undetected. Under these conditions, estimates of population trends should be interpreted with caution.

Trends Over Time and Social Correlates

Similar to patterns of criminal homicide and aggravated assault, rape rates in the U.S. have vacillated over time. UCR data indicate that rape rates increased from 1940 to 1945, remained fairly stable from 1950 to 1960, dramatically increased from the mid-1960s until the early 1980s, rose again from 1985 to 1992, and have decreased each year through 1995 (see Figure 3.1). The estimated 97,460 forcible rapes known to the police in 1995 represent the lowest number of rapes since 1989. This corresponds to a rate of 37.1 per 100,000. An estimated 34,650 persons were arrested for forcible rape in 1995, and an additional 94,500 people were arrested for sex offenses other than rape and prostitution (UCR 1995).

More than 430,000 rapes and attempted rapes were estimated in the 1994 National Crime Victimization Survey (Perkins and Klaus 1996). Contrary to trends based on police reports, victimization data indicate that the rate of rape victimization has remained quite stable

Figure 3.1
Rape Rates in the U.S. over Time

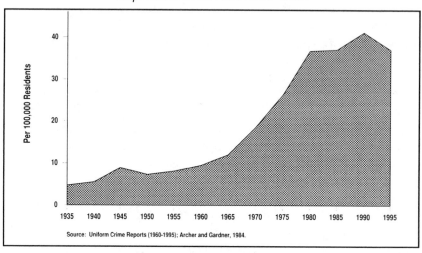

Source: Uniform Crime Reports (1960-1995); Archer and Gardner, 1984.

or actually decreased somewhat over the past two decades. Roughly 13 percent of adult women are estimated to be rape victims in their lifetime (Dobrin et al. 1996).

Official rape rates vary widely by region of the country, population size, and specific characteristics of geographical areas (see Figure 3.2). Rape rates tend to be higher in the Southern, Western, and Midwestern states. Southern states had the highest rape rate in 1995, and Northeastern states had the lowest rape rates (UCR 1995). Metropolitan areas and cities outside metropolitan areas had the highest rape rates, and rural counties had the lowest rates. Cities and neighborhoods with a high density of multi-unit dwellings, renter-occupied housing, ethnic heterogeneity, population mobility, low median family income, high unemployment, one-parent households, divorced females, and female-headed households have the highest rape rates (Miethe and Meier 1994; Warr 1988).

Official rape rates are considerably higher in the U.S. than in most countries. For example, the U.S. rape rate of 41.2 per 100,000 population in 1990 is twice as high as Australia's, four times higher than Rwanda's, six times higher than that of England and Wales, and more than 30 times higher than Japan's, Italy's and Egypt's (United Nation's Fourth World Crime Survey 1990).

A wide variety of explanations have been provided for the distribution of sexual assault over time and geographical bounda-

Figure 3.2
Characteristics of Cities and Neighborhoods with High Rape Rates

✓ Southern, Western and Midwestern States

✓ Large, Metropolitan Areas

✓ High Multi-Unit Dwellings

✓ High Renter-Occupied Housing

✓ High Ethnic Diversity

✓ High Population Turnover

✓ Low Median Family Income

✓ High Unemployment

✓ High One-Parent Households

✓ High Female-Headed Households

✓ High Density of Divorced Parents

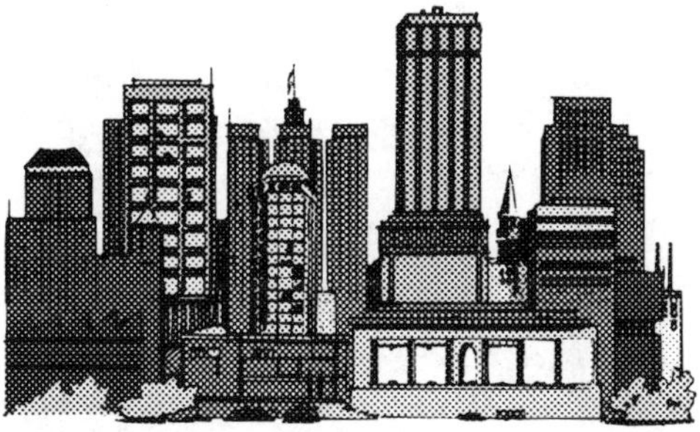

Source: Miethe and Meier (1994); Warr (1988); Uniform Crime Reports (1995)

ries. The decline of sexual morality in the U.S., the proliferation of pornography, and the persistence of prostitution, have, according to some observers, created a climate in which anything involving sex is perceived as acceptable. Others link high rates of sexual assault to gender inequality, arguing that rape is simply one of many means by which men exercise control over women. From this perspective, sexual assault is rooted in the economic and political domination of women (see Brownmiller 1975; Schwendinger and Schwendinger 1983). The high rate of sexual assault against American women is said to be symptomatic of their exploitation and domination. In contrast, an evolutionary or biological perspective presents rape as instinctual behavior, evolving over time as a means of perpetuating the species. From this perspective, prehistoric sex drives encourage modern men to have intimate relations with as many women as possible (Ellis 1989). Such an evolutionary or biological approach, however, is unable to account for the major variation in sexual assault rates over time and geographical boundaries. If sex offenses were merely a matter of instinct, they would not vary over time and place.

Offender Profile

Based on police reports and victimization surveys, rapists are disproportionately male, young, and African American (see Figure 3.3). Nearly 99 percent of those arrested for forcible rape are male and this pattern has changed very little over time. The few women involved in forcible rape are often accompanied by male offenders and they play a lesser role in the criminal activity (Brown, Esbensen, and Geis 1995). Males account for over 90 percent of those arrested for other sex offenses such as adultery, incest, indecent exposure, sodomy against nature, and seduction (UCR 1995).

Figure 3.3
The Offender Profile in Forcible Rape

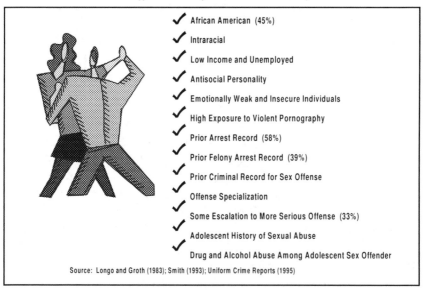

✔ African American (45%)

✔ Intraracial

✔ Low Income and Unemployed

✔ Antisocial Personality

✔ Emotionally Weak and Insecure Individuals

✔ High Exposure to Violent Pornography

✔ Prior Arrest Record (58%)

✔ Prior Felony Arrest Record (39%)

✔ Prior Criminal Record for Sex Offense

✔ Offense Specialization

✔ Some Escalation to More Serious Offense (33%)

✔ Adolescent History of Sexual Abuse

✔ Drug and Alcohol Abuse Among Adolescent Sex Offender

Source: Longo and Groth (1983); Smith (1993); Uniform Crime Reports (1995)

Several factors explain why some men are predisposed to commit sexual assault. Based on traditional socialization practices in patriarchal societies like the U.S., young boys are taught to be aggressive, tough, and dominating, and are led to believe that women want to be dominated or that certain special circumstances justify violent behavior against them (Burt 1980; Reiss and Roth 1993). For particular males who suffer from sexual insecurity, sex offending provides a means of enhancing their self-image and masculine identity (Russell 1975). Research that shows that men who hold more traditional sex-role stereotypes are more likely to use sexually coercive behavior supports this learning approach (Mosher and Anderson 1987).

More than four out of every 10 persons arrested for forcible rape are under 25 years old and nearly one out of five is under 18 years old. Persons aged 15 to 19, followed by 20 to 24-year-olds, are the most common age groups for arrested rapists (UCR 1995). Persons involved in intrafamilial sexual assaults, exhibitionists, peepers, and child molesters appear to be older, and gang rapists are often younger than rapists in general.

Over the last three decades, the proportion of reported rapes committed by teenagers and younger children has increased considerably. About 3 percent of rapists arrested in 1961 were under 15 years old, compared to about 6 percent in 1995 (UCR 1961, 1995). The number of reported rapes involving offenders under 10 years old has tripled over the last 25 years. A total of 72 children under 10 years old were arrested for forcible rape in 1995. Young sex offenders are extremely hostile and violent individuals with extensive histories of sexual trauma in their own lives.

The racial distribution of arrested rapists has remained fairly stable over time. About 54 percent of arrestees are White, 45 percent are African American, and the remaining 1 percent are of other races (UCR 1995). Similar to homicide and aggravated assault, the vast majority of rapes are intraracial. Amir's (1971) finding that arrested rapists are often unemployed and of low socioeconomic status is supported by the higher rate of forcible rape in neighborhoods with high unemployment and lower family income (Miethe and Meier 1994).

There is wide debate about whether exposure to pornography is part of the offender's profile in sexual assaults. The current wisdom is that the empirical link between pornography and sex crimes is, in general, weak or absent (Reiss and Roth 1993). However, exposure to explicit materials with both violent and sexual content has been linked to sexually aggressive behavior in men (Donnerstein, Linz, and Penrod 1987; Meese 1986). The riveting confessions of Wesley Allen Dodd, who raped and tortured two young boys in Washington state before killing them, and Ted Bundy, the serial murderer who sexually abused many of his victims, contain explicit mention of how viewing pornographic materials was a major precipitating factor in the onset of their criminal careers. Through the process of behavioral modeling (Bandura 1973), media images of sexual torture and brutality can become real-life fantasies that are perpetrated against actual victims.

Another aspect of the offender profile in sexual assaults involves differences in individuals' psychological attributes. Studies of incarcerated rapists indicate that a large percentage of them suffer some type of personality disorder, but psychoses and major mental illnesses are actually rare among sex offenders (Reiss and Roth 1993). Traits include hostile and sadistic feelings toward women, antisocial personality, and a masculine identity crisis that makes them largely oblivious to the sufferings of their victims (Gebhard, Gagnon, Pomeroy, and Christenson 1965). An anti-social personality is present in anywhere between 40 and 80 percent of sex offenders (Prentky and Quinsey 1988). Groth and Birnbaum (1979) contend that most rapists are emotionally weak, insecure individuals who want to possess, control, and dominate women. Based on the observations of 500 convicted rapists, these authors maintain that rape is always a symptom of some psychological dysfunction, either temporary or chronic. Perpetrators of sexual homicide are more prone to be diagnosed with serious psychopathologies than other criminals.

The criminal histories of sex offenders are wide and varied. Like other criminals, some rapists are first-time offenders and others are multiple or serial rapists. However, the clear majority of adjudicated sex offenders in most studies commit multiple sexual offenses and have prior criminal records for some type of sex offending (Fehrenbach et al. 1986; Groth 1977; O'Brien 1989; Rosenberg and Knight 1988). "Hands-off" offenses (such as exhibitionism and voyeurism) are the most commonly committed prior sexual offenses. More than two-thirds of rape suspects in the 75 largest U.S. counties had a prior arrest record, and more than one-third had a prior felony arrest (Smith 1993).

Offense Specialization and Escalation

Clinical samples and small studies of sex offenders in a particular jurisdiction reveal signs of both offense specialization and an escalation of a criminal career for some sex offenders. Adolescent sex offenders, for example, are often victims of sexual assault themselves and engage in a variety of deviant sexual practices (such as exhibitionism and voyeurism) prior to committing sexual assault. Drug and alcohol use, truancy, and other behavioral problems are common among adolescent sex offenders. Peepers and exhibitionists follow two patterns: Some specialize in these behavioral patterns in a somewhat ritualistic manner, whereas others engage in these non-contact sexual offenses as a developmental precursor to violent sexual assault (Davis and Leitenberg 1989). Child molesters, by definition, specialize in offenses against particular types of victims. Rapists have the highest risks of reoffending for the same crime than any other type of violent offender (Beck and Shipley 1989).

Escalation of violent sexual offenses occurs in a sizable minority of cases. Longo and Groth (1983), for example, found that about one-third of convicted adult offenders showed evidence of a progression from nonviolent sexual crimes as adolescents to more severe sexual assaults as adults. This pattern was more common in the histories of child molesters than in rapists.

Planning and Spontaneity

There are two common images of sex offenders. One image is the sexual predator who, with cold calculation and methodical planning, stalks an unsuspecting victim. The other image includes sexual assaults that spontaneously erupt in dating and social situations between known parties. Although the typical sexual assault is best characterized by spontaneity and little offense planning, offenders exhibit some elements of both planning and spontaneous action in sexual assault situations.

The level of planning exhibited by sex offenders is rather casual and low level. Rudimentary planning may involve gaining some brief knowledge of the victim's routine and lifestyle, the selection of a particular location that provides cover for the criminal offense and accessibility to victims, and preliminary assessment of the victim's level of protection or guardianship. A prior victim-offender relationship and the use of drugs and alcohol by the offender, victim, or both parties are some contextual factors that may increase the spontaneous emergence of sexual assaults in particular situations.

Victim Profile

National victimization surveys and police reports provide data on the characteristics of sexual assault victims. Victims of these crimes are typically women, young, unmarried, and economically disadvantaged. Males accounted for only 8 percent of the victims of rape, and more than half of rape victims are under 18 years old. Girls under 12 are victims in about one-eighth of all reported rapes, and a sizeable minority (20 percent) of these victims are sexually assaulted by their fathers (Brown, Esbensen, and Geis 1995). Based on NCVS data for 1994 (Perkins and Klaus 1996), the risks of rape victimization for women is highest (and lowest) for the following groups: African Americans (Caucasians), 16- to 19- year-olds (50 or older), family income less than $7,500 ($50,000 to $75,000), and central city residents (rural residents).

Situational Elements and Circumstances

The circumstances of sexual assault include offender motivation, the victim-offender relationship, and the situation dynamics of the crime. Each of these elements is summarized in Figure 3.4 and described below.

Figure 3.4
Situational Elements in Sexual Assault

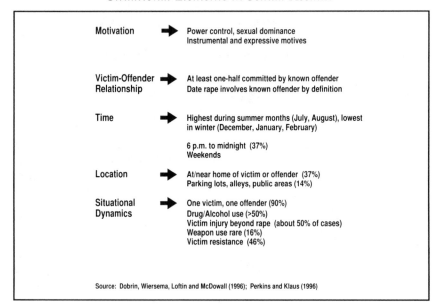

Motivation	➡	Power control, sexual dominance Instrumental and expressive motives
Victim-Offender Relationship	➡	At least one-half committed by known offender Date rape involves known offender by definition
Time	➡	Highest during summer months (July, August), lowest in winter (December, January, February) 6 p.m. to midnight (37%) Weekends
Location	➡	At/near home of victim or offender (37%) Parking lots, alleys, public areas (14%)
Situational Dynamics	➡	One victim, one offender (90%) Drug/Alcohol use (>50%) Victim injury beyond rape (about 50% of cases) Weapon use rare (16%) Victim resistance (46%)

Source: Dobrin, Wiersema, Loftin and McDowall (1996); Perkins and Klaus (1996)

The Motivation for Sexual Assault

At first glance, it seems rather obvious that sexual assaults are motivated by an instrumental goal or expressive desire of sexual conquest. However, most scholars believe that sex offenders are neither oversexed or undersexed, but rather, are emotionally insecure and weak individuals who are unable to handle the stresses and demands of life (Groth and Birnbaum 1979). The sexual aspect of sexual assault is the primary means in which these offenders attempt to exert power and control over others. Sanders (1983) considers rapists to be inadequate males whose feelings of inferiority push them toward anger and aggression against available weaker targets.

The image of rape as a violent act that is not sexually motivated has been called into question by several researchers. Felson and Krohn (1990), for example, argue that the rejection of the sexual motivation may be premature because most rapists prefer younger and presumably more attractive victims. The authors further contend that older offenders may be raping for motives of power or control, and younger offenders may be seeking sexual gratification. Under these conditions, elements of dominance, control, and sexuality form the basic motivation for sexual assaults.

According to the distinction between instrumental and expressive motivations, it is clear that sex offending involves both. Under Groth's typology of rapists, the "power" rapists and "sadistic" rapists are motivated by instrumental concerns, whereas "anger" rapists are expressive offenders. Specifically, the power rapist's goal is to possess and control his victim's sexuality, to dominate her and preserve his manhood by sexual conquest. The sadistic rapist's motive is also instrumental in that he uses ritualism and torture to achieve the goal of degradation and brutalization of the victim (Groth and Birnbaum 1979). The anger rapist, in contrast, acts on the spur of the moment after an upsetting incident has caused him irritation or aggravation. For these offenders, the sexual element of rape is essentially an afterthought, a means of expressing and discharging pent-up anger and rage. The higher incidence of power rape among incarcerated offenders suggests that the instrumental motive is most common among these offenders.

The instrumental-expressive distinction becomes muddled when we examine date rape and felonious rapes. Date rapes are often viewed as spontaneous acts in the heat of passion that emerge out of an assortment of situational factors. This apparent expressive side of date rape, however, is countered by research that demonstrates that these offenders are power rapists whose ultimate, instrumental goal is to dominate and control women (Groth and Birnbaum 1979). Similarly, felonious rapes (those that occur during the commission of another crime like burglary or carjacking) are often treated as expressive crimes, even though the sexual act in these crimes may have been planned by the offender in his selection of the particular crime target. Under these conditions, different types of sex offending have both instrumental and expressive dimensions.

The Victim-Offender Relationship

There are clear differences in both the type and nature of sexual assaults based on the victim-offender relationship. By definition, sex offenses like incest and marital rape are committed by relatives, whereas date rape involves persons who are acquainted or have had some prior interaction. Serial rapists and exhibitionists, in contrast, may begin their criminal careers by victimizing family members and friends, but they gravitate to victimizing strangers for perhaps no other reason than to reduce their risks of apprehension.

Estimates of the prevalence of stranger and acquaintance rape are wide and varied. National victimization data in the 1980s indicated that about half of the rapes were committed by someone known to the victim (Zawitz et al. 1993), but this proportion increased to about two-thirds by 1994 (Perkins and Klaus 1996). A similar range of prevalence for rapes involving known parties has been found using police and court data (Bowers, Jefferson, Strand, and Grohmann 1991; LaFree 1989; LeBeau 1987). Large surveys of students on college campuses also revealed that the vast majority of rape victims knew their assailants (Koss 1981).

Several factors explain these discrepancies across studies. First, there are differences in definitions of rape and sexual assault; studies using wider definitions to include fondling and offensive touching provide higher estimates of the prevalence of sexual assault and its frequency by acquaintances and intimates. Second, there are differences in trends based on the data source, with victimization surveys indicating that rapes by known offenders are less likely to be reported to the police (Dobrin et al. 1996). Third, because of the problem with selective unreporting and the definitional ambiguity of what constitutes sexual assault, estimates vary widely across states and study contexts. Studies on college campuses, for example, may generate higher rates of sexual assault and attacks by acquaintances because of the greater concentration of persons in the riskiest age group for rape, increased sensitivity of college women to sexual activity, and the communal nature of college life that increases the range of contact between classmates and acquaintances.

The distinction between strangers and acquaintance offenders is not only important in whether a sexual assault will be reported, but also a major factor in how the case will be handled in the criminal justice system. Compared to cases involving strangers, rapes involving known parties are far less likely to result in an arrest by police, have higher chances of being dismissed by the prosecutor or judge, have higher acquittal rates by judge or jury, and, for those convicted, are more likely to result in probation or shorter prison sentences (see LaFree 1989; Miethe 1987; Williams 1976). Rapes involving known parties are also quite different from stranger attacks in the frequency of weapon use, the degree of injury to the victim, and the physical location of the offense.

Situational Dynamics

A variety of situational dynamics is involved in sexual assault situations. The primary factors include temporal and spatial aspects, the type of weapon use, co-offending patterns, and alcohol and drug use in the crime.

Temporal and Spatial Patterns. Sexual assaults occur in a social context defined primarily by time and physical location. According to UCR data, summer months (especially July and August) are the peak season for rapes known to the police, and rapes are most infrequent during the winter months (UCR 1995). More than one-third of sexual assaults occur between 6:00 p.m. and midnight (Perkins and Klaus 1996). A higher proportion of rapes occur on the weekend than on other days of the week, and more than one-third take place at or near the victim's home. Only a small proportion (less than one-fourth) occur in parking lots, parks, or alleys (Perkins and Klaus 1996). Stranger assaults, however, occur in open public areas and parking lots in about half of the cases (Bachman 1994).

Weapon Use. The typical sexual assault does not involve the use of weapons beyond the perpetrator's physical body. A firearm is present in only 6 percent of sexual assault victimizations, and other weapons like knives, sharp objects, and blunt objects are used in an additional 10 percent of these assaults (Perkins and Klaus 1996). Weapon use is estimated in 28 percent of sexual assaults committed by strangers but in only about 8 percent of those assaults involving acquaintance offenders (Dobrin et al. 1996).

Victim Resistance. Much has been written on the extent and effectiveness of victim resistance in sexual assault. Victims report engaging in physical actions for self-protection in about half of rape cases (Dobrin et al. 1996). Physical resistance is more common in cases involving known offenders than strangers. Passive or verbal resistance like arguing or reasoning with the offender occur in about one-third of rape victimizations (Dobrin et al. 1996). In terms of effectiveness, resistance is often associated with higher rates of attempted rather than completed sexual assaults, but is also associated with a greater risk of additional physical injury if the resistance is unsuccessful. Regardless of the type or level of victim resistance, more than one-quarter of assault victims sustain additional injuries during the criminal event. More than half of the victims who resisted thought their actions were "helpful" and about one-quarter thought it made the situation worse (Dobrin et al. 1996).

Co-Offending Patterns. The vast majority of sexual assaults involve one offender and one victim. Although gang rapes with multiple offenders and one victim receive much media attention, multiple offenders are found in less than 10 percent of rape cases (Bachman 1994). An estimated 78 percent of sexual assaults involving multiple offenders are committed by strangers (Dobrin et al. 1996).

Alcohol and Drug Use. Drug and alcohol use is a common factor in homicides and aggravated assault, and sexual assaults are no different. Almost half (42 percent) of those in prison for sexual assault report that they were under the influence of alcohol or drugs when they committed their offenses (BJS 1993). In incidents in which victims are able to make inferences about offender's drug and alcohol use, nearly two-thirds perceive their attackers to be under the influence of drugs or alcohol (Dobrin et al. 1996).

Target-Selection Strategies

The "reasoning criminal" (Cornish and Clarke 1986) makes a series of rational choices about crime commission and target selection. As is true of other crimes, some sexual assault offenders select their victims on the basis of convenience and familiarity and the level of protection or guardianship.

The factors of convenience and familiarity may explain why most victims know their offenders in sexual assault cases. Incest and other types of intrafamilial sexual assaults are most easily explained by the physical proximity and convenience of victims to their attackers. It also makes intuitive sense that most sex offenders would prefer attacking unarmed and unprotected victims than guarded ones because protected targets decrease the chances of completing the attack and protected targets increase the offenders' risks of being hurt or killed during the attack. Other than the obvious fact that offenders select their victims because they are perceived as attractive, the particular victim characteristics considered "attractive" differ widely between sex offenders and the specific motivation for the crime.

The time, space, and situational features outlined above do not provide an adequate description of the situational dynamics and the interplay between victims and offenders in sexual assault cases. The following narratives taken from Las Vegas police reports provide a more thorough description of the dynamics involved in sex offenses:

- At approximately 6:15 p.m. the victim was hitchhiking and picked up by an unknown male suspect. The victim told the suspect "I'm not a hooker" and the suspect asked the victim if she wanted to go have a beer. The suspect grabbed the victim, punched her on top of the head, pulled her pants down to her ankles, held her down, and unzipped his pants. The suspect touched the victim's genitals with his right hand but did not penetrate. The victim hit the suspect in the nose with her elbow, fought off the suspect, and honked the horn. The suspect punched the victim again and threw her out the passenger door.

- The suspect offered help to the victim after she was kicked out of her car and abandoned by her husband. The suspect took the victim to his trailer. Once at his home, the suspect refused to let the victim go and forced her to submit to multiple acts of sexual penetration. The victim was able to escape and get help.

- The victim and suspect have been neighbors for 11 years. The suspect came over to the victim's home to use the phone. The suspect then grabbed the victim and carried her to the bedroom where he raped her. The victim has been stalked for about 10 months and now fears that the neighbor is the stalker.

Sexual Assault Syndromes

Sex offenders take various forms. "Hands-off" offenders such as obscene phone callers, exhibitionists, and voyeurs exhibit different behavioral patterns from violent sexual predators. Child molesters differ from each other and from other sex offenders in their *modus operandi* and target-selection processes. The sexual assault syndromes presented below illustrate some of the similarities and differences between these types of offenders.

Serial Sexual-Homicide Offenders

Studies of serial murders indicate that sexual desires and fantasies often underlie the offenses (Hickey 1991; Ressler, Burgess, and Douglas 1988). A variety of sexual perversions and mutilations of the victim's corpse are typical elements in serial murder. Some serial offenders have removed and saved the sex organs of their victims, and others receive sexual gratification from touching or eating the victim's fecal matter and urine (Hickey 1991). Serial murders have killed elderly persons of the opposite sex for sexual purposes, shot their victims in the head while they performed oral sex, tore off the victim's nipples with their teeth, sodomized children with various objects, and had sexual relations with the dead bodies. Accomplices to serial killers often admit to watching another offender rape or sodomize the victim (Hickey 1991).

The serial sex murderer is often portrayed in the media as a deranged sexual psychopath who methodically stalks and hunts his prey. While this public image may fit some of these offenders, serial sex murderers use a variety of approaches to lure and attack their victims. The social profiles of their victims also vary widely. Some serial sex killers target only particular types of people (such as redheads, young boys, or prostitutes), whereas others are opportunists who victimize whomever happens to be available and accessible. The following examples of serial sex murderers illustrate the diversity of the *modus operandi* and behavioral histories of these offenders (see Hickey 1991; Serial Killer Hit List (WWW) 1996):

- Jeffrey Dahmer's victims were primarily young, gay, minority men lured to his apartment from bars and the streets. He often used drugs to overcome his victims, cannibalized them, and sexually abused their corpses. He killed at least 17 people, and was killed in prison.

- Ted Bundy sometimes used an arm sling and other props to get women to help him with groceries and fake car problems. He bludgeoned, sexually assaulted, and bit many of his victims. His victims were primarily young women with dark hair in the states of Washington, Utah, and Florida. Bundy was linked to more than 20 murders and executed in Florida.

- Henry Lee Lucas began his murder career by knifing his mother in the back and raping her dead body. After serving 10 years for this murder, in the mid-1970s he joined Ottis Toole in a killing spree. Toole was a cannibal and Lucas was a necrophile who preferred sex with mutilated bodies and live or dead animals. Many of their victims were hitchhikers. The pair confessed to more than 500 murders, but many of their claims were later recanted.

- John Wayne Gacy dressed up in clown costume to entertain young boys at local hospitals. However, his victims either worked for him in a construction business or were picked up from gay hangouts. He lured them to his home, where he handcuffed and sodomized them, then bludgeoned and strangled them. Thirty-three bodies were found in a crawl space under his house. Gacy was executed in Illinois in 1994.

- Police Officer John Gerard Schaefer used his badge to lure young women off the highway. He was convicted of two murders in Florida in 1973. The victims were tied to trees in the woods while he went to work and were subsequently raped, tortured, and mutilated. He is believed responsible for 30 additional killings.

- The Boston Strangler, Albert DeSalvo, raped and strangled 13 women in the mid-1960s. He left the naked corpses carefully and provocatively posed with the strangulation cords tied in bows around their necks.

- Alton Coleman teamed up with Debra Brown in a crime rampage across the Midwest in the summer of 1984. Coleman was diagnosed as having pansexual propensities—a willingness to have sexual intercourse with any object, women, men, or children. Coleman has been linked to eight murders.

- Antone Costa reputedly killed 20 women whom he befriended and supplied with drugs, then had sex with their mutilated corpses. These killings took place across the U.S. in the early 1970s.

- Robert Hansen was linked to 17 murders in Alaska from 1973 to 1983. His victims were prostitutes and topless dancers whom he flew to a remote cabin hideaway. After raping his victims for several days, he released them in the woods and hunted them down with a high-powered rifle.

Contrary to the view of escalating criminal careers, studies of serial rapists find that the serial sex murderer is not a common pattern among serial rapists. In fact, analyses of the careers of serial rapists indicate that for most there was no significant change between the first, middle, and last offenses in the amount of force used, the pleasure experienced by the rapists, the gravity of victim injuries, or the duration of the physical assault (Warren, Hazelwood, and Reboussin 1991). The researchers, however, did find a small minority of extremely prolific serial rapists who escalated their use of violence over successive offenses. This group of sex offenders is most similar to serial sex murderers.

The serial sex murderer is also different from other sexual murderers in both psychological profile and motivations. "Happenstance" sexual murders that occur during carjackings or burglaries, for example, are not primarily motivated by sexual desires or fantasies, whereas in many cases the serial murderer's explicit goal is sexual dominance and degradation of the victim. The serial sex murderer often seeks out particular types of people to sexually dominate and control. The attractiveness and accessibility of the property, rather than the physical attributes of the victim, are more important precipitating factors in sexual assaults that occur during the commission of other crimes. Fortunately, both types of sexual homicides are relatively rare in the U.S., with only about 6 percent of homicides involving sexual assault (UCR 1995).

Child Molesters

Child molestation involves sexual relations between adults and children. Pedophiles are a particular type of child molester who have a definite sexual preference for children, but incest is often put in a different category because the offenders are members of the immediate family. Child molesters vary widely in their victims' characteristics and how they select their targets, the extent of specialization in child victims, and their sociodemographic characteristics. Several typologies of child molesters have been proposed in the literature.

One basic classification divides all child molesters as either "situational" or "preferential." Situational child molesters do not exhibit a particular sexual preference but are often opportunists who engage in sex with children for varied and complex reasons (Lanning 1987). Preferential child molesters, however, have a clear sexual preference for children. Pedophiles are often preferential child molesters who have extensive collections of child-oriented materials and pornography. Both preferential and situational child molesters are characterized as emotionally weak and immature offenders who desire to dominate and control others. An examination of traits of child molesters in Japan reveals that about one-half of these offenders are gloomy, lonely, and introverted people (Tamura 1992). For both preferential and situational offenders, their interest in children appears to represent a substitution for feelings and difficulties in contacting adult females.

Most pedophiles are men and many are married and have their own children. They do not usually have a homosexual identity, even though many of their victims are boys (Lesieur and Welch 1991). These child molesters exist in all socioeconomic, occupational, racial, and age groupings. In terms of general personality traits, pedophiles are often unable to establish genuine interpersonal relationships, have low self-esteem, and feel isolated and helpless (Groth 1978). Poor impulse control, defined as the inability to delay gratification, is a crucial factor underlying pedophiles' behavior.

Contrary to the stereotypical portrayal of child abduction and sexual assault by strangers, the vast majority of child molesters (ranging from 70 to 95 percent) are either acquaintances, family friends, or distant relatives of the victim (Groth 1978). Perpetrators of these assaults may use their relationships to the families as a way of enticing and luring victims to do things they would not otherwise do. Many of the warnings given to children, like "don't talk to strangers," are not applied to family friends and relatives. The offenders' relationships to the families also provide them with greater leverage to threaten children into silence. Physical threats become far more salient to young children when they are made by people with whom the family interacts on a daily basis. When parents are unwilling to suspect friends and family members of abusing their children, and kids are either unaware of the sexual abuse or too scared to report it, it is little wonder that much child molestation remains undetected.

One type of pedophile that has received much attention is the "saint." This offender is a person who has developed a reputation for serving the youth of the community (Shook 1988). Priests, teachers, coaches, doctors, and other persons of high respectability or social status are the perpetrators of these sex offenses. The sexual victimization of children by these persons is often veiled by expressions of affection (Howell 1982). Our strong outrage toward these offenders is linked to the victimization of children and the violation of a sacred trust that is bestowed to persons in positions of power.

Several other types of pedophiles have been identified. Rossman's (1980) classification of pederasts (pedophiles who engage exclusively in man-boy relationships) includes: (1) the *temporary* (or substitute) pederast who turns to boys as a source of sexual excitement and gratification due to the absence of a female partner; (2) the *criminal* (or exploitive) pederast who preys on youth and has a long history of predatory acts; (3) the *promiscuous* (or cruiser) pederast who often uses the services of child prostitutes; (4) the *careful* pederast who employs a middleman to minimize the chances of being arrested; and (5) the *responsible* pederast who is so fearful of apprehension that he avoids all physical contact with boys, instead collecting child pornography to enhance his sexual fantasies (Lesieur and Welch 1991:187). The relative prevalence of each of these types of pedophile is unknown.

Adolescent Sex Offenders

A growing national problem has been the increase in sex offending by adolescent boys. One hears on nearly a daily basis stories of a young adolescent or a group of them sexually assaulting another child. However, the actual prevalence of predatory sex offenses involving adolescent boys is unknown.

A large number of studies identify the characteristics of adolescent sex offenders (see, for review, Davis and Leitenberg 1989; Fehrenbach, Smith, Monastersky, and Deisher 1986). Knight and Prentky (1993) found eight major discriminating dimensions for these offenders: (1) family environment, (2) sexual history and adjustment, (3) social competence, (4) behavioral problems, (5) neurological and cognitive problems, (6) school achievement, (7) level of force and physical injury to victims, and (8) ethnicity of perpetrator.

Although the evidence is mixed and inconclusive, a modest relationship appears to exist between an abusive family relationship, prior sexual abuse, and adolescent sex offending. Fehrenbach et al. (1986), in the largest study of male adolescent sex offenders, found that more than 10 percent of them report a history of sexual abuse, primarily indecent liberties and rape. Physical abuse within the family was reported by nearly 20 percent of the offenders. Severe family dysfunction and disturbances through alcoholism, parental suicide, and parental sexual abuse are also common among adolescent sex offenders (Hsu and Starzynski 1990). Other researchers conclude that family dynamics, especially how the family responds to the adolescent's sexual offenses, are crucial in the persistence and escalation of these offenses (Groth and Loredo 1981). However, the causal significance of these family factors is negated by the presence of adolescent sex offenders in families not characterized by prior sexual abuse and dysfunction.

The most common personality anomaly attributed to adolescent sex offenders is low social competence or deficiency in social skills. Low social competence is indicated by the high proportion of these offenders who report having no friends at all, feelings of powerlessness, and an underachiever attitude or general lack of motivation (Groth and Loredo 1981; Groth 1977). These sex offenders also tend to have prior contact with mental health practitioners and often are diagnosed with conduct disorders (Prentky and Knight 1986). Neurological and cognitive deficits are associated with violent behavior, but do not apparently discriminate between adolescent sex offenders and other groups of delinquent youth (Prentky and Quinsey 1988). Many sex offenders and delinquent youth fail to achieve the grade-level placement for their age (Fehrenbach et al. 1986).

A number of other contributory factors explain adolescent sex offending. These factors include (a) the withholding of parental nurturing and intimacy from young boys to foster "tough" masculinity, (b) the failure to encourage boys to express their empathy in interacting with young children, (c) the development of negative attitudes toward women, (d) the reinforcement of dangerous myths regarding women's attitudes toward coerced sex, and (e) the absence of developmental experiences that help the adolescent resolve emotional needs through constructive behaviors (Finkelhor 1986). Unfortunately, like other types of sex offenses, adolescent sex offending has a complex etiological structure. Conflicting evidence can be found for each of the presumed causal factors underlying this type of sex offending.

The motivations and situational factors underlying adolescent sex offending are quite different for acts involving single and multiple perpetrators. Various needs such as to "fit in," "be one of the guys," or "show one's manhood" may motivate gang rape and predatory sexual assaults by multiple youth offenders. The group context may encourage and facilitate the completion of sexual offenses that the adolescent would not have committed alone. In contrast, the motivations for sexual assaults involving one victim and one offender are more varied and complex. Although most adolescent sexual offenses are committed by an isolated offender, a distorted desire to win peer approval may explain some of their behavior.

Date Rape and Intrafamilial Sexual Assault

Over the last two decades, we have become increasingly aware of sexual assaults that occur between acquaintances in a social setting and between immediate family members. The sexual offenses referred to as date rape, incest, and marital rape are similar in that the offenses are committed by nonstrangers. Serious legal attention has been given to these crimes only recently.

Date Rape. Date rape is a general term used to describe sexual assaults that occur between persons who know each other within the context of a dating relationship. Five types of date or courtship rape have been proposed to capture the diversity of the time and nature of these sexual assaults (Shotland 1992). *Beginning date rapes* occur during a couple's first few dates and *early date rapes* happen after several dates but before a couple has established sexual ground rules. *Relational rape* takes place after these sexual ground rules have been established. The remaining types involve *rape within sexually active couples* and *rape within sexually active couples who previously had sexual relations*. Date rapes in general, but especially those in which the victim and offender had a prior sexual relationship, often go unreported to the police.

A number of risk factors for date rape have been identified by researchers. These risk factors include: (a) males' initiating and taking a dominant role during a date, (b) miscommunication regarding sex, (c) heavy alcohol or drug use, (d) "parking," (e) male acceptance of traditional sex roles, interpersonal violence, adversarial attitudes regarding relationships, and rape myths, and (f) perpetrators' previous experiences as victims of childhood or adolescent sexual abuse (Lundberg-Love and Geffner 1989; Muehlenhard and Linton 1987). Many of the prevention strategies for date rape involve the dissemination and recognition of these warning signs.

Several large studies have been conducted to assess the prevalence of rape on college campuses. Koss (1981, 1992) found that about 15 percent of the women surveyed experienced an act that met the legal definition of rape, and the vast majority of them were acquainted with their assailant. Over half of date rapes are committed on first dates. In the majority of date rapes, the victims and offenders have been drinking or taking drugs just prior to the attacks. Less than one out of 10 victims report the sexual assault to the police or other authorities.

Incest. Long recognized as an act that occurs within the family context, incest is now considered a multi-dimensional problem from a social, legal, and mental health perspective (Rogers and Wettstein 1988). Defined as inappropriate sexual activity within the family, incest is often distinguished from other forms of sexual assault and molestation because of the victim-offender relationship and the repetition of the abuse that occurs with the same child. Incest includes relationships between parents and children, brothers and sisters, grandparents and grandchildren, and uncles and aunts with nephews and nieces.

The majority of incest cases involve sexual offenses by fathers against daughters. The dynamics of mother-son and sibling incest are thought to be quite different from father-daughter incest (Bavolek 1985). A weak marital relationship and a hostile mother-daughter relationship tend to foster rationalizations for father-daughter incest (Paveza 1988). In each type of incest, however, only particular family members may be involved (such as only one son or daughter) or a serial pattern will emerge (such as a father violating successive daughters through puberty and adolescence). The amount of force used in the sexual act may vary from simple requests to brutal attacks. Incest between siblings of similar ages often begins as mutual sexual exploration, whereas mother-son incest is more often characterized as a deviation from the stereotypical nurturing role of women. Because it may seriously disrupt the family unit, the vast majority of incest is unreported to other family members and the authorities. The experience of being an incest victim is often repressed in memory and discovered and recalled only later in life.

Several general traits and behavioral patterns are involved in the incest profile. According to a booklet published by Life Skills Education (1991), the following characteristics are common in incest cases:

- The average age of incest victims is approximately 11 years old, with the majority of victims experiencing their first encounter between the ages of 5 and 8.

- Incest is rarely a one-time incident. It is part of a pattern that continues over time and can involve various types of sexual activity.

- Incestuous families typically lack social skills and are often isolated from contact with community organizations and other families.

- The parents of incest victims are usually not happy with themselves or with each other.

- The incestuous father has emotional needs he cannot meet in interaction with adults, so he seeks more accessible and controllable intimate contact with his child.

- Negative value judgments about familial sexual relations emerge through familiarity with values of persons outside the home.

- Victims remain silent about incest out of fear of the consequences of disclosure.

- Adult survivors of incest experience psychological and relational consequences from the incest. Clinic treatment helps them address what has happened.

Marital Rape. As of 1992, marital rape is considered a crime in all but two states. Marital rape laws are designed to reserve the right of consent to sexual relations even between married persons. Estimates of the extent of sexual assault within marriage indicate that about 10 percent of wives have experienced a rape by their husband or ex-husband (Finkelhor and Yllo 1985; Russell 1990). These studies also reveal that spousal rape is more prevalent than stranger rape.

Similar to other sex offenses, marital rape is probably most common among emotionally weak and insecure males who want to dominate and control another person. Many spousal rapes are accompanied by brutal and sadistic beatings and have little to do with normal sexual interests (Finkelhor and Yllo 1985). Wife beating and spousal sexual assault are strongly related (Finkelhor and Yllo 1985; Russell 1990; Prescott and Letko 1977). It is likely that physical abusers of spouses exhibit many of the characteristics of marital rapists. For most victims of marital rape, sexual assault is not an isolated episode in their marriage. Finkelhor and Yllo (1985) found that 50 percent of the women in their study had been sexually assaulted by their spouses 20 times or more.

Sexual Assault Prevention and Intervention Strategies

Similar to other violent crime, efforts to control sexual assault have taken a variety of forms. Prevention and intervention strategies include the deterrent and incapacitative effects of punishment through the criminal justice system, rehabilitation and therapy efforts, and public awareness campaigns.

The Criminal Justice Response

Certain and severe punishment are the guiding principles underlying the deterrence doctrine. Unfortunately, analysis of police and court data on the criminal processing of sexual assault cases indicates that neither certain nor severe punishment characterizes the treatment of sex offenders within the criminal justice system.

One immediate problem with the certainty of punishment for sex offenders is that these crimes are notoriously underreported to the police. This is especially true of cases involving acquaintances and family members, the most prevalent offenders of sexual assaults. Few date rapes are reported to the police and, at most, only about one-third of all forcible rapes are reported (UCR 1995).

The low certainty of formal punishment for sex offending is also revealed in studies of case processing. Nationally, only about 51 percent of all rapes known to the police are cleared by arrest (UCR 1995). The likelihood of punishment is further diminished by the fact that more than one-third of rape cases are dismissed prior to trial or result in an acquittal (Langan and Graziadei 1995). Under these conditions, there is very little certainty of punishment for sex offenders.

The criminal prosecution of sexual assault has proven to be extremely controversial. The primary legal issue involves victim consent. As a necessary element for criminal liability, it must be shown that the sexual act was nonconsensual. Consent or its absence is usually inferred from an assortment of personal and situational factors: the prior relationship between the victim and offender, the location of the offense, and the amount of physical injury to the victim beyond the rape itself. The high rate of trial acquittals and pretrial dismissals in sexual assault cases, but especially those involving victims and offenders with a prior relationship, has been attributed to beliefs about victim consent (Miethe 1987; Williams 1976). The conviction of former heavyweight boxing champion Mike Tyson, the acquittal of William Kennedy Smith (a nephew in the Kennedy family), and the outcome of nearly all other rape cases are strongly affected by the circumstantial elements that relate to victim consent.

In terms of the severity of punishment for those who are convicted, about 87 percent of convicted rapists were given a prison or jail sentence, and the average imposed prison sentence was about 14 years (Langan and Graziadei 1995). National data on other types of sex offending are not available. However, given that offenses such as incest, voyeurism, and lewd and lascivious conduct are often misdemeanors and less serious offenses, the rates of imprisonment and period of confinement should be lower. According to data on felony convictions in state courts (Langan and Graziadei 1995), the proportion of convicted rapists who received a prison sentence (68 percent) is higher than all other crimes except murder (93 percent) and robbery (74 percent). The average maximum length of prison sentence for convicted rapists is only exceeded by convicted murderers. If severe punishment is a necessary condition for deterrence, these results provide some support for the possible general deterrent value of punishment for other potential sex offenders.

Certain and severe punishment is less likely in sexual assaults involving known parties than in cases involving strangers because of the underreporting of sexual assaults by known parties and the preferential treatment of rapists who know their victims throughout successive stages of criminal processing (LaFree 1989; Miethe 1987). Unfortunately, even for sexual assaults by strangers, legal sanctions will not usually deter others from sexual assault because of the low certainty of punishment.

The specific deterrent value of punishment for sex offenders is also brought into question by the high recidivism rate of these offenders. More than half of rapists released from prison are rearrested within three years of their release (Beck and Shipley 1989).

Offender Rehabilitation and Therapy

Various types of psychotherapy, drug therapy, and behavioral modification programs have been employed to rehabilitate and treat sex offenders. Different treatments have been applied to different types of sex offenders. None of the approaches, however, has provided a panacea to end sexual abuse.

One of the earliest treatments for sex offenders involves aversion therapy. Pedophiles and other convicted sex offenders were often treated with electric shocks to the genitals after viewing sexually explicit materials. Such an approach is assumed to abate sex offending by pairing inappropriate sexual arousal with pain. Unfortunately, shock therapy has been of limited effectiveness, primarily because this approach does not address the totality of factors besides sexual response that are predisposing and precipitating factors (such as low social competence, social isolation, low impulsive control) that underlie these criminal acts.

Another form of aversion therapy involves chemical castration through drug therapy. The most common type of drug treatment has been Depo-Provera. Depo-Provera reduces the production of testosterone, a hormone linked with aggression and the male sexual drive. Currently, it is administered only on a voluntary basis. Preliminary data suggest that the drug is effective for some sex offenders, but the use of volunteers makes it difficult to determine whether reduced recidivism rates among patients is due to the drug's effectiveness or the fact that those who volunteer to be chemically castrated may be those who really want help. Chemical or even physical castration may not reduce sexual assault because sex offending is often considered a violent rather than a sexual crime. However, the fact that Depo-Provera reduces testosterone—a hormone linked to aggressive behavior— provides some evidence for the potential effectiveness of this treatment modality.

Psychotherapy involves a variety of approaches in which clients and therapists discuss and attempt to identify the sources and causes of problem behavior. Under this approach, individual, group, or family counseling sessions are used to understand the motivations and situational factors that precipitated their sexual exploits. Often counseling sessions address the social isolation of the offenders and seek to develop more constructive means of dealing with their problems. The effectiveness of psychotherapy for sex offenders, however, has not been clearly established. The fact that current individual-based treatment approaches are primarily intervention rather than prevention programs also limits their effectiveness. There is wide variability in the duration and types of aversion and psychotherapy approaches used on sex offenders (see Maletzky 1991). Multi-treatment modalities have been commonly used as a rehabilitation strategy for sex offenders.

Opportunity-Reduction Strategies

A primary strategy for reducing sex offending in the U.S. involves efforts to decrease the opportunity for its occurrence. This goal has been accomplished primarily by increasing public awareness of the risk factors for sex offending and by the growing legislation regarding public notification of residential choices of sex offenders.

In one of the earliest studies of rape, Amir (1971) examined the social and interpersonal dynamics of sexual assault. Following Wolfgang's (1958) work on victim-precipitated homicide, Amir also examined the contributory role of victims in their sexual assault. Data from the Philadelphia police department indicate that a sizeable minority of rape cases involve careless actions on part of the victim like hitchhiking and going to bars with strangers. Although studies of victim-precipitated rape are widely criticized for blaming the victim (see Beirne and Messerschmidt 1991; Miethe 1985), it is undeniable that lifestyle changes by some potential victims can dramatically alter their risks of sexual victimization.

Efforts to promote victim responsibility are clearly revealed in many of the crime-prevention tips given to the public to reduce the risk of predatory crime. Opportunity-reduction suggestions are often disseminated by police departments, educational institutions, and social service agencies. Here is a representative example of the advice given to women to reduce their chances of date or acquaintance rape (Bucknell University, n.d.):

- **Be aware of controlling behavior in your date or relationship.** This includes intimidating stares, degrading jokes or language about women, refusal to respond to stated limits, refusal to accept "no" as an answer in a variety of contexts, insistence on making all the "important" decisions, extreme jealousy or possessiveness, and a strong belief in sex role stereotypes.

- **Define for yourself your sexual limits.** The first step in preventing abuse is to define your limits clearly to yourself and then to act quickly when a date or partner intentionally or unintentionally crosses your stated boundaries.

- **Set clear limits and be firm.** If you don't want to be touched, you can say "Don't touch me," or "Stop it, I'm not enjoying this."

- **Do not give mixed messages.** Say "yes" when you mean "yes," and "no" when you mean "no." Be sure that your words do not conflict with other signals such as eye contact, voice tone, posture, or gestures.

- **Be independent and aware on your dates.** Have opinions about where to go and appropriate places to meet.

- **Examine attitudes about money and power in the relationship.** Does your date have a sense of sexual entitlement attached to spending money on your relationship? If so, consider paying your own way or suggest dates that do not involve money.

- **Avoid secluded places where you could be vulnerable.** Meet in public places and suggest a group or double date if you are unsure about a new person in your life.

- **Trust your gut feelings.** If a situation feels bad or you start to get nervous about your date's behavior, confront the person immediately or leave as soon as possible.

- **If you feel pressured, coerced or fearful: protest loudly, leave, go for help.** Make a scene! Your best defense is to attract attention to the situation if you feel you are in trouble.

- **Be aware that alcohol and drugs are often related to acquaintance rape.** They compromise your ability and your partner's ability to make responsible decisions.

- **Be aware of inequalities in the relationship.** Does your partner perceive differences in terms of money, experience, and age as entitling him to power over you in the relationship? Someone who rapes chooses to enforce such power imbalances in a sexual context.

- **Practice self defense.** Knowing in advance how you would respond to a physical threat greatly increases your chances of escape. Any woman can learn self defense.

- **Challenge sexist attitudes that make rape acceptable.** Women can resist rape by challenging the attitude that women who are raped "deserve" to be victimized, and by intervening on behalf of women in danger.

The value of these opportunity-reduction strategies is that they increase public knowledge and awareness of risky and vulnerable situations. The approaches also directly address some of the widespread cultural values and norms that encourage sexual abuse. Any comprehensive effort to reduce sex offending, however, must unite general opportunity-reduction programs with specific treatment programs that address the particular needs of different types of sex offenders.

The final type of opportunity-reduction approach involves exerting greater control and community supervision over sex offenders. These community control efforts are most evident in the growth of laws regarding sex-offender registration and public notification of residency patterns. All paroled offenders have conditions for their release from prison, but sex offenders are often given the most severe restrictions for release. However, like increasing public awareness of risk factors, external restraints on sex offenders' behavior will only be minimally effective without extensive individualized treatment.

Summary

Sexual assault is met with much fear and disgust in American society. Sexual offenses vary greatly in frequency, distribution over time and space, characteristics of offenders and victims, and situational aspects. Although often viewed as motivated by exclusively sexual concerns, research on sex offenders clearly indicates the interplay between violence and sexual conquest as etiological factors. Sex offenders are commonly described as emotionally weak and insecure individuals who use their crimes to dominate and control others. However, sex offenders come from all social strata and are motivated by a variety of complex reasons. Differences exist between and within categories of serial sex murderers, child molesters, adolescent sex offenders, date rapists, and incestuous assaulters. Efforts to control these crimes include deterrence through formal legal sanctions, individual offender rehabilitation and treatment programs, and opportunity-reduction approaches. Current efforts to control sex offending exhibit limited success, but the union of specific treatment programs that address the particular needs of sex offenders and opportunity-reduction approaches that increase public awareness and knowledge about risk factors in sexual assault hold the most promise for crime prevention and intervention.

Chapter Four

Personal and Institutional Robbery

The holdup has a long history in American society, including wild-west bandits knocking off stagecoaches and trains, bank jobs by John Dillinger, physical attacks on unsuspecting strangers on the street, car thefts at gunpoint, commercial airplane hijackings, and quick hit-and-run thefts from modern convenience stores. Regardless of its particular form, the two major elements of robberies are the unlawful taking of property and the threat or use of physical force to accomplish that theft. As described in this chapter, different types of robberies vary in their frequency, the characteristics of offenders and victims, the motivations for offending, and how they can be controlled.

Definitions of Crime Types

Robberies are acts of property theft involving the use or threat of physical force. According to *Uniform Crime Reports* (UCR 1995), robbery is defined as "the taking or attempting to take anything of value from the care, custody, or control of a person or persons by force or threat of force or violence and/or by putting the victim in fear." Police reports classify robberies on the basis of location. Location classifications include: (a) street or highway, (b) commercial house, (c) gas or service station, (d) convenience store, (e) residence, and (f) bank. Street or highway robberies are commonly referred to as "muggings," whereas "institutional" robberies are those committed against commercial or financial establishments. "Personal" robbery includes muggings and forced thefts from persons in a residence or other noncommercial location.

Whether robbery should be classified as a violent or property crime is subject to interpretation. Similar to such violent crimes as homicide and forcible rape, robbery involves the use or threat of force against the person. When the victim is physically assaulted with a weapon during the commission of the theft, it is clear that such a robbery is a violent crime. However, the ultimate goal of robbery is to take another's possessions, suggesting that it should be considered a property crime. Under these conditions, it is best to treat robbery as both a violent crime and a property crime.

Thefts of property from the person such as purse snatching and pocket picking are officially classified as larcenies rather than robberies (UCR 1995). Pickpockets and purse snatchers are similar to muggers in that they make direct contact with their victims, but they do not typically subdue or physically assault them during the commission of the crime.

Compared to other crimes, the characteristics of robbery are different in several respects. First, robbery is more likely than other violent crimes to involve gun use, multiple offenders, and victims and offenders who are strangers. Second, the average yield from a robbery is nearly $900 (UCR 1995), a substantially higher monetary loss than in most other property offenses such as larceny and burglary. Third, because cash and credit cards are the items most commonly stolen in robberies, the need for a fence to buy stolen property is less of a concern in robberies than in other property offenses.

Trends over Time and Social Correlates

Robbery rates in the U.S. have risen and fallen erratically over the last 60 years. Robbery rates per 100,000 population were relatively stable from 1933 to 1965, dramatically rose until the early 1980s, then dropped in the mid-1980s, increased again until 1991, and have decreased over the last four years (see Figure 4.1). An estimated 580,545 robberies were reported to the police in 1995, representing a rate of 221 robberies per 100,000 population (UCR 1995). More than 500,000 robberies have been reported to the police every year since 1985. In contrast, national victimization data estimate that about 1.3 million personal robberies occurred in the U.S. in 1994 alone (Perkins and Klaus 1996).

Figure 4.1
Robbery Rates in the U.S. over Time

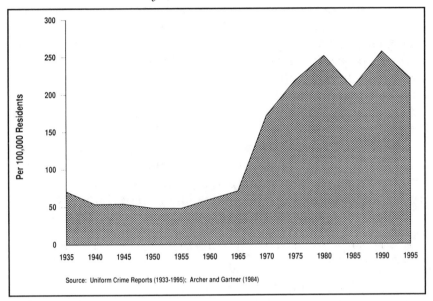

Source: Uniform Crime Reports (1933-1995); Archer and Gartner (1984)

Of the different kinds of robberies, bank robberies often grab the most media attention because they involve greater monetary losses and place more people's safety in jeopardy. However, banks are by far the least frequent target and account for less than 2 percent of all robberies (UCR 1995). More than one-half of all robberies (54 percent) are street muggings. The proportions of robberies that are muggings and bank robberies have remained stable over time. The growth in the number of convenience stores over the last several decades has dramatically increased their accessibility as a robbery target and their rate of victimization. Nonetheless, a convenience store was the target of only 5 percent of robberies in 1995 (UCR 1995).

Robbery rates vary widely by region of the country, population size, other sociodemographic characteristics of cities and neighborhoods, and by country. Robbery rates per 100,000 population are highest in the Northeast, followed closely by the West, and lowest in the Midwest (see Figure 4.2). Nearly two-thirds of the robberies in the Northeastern States are street muggings compared to only about 50 percent in Western and Southern States (UCR 1995). Bank robberies are about twice as likely in the Western States (especially Southern California) than in any other region of the country. Robberies of convenience stores and residences are most common in Southern States.

Although large urban areas have far higher robbery rates than smaller cities and towns (UCR 1995), the prevalence of different types of robbery varies by population size. For example, nearly two-thirds of robberies in cities with more than 250,000 residents are street muggings, but this type of robbery becomes less common as cities decrease in population size (UCR 1995). Convenience store robberies and bank robberies make up a higher proportion of robberies in small cities than in large urban areas.

Studies of robbery rates across cities and neighborhoods within them reveal several other crime correlates. Specifically, robbery rates are often higher in geographical areas with high ethnic heterogeneity, high population turnover, low family income, high unemployment, and high levels of single-parent families (Miethe and Meier 1994).

Figure 4.2
Characteristics of Geographical Areas with High Robbery Rates

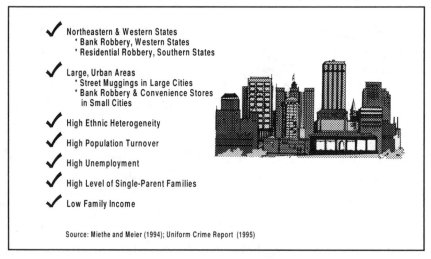

✔ Northeastern & Western States
  * Bank Robbery, Western States
  * Residential Robbery, Southern States

✔ Large, Urban Areas
  * Street Muggings in Large Cities
  * Bank Robbery & Convenience Stores in Small Cities

✔ High Ethnic Heterogeneity

✔ High Population Turnover

✔ High Unemployment

✔ High Level of Single-Parent Families

✔ Low Family Income

Source: Miethe and Meier (1994); Uniform Crime Report (1995)

Robbery rates vary greatly in different cities. The 10 U.S. cities with the highest robbery rates per 100,000 population for the period 1992 to 1994 are: (1) Newark, New Jersey, (2) Miami, Florida, (3) Baltimore, (4) St. Louis, (5) Atlanta, (6) Chicago, (7) Detroit, (8) Washington, D.C., (9) Oakland, and (10) Tampa, Florida. These data illustrate the strong regional differences in robbery and the fact that cities with the highest robbery rates are not necessarily the largest.

Cross-national comparisons indicate that the U.S. has a higher robbery rate than all other industrial countries (Kalish 1988). The closest countries to the U.S. rate of 205 per 100,000 in 1984 were Venezuela (161), Spain (147), Northern Ireland (119), and France (106 per 100,000). In contrast, the robbery rate in Japan in 1984 was 1.8 per 100,000, more than 100 times lower than the U.S. rate.

Several factors may account for the geographical distribution of robbery and changes in robbery rates over time. The higher rate of robbery in large cities, for example, is often attributed to the higher concentration of motivated offenders in urban areas, the greater anonymity provided to potential offenders, and/or more physical opportunities to victimize individuals and businesses (Miethe and Meier 1994). Increased robbery may also stem from increases in population growth and mobility. In contrast, increases in security surrounding financial institutions may displace robberies to less protected convenience stores and street muggings. High rates of robbery in urban areas and in socially disorganized areas within cities are often attributed to low economic opportunity, the diversity of languages and values, and the lack of youth supervision in these geographical areas (Miethe and Meier 1994; Sampson and Groves 1989).

Offender Profile

The sociodemographic profile of robbers is similar to that of other violent offenders. Compared to their distribution in the population, arrested robbers are disproportionately male, African American, and young (see Figure 4.3). Whether most persons who commit robberies share these same characteristics, however, is unknown because many robberies (especially those involving persons who know each other) are not reported and only about one-fourth of the offenses known to the police result in an arrest (UCR 1995).

Males are far more likely to be arrested for robbery than females, and gender differences in robbery arrests have remained quite stable over time. Males comprised about 95 percent of the arrested robbers in 1960 and about 91 percent in 1995. Police reports from Las Vegas indicate that high rates of robbery for men hold for different types of robbery, including street muggings, bank robberies, carjackings, and forcible thefts at convenience stores. Women robbers are far more likely to victimize persons they know than strangers and also tend to commit their offenses with male accomplices (Harlow 1987). Robbery arrests for women have increased during the five-year pe-

Figure 4.3
Offender Profile of Persons Arrested for Robbery

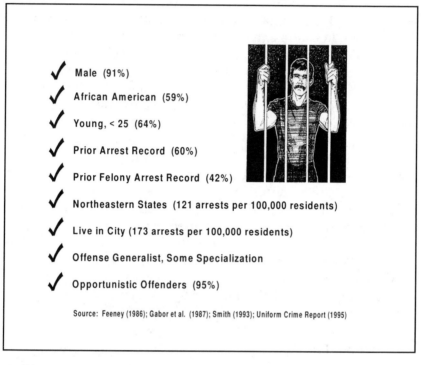

✓ Male (91%)

✓ African American (59%)

✓ Young, < 25 (64%)

✓ Prior Arrest Record (60%)

✓ Prior Felony Arrest Record (42%)

✓ Northeastern States (121 arrests per 100,000 residents)

✓ Live in City (173 arrests per 100,000 residents)

✓ Offense Generalist, Some Specialization

✓ Opportunistic Offenders (95%)

Source: Feeney (1986); Gabor et al. (1987); Smith (1993); Uniform Crime Report (1995)

riod between 1990 and 1994, but decreased for men during the same time period (UCR 1994).

Nearly 60 percent of those arrested for robbery are African American, and this proportion has also remained fairly stable over the last three decades. Compared to their population distribution, African Americans are overrepresented in arrests for various types of robbery, including bank robberies, street muggings, and carjackings.

Nearly one-third of arrestees for robbery in 1995 are under 18 years old, and about two-thirds of all robbers are under 25 years old (UCR 1995). Arrests of persons 18 years of age or older decreased over the last 5 years, but the number of robberies committed by juveniles rose dramatically. About half of carjackings involve offenders in their 20s (Rand 1994). Muggers are often younger than robbers of commercial establishments. When multiple characteristics are considered simultaneously, persons who are young, male, African American, and urban dwellers are the most common arrestees of robbery.

Court data on felony defendants in the 75 largest U.S. counties provide some details about the criminal background of robbers. Specifically, about 42 percent of the robbery offenders have a prior felony arrest, and nearly 60 percent have an arrest record when prior misdemeanor arrests are included (Smith 1993). Compared to other violent offenders, robbers are slightly less than murderers, rapists, and assault offenders to have a criminal history.

Offense Specialization and Escalation

An important question for understanding and preventing robbery involves offense specialization and the patterns of criminal careers. In other words, what are offenders' crime histories? Do they start their careers by committing a robbery and continue that trend? Is there a gradual escalation from petty thefts and drug offending to armed robbery? Or do robbers exhibit no consistent pattern of escalation or specialization?

Research on robbers' criminal careers indicates that their criminal histories are long and varied. Gabor et al. (1987) report that their sample of 39 armed robbers had 779 convictions, of which 460 were for armed robbery or offenses related to armed robbery (such as the illegal use or possession of a firearm). The other offenses were primarily thefts, burglaries, and frauds. Tunnell (1992) indicates that 46 convicted robbers in Tennessee reported that they had collectively committed about 2,000 robberies. Greenwood (1982) found that some criminals had committed as many as 53 armed robberies in a year. Although these studies overestimate robbers' level of criminal activity because they rely upon inmate samples, they clearly illustrate the extent of robbers' criminal careers.

Most robbers are generalists rather than specialists, but there is some evidence of a gradual escalation of violence that culminates in robbery. Gabor et al. (1987), for example, report that chronic offenders who start criminal activity in their preteen years tend to escalate from simple theft, to auto thefts and burglaries, and then robberies. The robbery careers of these offenders often start in late adolescence or adulthood. The typical robber doesn't specialize because taking money or property directly from a person by force is only one of several ways in which they can fulfill their desires for money and excitement.

Planning and Spontaneity

A common image of robbery is that it involves meticulous planning and calculation. From the perspective of a "reasoning criminal" (Cornish and Clark 1986), the decision to initiate robbery and continue it and the selection of the particular target involve a multiplicity of strategic and tactical choices. The reasoning criminal decides (a) when and where to commit the robbery, (b) whom to victimize, (c) what type of weapon, if any, to use, (d) how to escape, (e) how to overcome resistance, and (f) when to move on to other illegal or conventional lines of employment.

Contrary to the image of a reasoning criminal, interviews with convicted robbers reveal that the typical offender is an opportunist who reports little planning at all and had not even thought about being caught. Feeney (1986) found that most convicted robbers did no planning at all, and another third did low-level, rather casual, planning. For example, some calculation was involved in thinking about where to leave a getaway car, using a partner, or whether to use a weapon, but most of this planning took place the same day of the robbery and frequently within a few hours of the offense. Other "planners" simply followed an existing pattern for their offenses—they did little new planning because they already had an approach they liked (Feeney 1986).

The small minority of robbers (less than 5 percent) who planned in any detail are distinct in several ways. First, adults are thought to plan more than juveniles, and commercial robberies are twice as likely to involve extensive planning as personal robberies. These planning activities include stealing getaway cars, planning escape routes, detailing each partner's actions, evaluating contingencies, and observing the layout of prospective targets (Feeney 1986). Second, the likelihood of planning increases as the number of robberies committed increases—calculation is more common for offenders more firmly entrenched in the criminal lifestyle. Third, first-time robbers are generally more concerned about apprehension than are seasoned robbers. The risk of getting caught is often interpreted by seasoned offenders as simply one of the costs of committing a crime.

Some level of premeditation is often associated with the decision to use a weapon or force against the victim. By carrying a firearm during a robbery, one has already made a specific decision about the likelihood of using force to commit the crime. However, the substantial minority of robbers who made the decision to carry weapons also made deliberate decisions not to take full advantage of them. Approaches included carrying an unloaded gun, using a toy gun, or pretending to have a weapon. Most of these rational offenders wanted to make sure that no one was injured from an accidental shooting or reasoned that the penalty would be less severe if they were caught (Feeney 1986).

The level of planning is the major factor that distinguishes between two types of robberies identified in the comprehensive study by Conklin (1972). Specifically, *professional robbers* are those who "manifest a long-term commitment to crime as a source of livelihood, who plan and organize their crimes prior to committing them, and who seek money to support a particular lifestyle that may be called hedonistic" (Conklin 1972). Planning and skill are the trademarks of the professional robber. Other persons are assigned specific roles in order to steal large amounts from commercial establishments. In contrast, *opportunist robbers* steal to obtain small amounts of money when an accessible and vulnerable target presents itself. They most often prey upon "elderly ladies with purses, drunks, cab drivers, and people who walk alone on dark streets" (Conklin 1972:70).

It is important to recognize, however, that some robbers are keenly aware of their victim's habits and exercise a great deal of planning. Those engaged in detailed planning sometimes went to the trouble of renting apartments overlooking potential sites, both to enhance their observations and to avoid arousing suspicion (Gabor et al. 1987). Mapping out an escape route and the acquisition of weapons and disguises were also part of their planning:

> . . .Two days before, I bought surgical gloves and a nylon stocking, I stole a car, and with my surgical gloves I changed the plates three times . . . . (Gabor et al. 1987:60)

Victim Profile

Victims of personal robbery exhibit many of the same characteristics as offenders and victims of other violent crimes. Although all people are potential crime targets, risks of robbery victimization are greatest among males, young persons (under 25), African Americans and Latinos/Latinas, single persons (including those never married, divorced and separated), those earning low incomes (less than $7,500 per year), renters, those who live alone, frequent movers, and urban residents (see Figure 4.4).

Figure 4.4
The Victim Profile in Robbery

Highest	Lowest	Ratio of Highest to Lowest
Male	Female	2.0
African American	White	2.9
Latino	Non-Latino	1.8
Young, 12-24	> 65	8.4
Family Income < $7,500	> $7,500	2.6
Urban Resident	Rural Resident	4.2
High School Graduate	> High School Graduate	1.3
Single, Never Married	Married	2.1
Renter	Owner	2.4
Live in Multi-Family Unit	Live in Single-Family Unit	2.4
Live Alone	Live with others	1.3
Moved in Last 5 Years	No Moves	1.8

Source: Miethe and Meier (1994); Perkins and Klaus (1996)

The differences in robbery risks across different social groups are often large. The robbery victimization rate for men, for example, is about twice as high as the rate for women, and nearly three times higher for African Americans than whites (Perkins and Klaus 1996). The media often portrays senior citizens as mugging victims, but the victimization rate for persons over 65 years old is actually about eight times *lower* than for persons under 25 years old. Robbery rates are about four times higher for urban residents than rural residents, whereas those whose annual income is less than $7,500 are at least twice as at risk than those with incomes over $50,000 (Perkins and Klaus 1996). These differences across social groups, however, would be even greater if adjustments are made for the relative exposure of people to risky and vulnerable situations (see Miethe and Meier 1994). For example, persons who are urban residents, young, and male generally spend more time in risky and dangerous public activity than their respective counterparts. Adjusting for this differential exposure to potential offenders would greatly enhance the risks of robbery victimization for these persons.

One dominant explanation for the social distribution of robbery victimization incorporates a routine-activities or lifestyle perspective (Miethe and Meier 1994). According to this perspective, individuals' routine daily activities and lifestyles are important for understanding victimization risks because they represent one's exposure to risky and dangerous public settings, increase the attractiveness of the person as a potential crime victim, and decrease their personal safety or guardianship. The higher risks of robbery for males, the young, and single persons, for example, are often attributed to higher levels of non-familial public activity and higher exposure to risky and vulnerable situations like taking public transit, frequenting drinking establishments, and engaging in nighttime public entertainment.

The contributory role of the victim in robberies has been studied under the term "victim-precipitation" (see Curtis 1974; Fattah 1991; Normandeau 1968). Victim-precipitated robberies are those in which the victim is judged as careless in the handling, carrying, or displaying of money and personal property while in public places. A national study of 17 U.S. cities (Curtis 1974) and a separate study of robbery in Philadelphia (Normandeau 1968) show that about one of every 10 robberies is precipitated by victims' careless behavior. By flashing bills in public places, wandering in dangerous parts of the city at night, or giving subtle cues that one is an attractive target (such as constantly checking wallets or purses and their location), persons may inadvertently increase their risks of personal robbery. A higher level of victim precipitation would be found if a wider range of imprudent behavior are included.

Cross-national data confirm U.S. trends of victim precipitation in robbery. In a study in Nigeria, Nkpa (1976) concludes that fewer than half of robbery victims are completely innocent. The majority of victims create dangerous situations by being imprudent, negligent, or performing illicit behavior that place them in more vulnerable positions. McClintock and Gibson (1961:23) note in London that:

> . . . [E]xamination of the behavior of the offenders and the victims leaves little doubt that a number of the offences would have been

prevented if certain elementary precautions had been taken to avoid giving obvious opportunities to potential offenders . . . victims walked across parks or commons or along lonely ill-lit streets very late at night or during the early hours of the morning, instead of taking a longer route along a main thoroughfare. There were also those robberies which followed some preliminary association for sexual purposes, and there were a number of other incidents in which the victims behaved unwisely.

Although potential victims may increase their robbery risks by their actions and personal characteristics, the selection of the robbery target is often based purely on chance or a set of situational factors. Take, for instance, some robbers' descriptions of their target-selection criteria (Gabor et al. 1987:57-58):

> . . . It was a Sunday. I didn't know where to go to get some money. I had a gun but no bullets . . . . I saw a convenience store. On Sunday, you don't have much choice. I didn't look at the risks. I needed money. . . .

> . . . I hit the first bank I ran into because I didn't have much time; not much time to look around.

> . . . luck put us in an ideal spot. In passing in front of a place, we saw an armored truck parked. It was a perfect corner for it, an ideal spot for the getaway. . . .

> . . . we spotted it [the target] for many nights at the same hour. We were looking for stores with lots of people, lots of customers, and therefore lots of money. . . .

> . . . There must be a small street close by to park a car and to remove the disguises afterward. . . .

Because the nature of their work exposes them to dangerous persons and places, people in certain occupational groupings are most susceptible to robbery victimization. These include taxicab drivers, convenience-store workers, bus drivers, pizza-delivery personnel, liquor-store employees, tavern workers, casino or gaming staff, and small motel workers. Robberies committed against these persons often occur at night and when few customers and fellow employees are present. Some efforts have been made to decrease the attractiveness of these persons for victimization—for example, posting signs indicating the small amount of on-hand cash, using time-delayed safes, and increasing surveillance equipment. However, the nature of their work environment and their exposure to particular people and situations still make them prime targets for robbery victimization.

Figure 4.5
Situational Elements in Robbery

Motivations	➡	Money (1/2), Anger/Disturbance (1/4), Accidental Robbery While Committing Other Crime (1/4)
Victim-Offender Relationship	➡	77% Strangers, 23% Known
Type of Weapon	➡	41% Firearm, 40.7% Strong-Arm, 9.1% Knives, 9.2% Other Weapon
Victim Injury	➡	1/3 Some Injury
Group Context	➡	Multiple Offenders in Majority of Robberies (51%)
Alcohol/Drug Use	➡	2/3 Robbery Arrestees Tested Positive For Drug Use 1/2 Robbers Report Daily Use of Illegal Drugs
Temporary Patterns	➡	Nighttime, 6 p.m. to Midnight (43%) Late Summer and Fall Months
Physical Locations	➡	Low Income, High Unemployment, High Population Turnover, High Ethnic Diversity, High Percentage of Single-Parent Families

Source: Feeney (1986); Harlow (1987); Perkins and Klaus (1996); UCR (1995)

Situational Elements and Circumstances

The situational elements of robbery include the perceived motivation for crime commission, the victim-offender relationship, the physical location and temporal aspects of the crime, and other aspects of the crime event. Each of these situational elements is summarized in Figure 4.5 and described below.

The Motivation for Personal and Institutional Robbery

At first glance, robberies seem to be easily explained by the offenders' desire for money. Willie Sutton's classic response that he robbed banks because "that's where the money is" clearly conveys this instrumental motivation. However, a closer examination reveals that robbery, like other acts of personal violence, is motivated by a variety of concerns.

Contrary to the popular image of robbery as solely motivated by financial needs, only about one-half of convicted robbers said that their crime was driven by the desire for money (Feeney 1986). About one-fourth wanted something other than money, and another one-fifth were involved in "accidental robberies," like burglaries, fights, or other acts not originally intended to involve both theft and violence. Offenders wanted money for a variety of reasons, ranging from drugs to rent and food. Two of the convicted robbers in Feeney's study (1986:56-57) described their financial needs this way:

> . . . I needed the money for food. I tried welfare. I tried to borrow from all the people that I could borrow from. I didn't have any sources of money. I was just flat broke. I was getting it out of savings and borrowing money from my mother, but I was getting kind of run out because she was starting to need more. I didn't even think about how much I wanted to get. I just felt that anything I got would help. It was better than nothing. . . .

> . . . I had a little $1.65 job working 20 hours a week, which wasn't very much, but I was still trying to make it on the legit side, but there just wasn't nothing open to me. I don't mind working, but $1.65 is kind of ridiculous. . . . [Robbing] was the only thing open to me at the time. . . .

Robbers mention monetary gain and the ease with which it can be obtained as primary reasons for selecting this crime over other offenses. The comparative advantages of robbery are explicitly mentioned by these offenders (Gabor et al. 1987:63):

> . . . with burglary you have problems selling goods like televisions and stereos. People don't want to pay you the right price. . . . [in] armed robbery you don't have problems; you get the money right away. . . .

> . . . it [fraud] is inconvenient because it's complicated; [you] need equipment, machines. . . .

> . . . It's the fastest and most direct way to get money. There's no thrill in getting it. It's for the cash, the money, that I do it. . . .

> . . . one armed robbery pays about as much as 20 burglaries. . . .

Financial motives are most evident in bank and commercial robberies, whereas anger and previous disturbances often motivate personal robberies. Strictly economic motives may play only a secondary role for robberies involving juveniles. In fact, these offenses are often used to enhance one's reputation and status within delinquent peer groups, indicating that the juvenile is tough, resourceful, and streetwise. Katz (1988) suggests that a variety of "seductions" underlie robbery. The seductions of excitement and novelty in a life of despair are expressed by the following robbers interviewed by Feeney (1986:58-59):

> . . . I get a kick out of it, really. Watch people's faces when they see you. They're scared. I robbed because he gave me a smart answer. . . .

> . . . I don't know. It sounded easy and I guess we needed the money. We didn't really need it but we wanted to do something. Something to do. I don't know. . . .

> . . . Just to cause some trouble. Well, we just wanted to try that, you know. Goof around, you know . . . have some fun—jack up somebody. . . . We thought we were really big and stuff like that. . . .

> . . . I did it because I didn't care. I felt I didn't have anything to live for anyway so what the heck's the difference. . . ."

Many offenders use robbery as a means of empowerment or as a challenge through which they could prove themselves to their friends. These sentiments are clearly expressed by the following offenders (Gabor et al 1987:63):

> . . . when I have a gun in my hands nothing can stop me. It makes me feel important and strong. With a revolver you're somebody. . . .

> . . . Someone pushed me to take up the challenge. He told me I wasn't capable of doing an armed robbery. I said give me the gun. I'm going to do it. At 14 you don't realize what you're getting into. . . .

> . . . I was influenced . . . you want to show others you've done it. . . .

Finally, political motivations influence a small minority of robberies. Patty Hearst's kidnapping and her subsequent participation in bank robberies were politically motivated, and air hijackings are often planned for political purposes, including monetary ransom or hostage and prisoner exchanges.

The Victim-Offender Relationship

Both police reports and victimization data indicate that personal robberies typically involve strangers. More than 90 percent of the robberies known to the police in Las Vegas involve strangers and about four out of every five robbery victims nationally said their attacker was a stranger (Perkins and Klaus 1996). As true of other criminal offenses, robberies involving acquaintances and family members are underreported in both sources. Of violent crimes, robbery has the highest level of participation by strangers.

Personal robberies involving strangers and acquaintances are quite different in terms of their interpersonal dynamics and social and spatial distribution. Stranger attacks more commonly occur in public locations, involve multiple offenders, involve weapons, and often result in greater physical harm to victims than acts involving known offenders. Robberies that occur after personal assaults, thefts against rival gang members, and bad drug deals are common situations that involve "known" offenders. Victims are often co-conspirators in robberies among known parties. These situations include the truck drivers who fake robberies and share their cargo with the robbers, jewelers who attempt to cheat insurance companies with planned heists, or bank managers and convenience store operators who tip off others to security flaws in order to cover their own thefts (MacDonald 1975).

Situational Dynamics of Robbery Incidents

An assortment of situational elements influence the frequency of robbery and the likelihood that the crime will be successfully completed. These elements involve temporal and spatial aspects, weapon use, the group context of robbery, alcohol and drug use, and the sequential dynamics of robbery events.

Temporal and Physical Dimensions. Robberies are more common in particular seasons and at particular times of day. Late summer and fall months are the peak seasons for robbery, and these crimes are less likely to occur in the winter and early spring (UCR 1995).

Personal robberies occur more frequently during nighttime hours, especially between 6:00 p.m. and midnight (Perkins and Klaus 1996).

There are some apparent hot spots for robbery in terms of specific locations. Robbery rates, for example, are highest within specific areas of cities characterized by low socioeconomic opportunity, high population turnover, ethnic diversity, and a high proportion of single-parent families (Miethe and Meier 1994). Because they increase the potential yield of cash with little protection, physical areas outside automatic teller machines (ATMs) are a prime location for personal robbery.

Weapon Use. A firearm was the most common weapon in robberies, followed closely by "strong-arm" tactics and knives or cutting instruments (UCR 1995). City data from Las Vegas indicate that robbers of commercial establishments are the most likely to use or threaten to use firearms during the crime, whereas knives and blunt objects are the weapon of choice for street muggers and robbers of persons in their residences. Handguns are used in the majority of completed carjackings but in less than one of every five attempted carjackings (Rand 1994). A smaller proportion of robberies involve other weapons such as screwdrivers, lug wrenches, metal bars, shovels, pool cues, bricks, dog repellent, pieces of lumber, or broken beer bottles. The weapons in these cases are almost always something handy when the need arises rather than an instrument carried by careful design (Feeney 1986).

Victim Injury. The victim suffers serious physical injuries in one out of every 12 robberies (Harlow 1987). These serious injuries involve rape, knife or gunshot wounds, broken bones, and being knocked unconscious. About one-third of the robbery victims experience at least some injury in the attack (Perkins and Klaus 1996). The use of physical force and subsequent injury is more common in robbery cases in which the victims resisted (Katz 1988).

Co-Offending Patterns. Robberies are more likely than other violent crimes to involve multiple offenders. In fact, multiple offenders are present in about half of robbery victimizations (Harlow 1987). Elaborate bank heists with getaway-car drivers and quick drive-up robberies of convenience stores are the best examples of the group nature of robbery. Street and institutional robberies by juveniles are especially likely to involve multiple perpetrators. Peer pressure in this group context may often encourage robberies and other offenses that would not have occurred otherwise.

Alcohol and Drug Use. Drug and alcohol use is less common among robbery offenders than other violent offenders (Zawitz et al. 1993). Even so, national data reveal that about two-thirds of those arrested for robbery tested positive for drug use (NIJ 1993). About one-third of incarcerated robbers said they committed their offense to get money for drugs (BJS 1994). According to Conklin's (1972) typology, *addict robbers* display a low commitment to robbery and prefer less dangerous forms of property theft to acquire cash. They choose targets that present a minimum of risk, but will take greater chances when they are desperate for money. Addicts are not looking for a big score; they only want enough money to get their next fix. Similarly, the *alcoholic robbers* often commit their crimes when in a disoriented state, attempting to get more money to buy liquor. Their crimes are rarely planned and they give little thought to victims or the likelihood of success or escape.

The Temporal Sequencing of Robbery Episodes

All criminal events have a beginning, middle, and end. Regardless of the particular form of robbery, the initial contact between victims and offenders is usually short and direct; the typical robbery is completed within a few minutes. MacDonald (1975) indicates that in many armed robberies few words are spoken, offenders waste no time, and perpetrators leave the scene before the startled victims have time for reflection.

After making initial contact with victims, robbers are brief and to the point about their intentions. MacDonald (1975:62) summarizes some phrases echoed by robbers or written on notes:

 . . . This is a stickup, give me your money.

 . . . Give me your wallet and your money.

 . . . Open the cash register and give me the money.

Often these requests are immediately followed by threats to harm or kill to encourage cooperation, and victims are warned not to make any sudden movements. Perpetrators may order victims to sit down, lie on the floor, or go into another room.

A primary situational aspect that arises after initial contact involves victims' decisions to resist the attack or not. Resistance increases the chances of physical injury during an attack, but also increases the chances of thwarting the crime. Often, offenders anticipate possible resistance from victims and quickly discourage it with a variation on the following phrases (MacDonald 1975:65):

> . . . I want no shit, just give me the money.

> . . . Lay on the floor and don't try to be a hero.

> . . . Just give me all your money and no foolishness.

The final stages of the robbery event involve offenders' attempts to escape from the scene. Here, several different scenarios can emerge. One strategy for robberies of banks and convenience stores includes tying up the victims and witnesses or locking them up in a storage room or vault. Sometimes offenders will leave the victims in this condition, but in other cases the victims are executed by the perpetrators to avoid identification. Regardless of whether or not victims and witnesses are physically restrained, robbers often convey particular advice to their victims about pursuit and contacting police. As noted by MacDonald (1975:65-66), these final comments may include statements such as:

> . . . If you look at me or say anything, I'll come back and kill you.

> . . . Don't call the police or I'll come back and blow your brains out.

> . . . Don't call the cops for two hours. I'm an excon and I don't care. I'll just shoot you.

> . . . Go into the back room and count to 100.

> . . . Keep walking down the alley and keep your eyes straight ahead.

> . . . Don't follow me or I'll shoot you.

Target-Selection Strategies

Robbery targets are not usually selected at random. Instead, specific crime targets are selected by robbers because they have one or more of the following characteristics: (1) convenience and familiarity, (2) low protection or guardianship, and (3) high expected yield and target attractiveness.

The vast majority of robbers who are impulsive, spur-of-the-moment opportunists select their victims primarily out of convenience rather than because of meticulous estimates of the expected yield or risks of being caught. Despite the risks of recognition, convenience as a target-selection factor is also indicated by the fact that over a third of robbers attack victims in their own neighborhoods (Feeney 1986). When asked why they selected a particular target or site, typical comments by robbers are (Feeney 1986:62):

. . . Just where we happened to be, I guess. Don't know.

. . . Nothing else open at 2:00 a.m. Had been there before.

. . . We thought it would be the quickest, you know, it's a small donut shop.

An examination of the prevalence of different types of robbery and their average yields suggest that typical robbers consider all three elements in their target-selection decisions. For example, bank robberies provide the greatest yields (an average of $4,015), but the low rate of bank robbery is probably due to the fact that banks are highly protected and most offenders are not familiar with the interworkings of vaults and alarms. Convenience stores, on the other hand, offer smaller returns (an average of $400) but they are more convenient and offer less protection, factors which may explain why convenience stores are three times more likely than banks to be the sites of robberies (UCR 1995). The prevalence of street muggings may be explained by the simultaneous optimization of all three factors—street muggings are convenient, their personal victims are more likely to lack protection, and result in considerably large returns ($645 on average).

Robbery Syndromes

The combination of offenders, victims, and situational characteristics reveals several types of robbery syndromes. These syndromes are (1) offender-based classifications, (2) bank robberies, (3) convenience store robberies, (4) street muggings, (5) residential robberies, and (6) carjackings.

Offender-Based Classifications

Studies of robbers indicate that they differ widely in demographic characteristics, the extent of their criminal activities, level of offense specialization, and degree of planning. Using these categories, Gabor et al. (1987) identified four types of male armed robbers: the chronic, the professional, the intensive, and the occasional armed robber.

As the name implies, *chronic* armed robbers have the longest criminal histories, starting with their first offenses at an average age of 12 and their first arrests at the age of 14. Typical chronic offenders commit their first armed robberies at the age of 17 and remain active as robbers for seven to eight years (Gabor et al. 1987). These offenders report involvement in 20 to 25 armed robberies and many other offenses such as burglaries, drug offenses, and auto thefts. In executing offenses, chronics do not rigorously plan their offenses, but are almost always disguised, well armed, and prepared to discharge their weapons if necessary (Gabor et al. 1987:80). The typical yield from robberies is between $500 and $5,000 per incident, and the money is often spent quickly on drugs and entertainment.

Professional armed robbers are distinguished by meticulous detail in target selection and crime commission. Preparation for crimes may last from weeks to months (Gabor et al. 1987). Crime targets are selected carefully and kept under close surveillance. This greater planning also results in a higher average earning per robbery incident (between $1,000 and $5,000) than is true of other robberies. Professionals begin their criminal careers as early teens and commit their first armed robberies by the age of 16. Their careers in armed robbery typically last more than 10 years. Professionals' income from robbery pays for their daily living expenses and is usually deposited in a bank account (Gabor et al. 1987). Burglaries, auto thefts, and drug deals supplement their incomes. Although professionals are well-armed and sometimes carry automatic weapons, a weapon is discharged in only about one out of 10 cases.

Intensive armed robbers differ from the other classes of offenders in a variety of ways. They have minimal prior criminal records and suddenly commit a rash of five to 10 holdups in a short time frame. The crimes are often poorly planned and occur when offenders are in their mid-twenties. They often have accomplices and carry non-lethal weapons. The limited planning results in only a modest income from their offenses, averaging between $150 and $1,400 per incident (Gabor et al. 1987). Arrest and subsequent incarceration often terminate the robbery sprees.

Occasional armed robbers commit offenses only rarely, but they are active in other crimes. Occasional robbers generally begin criminal activity early but commit their first armed robberies when in their twenties. As opportunists, these offenders are rarely prepared for the crimes, lack disguises, and are not usually armed. The criminal careers of occasional armed robbers are short, spanning from several months to two years. After arrests, these offenders may feel that the returns from armed robbery are not worth the price that they may have to pay and thus turn to less violent and dangerous activities, such as fraud, drug dealing, or auto theft (Gabor et al. 1987). For occasional robbers, armed robbery is one episode in a long criminal career.

Bank Robbers

Bank robbers throughout history have received wide notoriety. The James-Younger gang, the Dalton brothers, and Butch Cassidy terrorized banking institutions and trains in the Wild West. Later, John Dillinger, Clyde Barrow and Bonnie Parker, "Pretty Boy" Floyd, "Baby Face" Nelson, and "Machine Gun" Kelly became household names during their robbery sprees in the late 1920s and 1930s. Modern bank robbers, however, are less visible and glamorized. Electronic surveillance equipment and greater security within financial institutions have decreased the active criminal careers of serial bank robbers. Because their crimes more often occur in the presence of witnesses and monitoring devices, chronic bank robbers are more likely to be apprehended than other types of serial offenders.

The physical security surrounding financial institutions requires more planning and calculation on the part of bank robbers than is expected from other thieves. Rational bank robbers consider a wide array of situational factors in the timing and selection of targets. These factors include (1) the number of customers or witnesses, (2) the physical presence and placement of security guards, (3) the location of teller booths, (4) the accessibility of exits and escape routes, and (5) the use and possession of a getaway car. Obviously, bank robbers differ widely on these factors. Some methodically scope out many potential sites and select the one with the highest expected yield and lowest risks, whereas others simply walk in with little preparation. Co-conspirators may use recently stolen cars to escape, other offenders flee on foot. After-hours bank robberies require greater sophistication to disable alarms and crack safes.

Not only are bank robberies a higher profile crime than other robberies, but they also are relatively unique in terms of offender and victim characteristics. Analysis of police data in Las Vegas indicates that bank robbers are older and more likely to be white than other types of robbers. One-half of the bank robbers in this jurisdiction are white compared to less than one-fifth of the street muggers, and the average bank robber is 28 years old whereas the average street mugger is under 24. Only about one out of every 20 bank robbers are under 19 years old, whereas nearly one-fourth of street muggers fall into this age group. Victims are injured in less than one-fifth of the bank robberies but in more than half of street muggings. Given the overrepresentation of women as bank tellers, it shouldn't be surprising to find that the clear majority of the individual victims of bank robbery are women. For other types of robbery, the vast majority of victims are male.

Professional robbers are most likely to target banks and financial and commercial establishments. According to Conklin (1972), professional robbers carefully plan their offenses, recruit others to perform assigned roles, and typically commit four or five robberies per year. Professional robbers are usually male, white, in their mid-twenties, and from middle- or working-class backgrounds.

Convenience Store Robbers

The growth of mini-markets and one-stop convenience stores has created new opportunities for robbery. Several structure features of convenience stores and their physical location and design also increase their attractiveness as crime targets. First, convenience stores are strategically located on major transportation arteries, making them visible and accessible to large numbers of potential offenders. This physical location also provides a quick exit into the urban jungle upon crime completion. Second, the physical design of most convenience stores enhances their appeal for victimization. These physical features include small size (so that offenders can quickly enter, scope out, and exit the entire complex with little effort), a limited number of employees to thwart an attack (usually only one or two), and a well-defined location behind the counter where money is stored. Third, most convenience stores in urban settings stay open 24 hours a day. The absence of other customers during late evening and early morning hours makes them especially vulnerable to attack. Although convenience stores have taken several steps to decrease their risks of victimization (for example, by adding staff and video-surveillance, moving the counters and cash register farther inside the store, and posting signs indicating the small amount of on-hand cash), the physical location and design of convenience stores still make them prime targets for economically motivated robberies.

The sociodemographic profile of convenience store robbers and victims exhibits similarities and differences with other robbery situations. Based on Las Vegas data, nearly all (more than 90 percent) of convenience store robbers are male and strangers to their victims, a slightly higher proportion than that for other robbery types. The average age of the offender (25 years old) and the rate of gun use (56 percent) in convenience store holdups are similar to other robberies, but the victims in convenience store robberies are generally less likely to be injured during the attack than other victims. The victims are alone in over three-fourths of the convenience store robberies, a higher proportion than in any other type of robbery except for carjackings. Typical robberies of convenience stores involve multiple offenders, often one inside the store and another driving a getaway car.

The *modus operandi* and situational dynamics in robberies of convenience stores are wide and varied. MacDonald (1975:84-85) describes some of the variation in these robbery approaches:

> . . . The offender, who has his car parked nearby, waits until any customers have left, then comes to the counter with some items from the shelves. When the employee opens the cash register to complete the sale, the robber pulls a gun and demands the money. . . .

> . . . The robber may not bother to wait until all customers have left the store; he may demand that the safe be unlocked; he may tell the employee to lie on the floor and remain there for five minutes or force the employee into the back room or cooler, shoot the employee, or kidnap him and kill him later. . . .

> . . . If customers enter the store during the robbery, the self-possessed stickup man will hide his gun from view and tell the employee to act naturally. . . . After the customers have been served, the stickup is resumed. . . .

Street Muggings

Street muggers most typically fit our image of predators, lurking in the background and lying in wait for unsuspecting targets. Like other robbers, muggers are often viewed as the ultimate rational calculators, weighing the relative pros and cons of selecting one victim over another.

Muggers vary widely in their method of contact with their victims. Some muggers casually approach their targets, asking for directions, spare change, or a cigarette light before they accost them. Others are more abrupt, grabbing victims while passing by or jumping out of structures and pouncing on them. Some muggers may stick a gun or other object in their victims' backs, order the targets to drop their wallets or purses, and keep walking. Other robbers may punch, kick, or pistol-whip their victims even without resistance (MacDonald 1975).

The *modus operandi* of street muggers seems to depend on the number of perpetrators. Multiple offenders may more easily intimidate their victims into submission by brute force, whereas lone muggers may have to exert greater social skills in getting close enough to the victims to commit their crime. Multiple offenders may also divide their labor. For example, one robber may take a victim down an alley to steal the watch, wallet, or money roll while the partner keeps watch at the corner of the alley and the street. The following strategy used by several muggers in Las Vegas further illustrates the diversity of approaches for crime commission (Las Vegas Police Reports, 1994):

> ... Two males drive slowly through parking lots in shopping centers. Female victims carrying groceries are approached from behind, the car passenger grabs the victim's arm and rips off her purse. Victims are slammed up against the moving car and the offenders quickly drive off. ...

The sociodemographic profile of muggers differs in substantial ways from other types of robbers. Compared to other robbers, street muggers are younger, have the highest concentration of minority offenders, and victimize a greater proportion of persons under 18 years old and the fewest victims over 65 years old. Muggers are least likely to use guns in the commission of a crime, but they are the most likely robbery group to physically assault their victims.

The financial motive for street mugging is often mentioned, but it is only one of many personal desires fulfilled by the crime. Some muggers report a high level of excitement while attacking their victims, some juveniles may perceive mugging as a status-enhancing tool in their peer groups. The small number of muggings reported between known parties often involve bad drug deals or disputes over personal debts.

Home Invasion Robbery

Home invasion robberies differ from other robbery situations in their place of occurrence and the higher proportion of victims and offenders who are known to each other. The majority of home invasion robberies are committed by strangers, but a substantial proportion involve ex-lovers, roommates, and co-offenders in other criminal activity. Home invasion robberies involve either deliberate thefts by force against victims or botched residential burglaries in which victims unexpectedly return. Home invasion robberies account for about 11 percent of all robberies known to the police (UCR 1995).

Although infrequent, some robbers specialize in the armed hold-up of home owners in wealthy neighborhoods (MacDonald 1975). Employees, so-called friends of the family, and even relatives of victims may provide these offenders specific details about valuable items in the homes, the physical layout of the dwellings, alarm systems, and information about the residents' routine activities and behavior patterns.

According to MacDonald, robberies in wealthy neighborhoods usually take place at night or in the early hours of the morning. Typical scenarios involve two or more men breaking into a home and blindfolding, gagging, and binding the victims. Professional home robbers often use masks and costumes to conceal their identities. Home invasion robberies in less affluent areas involve a variety of motives, including drug "rip-offs" and sexual assault. Here are some examples of these robberies provided by MacDonald (1975:92-97):

> ... A wealthy middle-aged couple are (sic) robbed at gunpoint by two masked men who inactivated a burglar alarm and then entered through the window. They escaped with jewelry and other property valued at $85,476. ...

. . . Late one night an elderly man answered a knock on the door of his apartment. The person at the door said "I'm the plumber and I came up to check your apartment for a leak due to water in the apartment below you." Both men checked the bathroom and the kitchen for leaks. When the apartment owner stooped down to look for a leak beneath the kitchen sink, the "plumber" choked him, warned him not to make a sound, handcuffed him, then placed a tape over his mouth after gagging him with a dishtowel. The man obtained a revolver but not the victim's coin collection which had been placed in a bank safety-deposit box. . . .

. . . One hundred boxing fans were invited to attend a party in a house following a heavyweight boxing fight between Muhammad Ali and Jerry Quarry. They received engraved invitation cards. When they arrived, the fans were stripped of money, jewelry, and clothing by masked bandits who obtained an estimated $200,000. . . .

Nothing about the offenders' sociodemographic characteristics clearly distinguishes home invasion robberies from other robbery situations. Similar to other robbers, these offenders, based on data from Las Vegas, are disproportionately male, nonwhite, and have an average age of 25. About one-half use a gun and a similar proportion hit the victim during the attack.

Carjacking

The newest form of robbery is carjacking, the commission of a robbery during the abduction and takeover of a motor vehicle. Carjackings take various forms. Victims may be told to vacate the car at gunpoint, or be kept in the car and later dumped. Some offenders run up to cars at stop signs and force the victims to give up their wallets, purses, or other possessions within the vehicle. In other situations, victims are forced off the road by other vehicles. Sometimes persons in private cars are held up while on a lover's lane, during an illicit drug or sexual transaction, or after giving rides to offenders posing as hitchhikers. In addition to those involving private automobiles, a number of other thefts of and from motor vehicles, including taxicabs, buses, large vans and tractor-trailer trucks, and armored cars, fall under the general category of carjacking. National data from victimization surveys estimate that an average of 35,000 carjackings occurred annually in the U.S. from 1987 to 1992 (Rand 1994).

Although some carjackings are conducted as part of organized fencing operations of stolen vehicles, typical carjackers lack this sophisticated network. Instead, like other robbers, carjackers attempt to get quick sums of money, credit cards, and easily liquidated property. Most stolen cars are simply used for transportation and escape.

The major exceptions to this pattern of minimal sophistication are thefts of tractor-trailer trucks and armored cars. Robberies involving these vehicles usually involve careful planning by groups of experienced professional criminals. Insiders are often used to better establish routines and routes. Members of criminal gangs may disguise themselves as a highway repair crew, set up road barriers, and actually tear up roadways with jackhammers (MacDonald 1975). Police and armored guard uniforms are also common disguises in these crimes. Such offenses often reap large financial rewards. Over a 15-month period in Boston, for example, six armored cars were looted for more than $1.5 million (MacDonald 1975). Nearly $2 million was stolen in an armored car heist in Las Vegas orchestrated by the driver and his girlfriend.

While the *modus operandi* and target selection processes are different, carjackers are similar to other robbers in their socio-demographic characteristics. These offenders are disproportionately male (87 percent), minority group members (55 percent), and the vast majority of them are under 30 years old (Rand 1994). A firearm is used in nearly 60 percent of the completed carjackings, two-thirds of these crimes occur at nighttime, and the victims and offenders are strangers in about 9 out of every 10 incidents (Rand 1994). Victims suffer some injury in nearly one-fourth of the carjackings. The rates of victim injury, stranger assaults, and nighttime offending in carjacking are all slightly higher than those in other robbery situations.

Robbery Prevention and Intervention Strategies

Three general approaches have been used to attempt to control personal and institutional robbery: the criminal justice response, social welfare and personal betterment programs, and opportunity-reduction approaches.

The Criminal Justice Response

The effectiveness of the criminal justice system in curbing personal and institutional robbery rests on the certainty and severity of criminal sanctions. There are several aspects of robbery that both increase and decrease the effectiveness of the criminal justice system in punishing this crime.

Reporting rates for personal robbery are higher than for any other crime (except motor-vehicle theft), involving about two-thirds of the completed robberies (Perkins and Klaus 1996). Nearly 9 out of every 10 carjackings are reported (Rand 1994). Institutional robberies also have a high reporting rate because of the physical threat posed to multiple victims and the loss of property.

Although a large proportion of robberies are known to the police, only about one-fourth of them are cleared by the arrest of a suspect (UCR 1995). This low clearance rate is surprising given that video surveillance equipment in financial and commercial establishments often provides a physical description of the perpetrator, and robbery is a high-impact crime, resulting in more extensive police investigation and attention than most other offenses. These factors, however, are offset by the fact that the majority of robberies are street muggings involving persons unknown to the victims. Under these conditions, the lack of visible recognition of the perpetrators by victims in robberies hampers the effectiveness of law enforcement in apprehending suspects.

Data on felony court processing reveal several trends about the severity of punishment for robbery. First, about two-thirds of robbery defendants in the 75 largest U.S. counties in 1992 were convicted, and felony convictions were about seven times more common than misdemeanor convictions (see Langan and Graziadei 1995). Felony convictions are only about four times more likely than misdemeanor convictions for other felony defendants. Second, among those convicted in state courts, almost 9 out of 10 robbers receive a jail or prison sentence (Langan and Graziadei 1995). The average maximum length of prison sentence for convicted robbers was slightly less than 10 years. Considering "good time" and other release policies, the estimated time served in prison for robbery in 1992 was 4.5 years. Rates of imprisonment and the length of confinement for robbers are generally higher than for any other crimes except murder and rape.

Because most robberies have some elements of calculation and planning (no matter how superficial), the potential for threat of legal sanction to deter these offenses remains high. In fact, interviews with offenders suggest that the threat of getting caught and imprisoned plays a major role in their desistance from robbery. For example, when asked why they were giving up robbery, offenders interviewed by Gabor et al. (1987:72-73) gave the following reasons:

> . . . it [robbery] doesn't interest me; it doesn't pay. It's not worth the time you serve if you get caught. The sentences are too heavy. . . .

> . . . bank robbery doesn't pay. When you have a record, if you're caught for the same thing, it's clear that the sentence will be longer. . . .

> . . . one knows that if one is caught, he will spend the rest of his days in prison because he has already been in the penitentiary. . . .

> . . . the fear of doing time increases as I age; I see things differently. If I do more prison terms, I risk leaving at 30, 40 years [of age] or more. It doesn't interest me. . . .

Although it does not lead to law-abiding behavior, the threat of legal sanction may nonetheless persuade some robbers to reorient their criminal careers to less serious property offenses. Fraud and drug dealing are often mentioned as alternative choices for the following reasons (Gabor et al. 1987:74):

> . . . the fraud artist has fewer problems than anyone. You don't hurt anyone, physically or psychologically. Occasionally they make large sums of money and they don't get long sentences. There are no arms, no threats, no violence. . . .

> . . . fraud, if someone is capable of doing it, the sentences are lighter; it isn't considered dangerous. . . .

> . . . dope today is maybe the most profitable and the sentences are much lighter. . . .

Through repeat-offender laws and units within police departments, chronic robbery offenders have been increasingly targeted by law enforcement efforts. Chronic robbers are often covered under "Three Strikes and You're Out" legislation, and special repeat-offender programs (ROP) are used to identify and rigorously monitor chronic predators in the community. Major reductions in robberies may be possible in some jurisdictions by developing these methods for identifying and tracking robbers with extensive criminal careers.

Social Welfare and Personal Betterment Programs

According to social-structural theories of crime causation like anomie (Merton 1938) and differential opportunity (Cloward and Ohlin 1960), robbery is considered a viable illegitimate route to success for those denied legitimate means to obtain money. The fact that typical robbers are socially and economically disadvantaged persons whose crimes are often motivated by financial gain suggests that these theories have some merit. From this perspective, effective reduction in robberies will occur when legitimate opportunities are provided for those who currently do not have access to legitimate means.

Social programs aimed at improving potential robbers' economic opportunities are a logical step in the development of reform policies. Job training and educational enhancement, especially among the urban minority poor, would increase the legitimate opportunities for these groups. Some robbers state that they would prefer to live "normal" lives with conventional jobs (Gabor et al. 1987). However, if potential offenders do not have access to rewarding and stimulating legitimate opportunities, they are unlikely to resist criminal temptation.

A focus on the economic motivations of robbery, however, neglects the wide variety of other motivations for offending. These include status enhancement, cheap thrills, revenge, and the recovery of personal property. For these motives, programs that emphasize prosocial behavior and alternative dispute resolution strategies may provide a more constructive way for offenders to handle their problems.

Opportunity-Reduction Strategies

The primary method of controlling robbery involves various types of opportunity-reduction activities, such as increased security measures, enhanced surveillance, and increased public awareness.

One of the most common strategies to combat robbery is to increase security and surveillance measures. Alarms may take various forms. Most banks, for example, have security alarms that can be activated at each teller's window while a robbery is in progress. Removal of "bait" money from a cash register or cash drawer automatically triggers one type of business alarm (MacDonald 1975). Many homes and commercial establishments have motion detectors that activate silent alarms, whereas some taxicab companies have a switch to turn off particular lights as a warning to police cars of a robbery in progress. As another protective action, metal detectors have dramatically increased security at airports, courthouses, and other public settings. Although security alarms are often used to thwart a crime in progress, metal detectors reduce the physical opportunity for a robbery to be initiated in the first place. The dramatic decrease in airplane hijackings over the last decade is attributable in large part to the success of metal detectors and other security measures.

Video surveillance equipment provides a visual message to potential offenders about the risks of detection and identification. Such equipment may be sufficient to thwart the motivations of typical opportunistic robbers. In fact, one study (Poyner 1988) found that the installation of videocameras on public transit buses reduced crime on those vehicles. These effects were observed even when the cameras were not operative. The presence of video monitoring equipment in banks and convenience stores may also diminish criminal opportunities. For those offenders not deterred by the mere presence of surveillance equipment, this equipment enhances the opportunity for law enforcement personnel to apprehend and convict suspects.

Institutions and individuals have also employed a variety of other strategies to increase the protection of valuables, increase the risks of detection, or decrease the yield from criminal activity. For example, transportation companies hauling valuable loads such as perfumes, cigarettes, and liquor have installed tamper-proof electronic equipment which immobilizes a truck if it deviates from a predetermined route (MacDonald 1975). A robbery "bait" pack, containing tear gas and a red dye inside a banded package of one dollar bills, explodes and taints the money supply, provides a smoke trail for police, and temporarily incapacitates the offender. Time-delayed safes limit the accessibility of money and valuables in commercial establishments, and door signs tell potential robbers that little money (usually less than $50) is on the premises. Firearms may be used to ward off robbery attacks, or food store chains and other commercial businesses may offer substantial rewards for information leading to the arrest and conviction of robbers. Redesigning the physical layout of buildings to improve lighting and remove unsafe locations within them is another common tactic to reduce the opportunity for robbery. These situational crime prevention measures are widely praised for their potential crime-reduction benefits (Miethe 1991; Clarke 1983).

Public-awareness programs are also designed to reduce the physical opportunities for institutional and personal robberies. These programs or strategies have taken various forms. MacDonald (1975:408-411) identifies some basic actions and telling signs that individuals and institutions can use to reduce robbery opportunities and facilitate early detection:

- Store owners should keep their store windows as uncluttered as possible so that police officers driving by can see inside the store.

- Check the identification, arrest records, and backgrounds of new employees.

- Home owners should have entrance lights and a strong front door with a peephole. Large shrubs should not be located near the door.

- Call utility and telephone companies to confirm the identity of employees when they make surprise visits.

- Never advertise possession of large sums of money nor discuss payroll or other money matters in public places.

- Keep as little money as possible in cash registers.

- Make bank deposits in daylight whenever possible. Vary the time and route of trips to the bank.

- Tell all your employees to carefully observe persons loitering in the building.

- Be on guard when two men enter a store together then immediately split up.

- People with credit cards usually carry them in a billfold or purse. The customer who quickly pulls a card from a shirt pocket may be a criminal.

- Cars parked near the rear entrance of a fast-food service outlet rather than in the lighted front parking lot may be there for a nefarious purpose.

By increasing public awareness of these subtle cues and strategies, it is believed that the opportunities for robbery victimization will be decreased. Unfortunately, given sufficient motivation for crime commission, a desperate robber can often capitalize on the wide variety of robbery opportunities that are still available in modern societies.

Summary

Personal and institutional robberies are different from most criminal acts in that they have elements of both violent crime and property crime. Although the most common robberies involve street muggings, robbery targets also include convenience stores, banks and commercial establishments, residences, and automobiles. Similar to other violent crimes, robbery rates have vacillated over time but exhibit a general upward trend, and tend to be higher in urban areas, particular regions of the country, and during nighttime hours. Robbery offenders are disproportionately male, young, and minority group members who often victimize strangers. Occasional, chronic, and professional robbers vary greatly in terms of their *modus operandi* and target-selection processes. Although few robbers are apprehended, the risks of detection and incarceration are often considered in offenders' decisions to desist in criminal activity or to undertake less dangerous and less serious property offenses. Public-awareness activities and increased security and surveillance measures may decrease the chances for opportunists to commit robbery. However, offenders that are sufficiently motivated to commit robbery are likely to do so even in the face of efforts to reduce criminal opportunities, to increase the risks and consequences of detection, and to decrease the expected yield from the robbery commission.

Chapter Five

Residential and Nonresidential Burglary

O ur images of typical burglars are wide and varied. On the one hand, professional burglars—like those portrayed in the recent movies *Mission Impossible* and *Sneakers*—are dashing, smooth, and sophisticated operators who steal with grace and style. These crafty thieves easily circumvent motion detectors and high-tech surveillance equipment. Alternative images involve residential burglars who often lack both grace and skill. These offenders enter homes with crowbars or by breaking windows and grab anything that is expensive and portable, without gloves, elaborate disguises, or sophisticated hardware. Entry and exit are quick. A wide assortment of offender types and behavioral patterns lie between the images of professional, commercial cat burglars and the somewhat bumbling, thug-like residential thieves.

Different types of burglars are described in this chapter. Like other crimes, burglaries vary greatly in their frequency, characteristics of offenders and victims, situational elements and circumstances, target-selection strategies, and methods of crime prevention.

Definitions of Crime Types

Burglary is the unlawful entry of a structure to commit a felony or theft (UCR 1995). The entry into the structure or dwelling does not have to involve force. Walking through the open front door of a residence to commit a theft, for example, is a burglary under this legal definition. Police reports classify burglaries according to their location and time of day, resulting in four distinct burglary classifications: (a) residential daytime, (b) residential nighttime, (c) nonresidential daytime, and (d) nonresidential nighttime. Because of the higher risk of contact with a person, nighttime residential burglary is often considered a more serious offense than daytime residential burglary. The greater potential of physical harm to workers and customers contributes to the greater perceived seriousness of nonresidential burglaries committed in the day than those at night.

Burglary differs from trespassing because it requires criminal intent beyond just breaking and entering. Unfortunately, this determination of criminal intent beyond trespass is highly subjective. If someone walks through an open front door and is confronted by the homeowner, for example, is he/she guilty of attempted burglary or criminal trespass? Would that assessment change if the suspect claimed that he/she had car trouble and entered the house just to use the telephone? Depending on the officer, this behavior may be classified as either criminal trespass, attempted burglary, or no crime at all. Official estimates of the number of burglaries under these conditions are highly unreliable.

Another problem with official estimates of burglary involves the UCR counting rule that only the most serious crime in a criminal event is recorded. In any residential or commercial robberies, for example, only the robberies are counted in official data even though the perpetrators have also committed burglaries by the unlawful entry of the structures. Unfortunately, some agencies may count the robbery and the burglary as separate crimes, whereas others follow the UCR counting rule. Although the uniform application of the "one crime per criminal event" rule by all reporting agencies decreases the national estimates of burglary, the selective use of this rule by different jurisdictions distorts these national trends.

Trends over Time and Social Correlates

Burglary rates over the last 35 years have increased and decreased (see Figure 5.1). Starting in 1960, burglary rates rose dramatically until 1980 and have generally decreased since. The national rate of 988 burglaries per 100,000 population in 1995 is the lowest rate since 1969 (UCR 1995,1969).

National victimization data estimate that 5.5 million household burglaries occurred in 1994 (Perkins and Klaus 1996). The propor-

Figure 5.1
Burglary Rates in the U.S. over Time

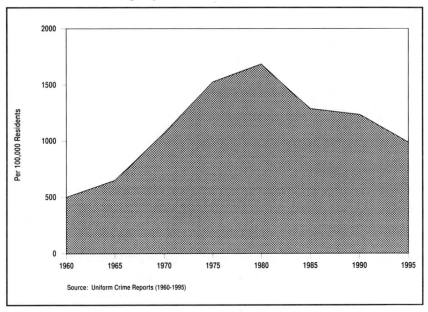

Source: Uniform Crime Reports (1960-1995)

tion of American households experiencing burglaries each year has continued to decrease over the last two decades. An estimated 5 percent of U.S. households were burglarized in 1994 (Perkins and Klaus 1996).

Changes in burglary rates over time have not been uniform across different burglary situations. Daytime residential burglaries have actually increased since the 1960s. Only about 16 percent of all burglaries in 1961 involved daytime thefts from residences, compared to about 40 percent of burglaries in 1995 (UCR 1961, 1995). The proportion of all burglaries that occurred at nighttime has decreased from nearly two-thirds in 1970 to less than half in 1995.

As with other crimes, burglary rates differ by region of the country, population size, sociodemographic characteristics of the geographical areas, and across countries. Burglary rates in Southern and Western states are substantially higher than those in Midwestern and Northeastern states. Burglary rates in large metropolitan areas are nearly twice as high as those in rural counties. Cities and geographical areas within them that have higher levels of ethnic diversity and residential mobility also have the highest rates of burglary (Miethe and Meier 1994). These differences in burglary rates across cities are commonly attributed to the adverse impact of mobility and diversity on the establishment and maintenance of community-based supervision and control of teenagers and young adults.

Internationally, the burglary rate in the U.S. is higher than most countries, though lower than that of some nations. Based on Interpol data for 1983 and 1984 (Kalish 1988), the following select countries have a higher burglary rate per 100,000 inhabitants than the United States: Netherlands, New Zealand, Denmark, Scotland, Australia, Sweden, England and Wales, Germany, and Canada.

Offender Profile

Compared to their distribution in the U.S. population, arrested burglars are disproportionately male, African American, and young (see Figure 5.2). Unfortunately, whether most burglars exhibit these characteristics is largely unknown because about one-half of burglaries are not reported to the police and fewer than 15 percent of those known to the police result in an arrest (Perkins and Klaus 1996; UCR 1995). If reporting and arrest decisions vary by offenders' sociodemographic profiles, inferences about the characteristics of burglars should be viewed with caution.

Based on police data, males are far more likely to be arrested for burglary than females and these gender differences have remained

Figure 5.2
The Offender Profile in Burglary

✓ Male (89%)

✓ White (76%)

✓ Young, < 25 (64%)

✓ Prior Arrest Record (75%)

✓ Prior Felony Arrest Record (64%)

✓ Little Offense Specialization

✓ Little Escalation in Seriousness

✓ Both Planned and Opportunistic Offenders

Source: Bennett and Wright (1984); Chaiken and Chaiken (1982); Smith (1993); Uniform Crime Reports (1995)

stable over time. About 95 percent of those arrested for burglary in 1970 were male, compared to 89 percent in 1995. African Americans are overrepresented by a factor of two in arrests for burglary and account for about 24 percent of those arrested for this crime in 1995 (UCR 1995). About one-third of burglary suspects known to the police are under 18 years old; almost two-thirds of them are under 25 years old. Trends in age differences in burglary arrests over time, however, are quite different than the pattern for violent crime. Specifically, the proportion of violent crimes involving persons under 18 years old has increased appreciably over time, whereas an increasingly smaller proportion of arrested burglars are juveniles.

Court data indicate that arrested burglars often have extensive prior criminal records. Nearly two-thirds of burglary defendants have a prior felony arrest and about three out of four have a previous misdemeanor arrest (Smith 1993). Burglars are more likely than any other major category of offenders to have prior arrest records and to have extensive criminal histories (Smith 1993).

Offense Specialization and Escalation

Several studies have examined whether burglars are specialists or generalists and the nature of their criminal careers. Is there a gradual escalation from petty thefts and drug offenses to burglary? Is burglary a stepping stone toward more serious violent behavioral patterns?

Data on the criminal records from convicted burglars indicate a wide range of behavioral patterns. In a study of more than 2,000 prison and jail inmates in three states, Chaiken and Chaiken (1982) found that the most common pattern of repeat offending by convicted burglars involved little specialization in burglary or other property offenses. Instead, typical burglars are also robbers, assaulters, thieves, and drug dealers. This behavioral pattern describes general predators who have no specific allegiance to burglary or any other type of crime. The second most common pattern discovered are burglars with histories of drug dealing, but who rarely commit violent crimes. Still another pattern involves low-level burglars with backgrounds in other types of property theft, fraud, forgery, and credit card crimes (Chaiken and Chaiken 1982). Although some burglars focus exclusively on property offending, the majority of convicted burglars are generalists with varied histories of violent crime, drug dealing, and property crime in their backgrounds.

A comparison of offense patterns over time also provides only limited evidence of escalation among burglars. Some burglars have histories of property theft and drug offending, but only a small minority of those with drug histories evolve into violent predatory offenders (Chaiken and Chaiken 1982:41). The most common pattern for burglar-dealers is the commission of the same type of offense in the two previous years. Nearly 80 percent of burglars who also committed other property thefts in a two-year period either maintained this offending pattern or had not previously engaged in major forms of crime.

Although burglars exhibit wide diversity in offending patterns over their criminal careers, there is considerable evidence that some burglars specialize in a particular type of burglary situation for short time periods. In fact, nearly half of all burglars may exhibit this pattern of short-term specialization (Maguire 1982; Shover 1991; Wright and Decker 1994).

Planning and Spontaneity

Burglaries often involve both spontaneity and detailed planning. Some burglaries are crimes of opportunity that involve no planning or premeditation. Residential and commercial thefts that occur when offenders take advantage of open windows or doors, grab visible and accessible property, or steal drugs or money while at acquaintances' homes are examples of these spontaneous burglars. In contrast, professional or even semi-professional burglars, by definition, are assumed to exercise great care and calculation in the target selection and the execution of the crime. The use of electronic equipment to disable alarms and crack safes and vaults presupposes a level of sophistication and planning.

Whether most burglaries are planned or opportunistic acts, however, depends in large part on the definition of these terms. Bennett and Wright (1984: 148), for example, define burglaries as opportunistic if the crime-commission decision is precipitated by the chance discovery of a suitable target *and* the offense is committed there and then. Burglaries are planned when there is a time gap between the selection of the target and the commission of the offense. The situation becomes more complex because Bennett and Wright (1984) further define two types of planned offenses. Opportunistic-planned burglaries are those in which there is a chance discovery of an opportunity and the offense is committed sometime later, whereas search-planned burglaries involve situations in which the decisions to offend, target selection, and the criminal acts all occur at different times. Bennett and Wright (1984) conclude that the majority of burglars are one of the two types of planners and few are strictly opportunistic offenders.

Other researchers find support for the characterization of burglaries as opportunistic and spontaneous acts. Walsh (1980), for example, found that most burglars he interviewed did not know anything about the dwelling they burglarized or the people who lived there. Reppetto (1974) argued that most burglars, especially young offenders, do not necessarily set out to commit a crime, but rather act on impulse when an opportunity presents itself. Maguire (1982), however, found little evidence that burglars simply respond to opportunities. Instead, most burglars make their opportunities by searching for suitable and available targets. The search for potential crime targets, by definition, implies some level of planning or calculation, casting doubt on an exclusively opportunistic conception of burglary.

Victim Profile

Two different classes of victim characteristics are present in burglaries. One type involves the sociodemographic profile of the residents and their routine activities or lifestyles. The other type of victim characteristics includes the physical structure of the building and its surrounding areas. The frequencies of both types of victim characteristics are summarized in Figure 5.3.

The National Crime Victimization Survey provides the most comprehensive data on residential burglary victims. These data reveal that ethnic and racial minorities, the poor, urban dwellers, and renters have the highest rates of burglary victimization (Perkins and Klaus 1996). From studies of particular cities, we know that people at greater risks of burglary are those who are single, better educated, frequent movers, and currently living in a multi-unit dwelling (Miethe and Meier 1994). At-risk persons are also those who leave their homes vacant during evening hours and own expensive and portable consumer goods.

From a routine activity or lifestyle perspective, many of the high-risk sociodemographic characteristics of burglary victims are attributed to differences in lifestyles that increase their exposure to risky situations, increase their attractiveness as crime targets, and decrease the protection or guardianship of their property. Those who

Figure 5.3
The Victim Profile in Household Burglary

	Highest	Lowest	Ratio of Highest to Lowest
National 1993			
	African American	White/Other	1.4
	Latino	Non-Latino	1.3
	Family Income <$7,500	> $50,00	2.0
	Urban Resident	Suburban/Rural	1.4
	Renter	Owner	1.5
Seattle 1990			
	Live Alone	Live with others	1.1
	Single/Separated/ Divorced	Married/Widow	1.4
	Moved in Last 5 Years	No Moves	1.2
	Live in Multi- Family Unit	Live in Single- Family Unit	1.1
	Household Head, 30-59 yrs. old	> 60 yrs. old	1.6
	Some College Education	< High School Education	1.3

Target Selection Factors

✓ Property in Isolated Locations

✓ Low Surveillability of the Structure

✓ Low Signs of Occupancy

✓ High Accessibility

Source: Bennett and Wright (1984); Cromwell et al. (1991); Miethe and Meier (1994); Perkins and Klaus (1996)

live alone or are not currently married may spend more time in public settings away from their homes, thereby decreasing the personal protection or guardianship over their dwellings. Owners of expensive and portable consumer goods may inadvertently display particular trappings of wealth to potential burglars that increase their attractiveness as crime targets.

The physical characteristics of dwellings and commercial establishments that are most likely to be victimized have also been examined. Properties in isolated, remote locations within cities have the highest risks of burglary victimization. For example, houses' chances of being burglarized increase if they are adjacent to woods, parks, abandoned railroad tracks, or are located away from the street (Hakim and Buck 1991). Of the different types of commercial settings and buildings, office parks are the most likely targets, followed by retail establishments and single office buildings. Parkland, golf courses, school grounds, and industrial property are especially enticing locations for burglars because they bring unfamiliar people in the neighborhood, enabling burglars to blend in with other unfamiliar faces, and provide them a legitimate reason for being in the area (Rengert and Wasilchick 1985).

Other physical characteristics conducive to burglary have been identified in interviews with offenders. Bennett and Wright (1984), for example, found that burglars use a variety of cues in selecting their targets. The most important of these factors are "surveillability," signs of occupancy, and accessibility.

Surveillability refers to the extent to which a structure is overseen and observable by neighbors or passersby (Cromwell et al. 1991). Poor lighting, decorative walls, shrubs, blind doorways, and fences may block the public visibility of entry points into structures and offer cover for burglars. Signs of occupancy that may deter burglars include internal lighting, cars in driveways or garages, seeing residents in the homes, and noise or voices emanating from the structures. These features are important because most burglars avoid occupied structures out of fear of a possible confrontation with victims (Cromwell et al. 1991). A build-up of junk mail or newspapers is but one of many obvious visual cues that dwellings are temporarily vacant. Accessibility refers to ease of entry into structures without detection. Burglar alarms, window and door bars, security entrances, and dogs give immediate cues to potential burglars about how accessible structures are. The higher risk of burglary for residents who live on cross streets and continuous roads rather than dead ends or cul-de-sacs is often attributed to the greater accessibility of major streets (Rengert and Wasilchick 1985).

Although it makes intuitive sense that physical aspects of buildings should increase their risks of burglary, empirical research has often demonstrated mixed results. For example, some studies report that houses with extra locks on doors and windows are less likely to be burgled (Rengert and Wasilchick 1985; Scarr 1973), but other research shows that these target-hardening strategies do not necessarily decrease the chances of burglary (Bennett and Wright 1984; Miethe and Meier 1994; Reppetto 1974). If offenders are sufficiently motivated, most window and door locks can easily be removed with crowbars or screwdrivers. Dogs and alarms show no direct effectiveness in reducing crime. The following comments made by convicted burglars illustrate the diversity of opinions about the deterrent effect of these factors in reducing burglary:

. . . Police take 15 to 20 minutes to respond to an alarm. Security [private security] sometimes gets there a little faster. I'm gone before any of them get there (Cromwell et al. 1991:29).

. . . Why take a chance? There's lots of places without alarms. Maybe they're bluffing, maybe they ain't (Cromwell et al. 1991:30).

. . . Alarms only cover a certain area. You can usually get in some other way (Bennett and Wright 1984: 80).

. . . It gets the adrenalin going. The thought of being able to outwit who put the alarm there (Bennett and Wright 1984: 80).

. . . I don't mess with no dogs. If they got dogs I go someplace else (Cromwell et al. 1991: 31).

. . . Big dogs don't bark much. I talk to them through the fence or door and get them excited. Then I open the gate or the door and when they charge out, I go in and shut the door behind me. They are outside and I'm in. Little dogs yap too much. They [neighbors] look to see what they are so excited about. I don't like the little yapping dogs (Cromwell et al. 1991: 32).

. . . If you go in and a dog is there you just close the door. If they run at you, you kill it (Bennett and Wright 1984: 85).

. . . If you look after them and give them a bit of grub, they [dogs] are not going to bother you (Bennett and Wright 1984: 85).

Situational Elements and Circumstances

The circumstances surrounding burglary involve the motivations for its commission, the victim-offender relationship, and situational dynamics. Data on the prevalence of these situational elements are summarized in Figure 5.4 and described below.

The Motivation for Burglary

Like other crimes, burglary is motivated by a variety of instrumental and expressive concerns. However, the primary motivation expressed by burglars for their crime is a need for money (Rengert and Wasilchick 1985; Reppetto 1974; Scarr 1973). This financial motivation is usually based on more than subsistence needs like food, shelter, and transportation. In fact, most burglars report using their proceeds for "party pursuits" like purchasing drugs and alcohol, to support gambling habits, and to maintain a "fast, expensive life" (Cromwell et al. 1991; Shover 1991). The majority of burglars say that they would give up burglary if all their financial needs were satisfied (Reppetto 1974). The need for money is not only the primary motivation for the decision to commit particular burglaries, but is also instrumental in explaining the frequency of their offenses. The financial needs of burglars with drug habits, for example, make them especially likely to reoffend. Financial gains from burglary allow some offenders to act like "high rollers" and "big spenders." One burglar said:

> . . . It's important to keep up a front, to have money and for people to know you have money. Looking good is important. You can't get women if you don't have some bread (Cromwell et al. 1991: 21).

A smaller but notable proportion of burglars mention excitement and thrills as the motivation for their crime (Bennett and Wright 1984). This motivation is more commonly expressed by younger and less experienced burglars. Some burglars even claim that they select occupied buildings for their crime because they are more "fun" to burgle and give them the opportunity to physically abuse people. For these thrill offenders, burglary provides a level of excitement not apparently available in the mundane activities of everyday life.

Burglars identify an assortment of other motivational factors, including revenge, challenging fate, intoxication, and, among younger offenders, peer approval and status enhancement. Revenge usually takes the form of "trashing" victims' homes because the residents disrespected or snitched on the offender. Others may use burglary to challenge fate and to enable them to make things happen in their lives (Bennett and Wright 1984). As noted by several burglars, alcohol often provides the "courage" to commit the offense and minimizes their fear of its consequences (Bennett and Wright 1984: 38):

Figure 5.4
Situational Elements in Burglary

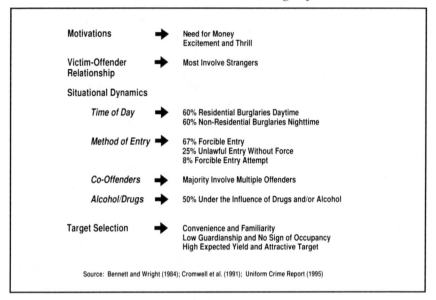

Source: Bennett and Wright (1984); Cromwell et al. (1991); Uniform Crime Report (1995)

. . . It's just because I'm drunk that I do them. It [burglary] is risky, but when you've had a few too much to drink, you don't think about the consequences. You just don't worry about it.

. . . I would be out drinking and the idea would just build up. I can't explain it really. When I've had a drink, then I'm prepared to take risks. I'm not really fit to do a burglary.

. . . It takes a fair while to get up courage to do it. Drinking gave me that extra bit of courage I needed.

The Victim-Offender Relationship

Most burglaries involve persons who are strangers to their victims. The major exceptions to this pattern are revenge burglaries and break-ins committed by drug users to steal from known drug suppliers. Victims and offenders may be related, if only indirectly, in burglaries involving "tipsters." These situations involve workers and acquaintances of potential burglary targets who disclose information to other criminals about occupancy patterns, safety precautions, and expensive goods within homes or buildings. Professional burglars often receive information about criminal opportunities through a "tip-off" but even novices may learn about potential crime targets during casual conversations or by overhearing conversations of others (Bennett and Wright 1984). Maids, gardeners, and other people in service occupations (such as repair, carpet cleaning, pizza delivery, plumbers, or carpenters) enter many homes daily and may inadvertently assist burglars by mentioning something about certain buildings or their property. Some burglars will even make special efforts to establish contact with employees in these businesses to obtain inside information (Cromwell et al. 1991). Although tipsters are used by many successful burglars (Shover 1973), the majority of burglars are strangers to their victims and do not use insiders for specific information.

Situational Dynamics

A number of situational elements define the nature of burglary and its social, spatial, and temporal distribution. Particular situational elements of burglary involve its temporal pattern, method of entry and exit, its group context, and alcohol and drug use.

Temporal Patterns. The proportion of both residential and nonresidential burglaries that occur during daytime hours has dramatically increased over the last three decades, now accounting for nearly 60 percent and 40 percent of these respective crimes (UCR 1995). If burglars want to avoid contact with personal victims, it is often necessary for them to monitor the routine activities and patterns of their potential victims. However, by committing their crimes during daytime hours, even novice burglars may anticipate that most houses will be empty.

The fear of confronting victims may explain why weekday hours between 10:00 and 11:00 a.m. and from 1:00 to 3:00 p.m. are the most active periods for burglary (Cromwell et al. 1991; Rengert and Wasilchick 1985). More advanced and professional burglars may exhibit greater versatility and strike when they are certain that their particular targets are unguarded. Nighttime burglars are more likely to know their victims and their particular schedules.

Method of Entry. Offenders' methods and skill in entering the structures they burglarize vary widely based on their particular backgrounds. Although about two-thirds of burglaries are forced entries(UCR 1995), novices shatter glass or use crowbars to break locks; more advanced burglars quickly and cleanly remove window panes or simply pop door locks and replace them after exiting the structure. The value of this skilled approach is expressed by one burglar:

> . . . I always put the pane back in and I don't disturb anything in the house. Sometimes the burglary doesn't even get reported. If I take small stuff, like jewelry, sometimes the people don't even miss it for a week or two and when they do, they think they lost it or something (Cromwell et al. 1991: 26).

Contrary to the image of cat burglars scaling buildings and skillfully entering through roofs or windows, nearly half of burglaries involve unlawful entry through the front, back, or side doors (Bopp 1986). Sliding glass patio doors are a popular way of entering residences because they can be easily and quietly popped out of their sliding tracks. Other burglars use large pliers to twist off doorknobs, recruit their own or other small children to crawl through pet doors and other small openings, climb through air conditioning ducts, or remove skylights and enter through roofs. Heroin addicts and other drug abusers often kick down a door or smash a window with little apparent concern for noise (Cromwell et al. 1991).

Co-Offending Patterns. Burglaries are often committed by sole offenders or small teams. Large-scale burglary rings involving multiple offenders are usually professional jobs. Team burglaries capitalize on task specialization and the division of labor. Specialized roles may include lookouts or "points" who watch for visitors during heists, electronics experts who crack safes and defuse alarms, and "muscle" who carry the goods and incapacitate possible victims. Although the skills necessary for committing most burglaries are rather minimal, lone burglars often operate at a disadvantage in the ability to quickly identify the location of valuables and security equipment within structures.

Aside from facilitating the practical demands of stealing, there are several additional reasons why burglaries usually involve more than one offender(Pope 1977; Shover 1991). First, co-offenders may bolster courage and feelings of invincibility. Second, face saving may require reluctant young offenders to go along with the crowd. Third, offenders in a group context may feel they have greater chances of success because others may be able to cover up their mistakes and miscalculations in the commission of the crime. Fourth, it may be reassuring for some offenders to know that, if they are arrested, they will not have to endure punishment alone (Shover 1991). Under these conditions, it is not surprising that co-offending is often the preferred mode of crime commission, especially for young and novice burglars.

Alcohol and Drug Use. Alcohol and drug use play a major role in the commission of crime, and burglary is no exception. As liquid courage that reduces inhibitions and impairs judgment, alcohol and drug use often precipitates burglary events. About 10 percent of burglars report that alcohol was a direct cause of their offending (Bennett and Wright 1984), whereas other studies indicate that as many as 50 percent of burglars were under the influence of alcohol or drugs (Bopp 1986). When the desire to obtain drugs and alcohol are also considered as criminal motivations, the proportion of burglaries that are alcohol- or drug-related increases.

Target-Selection Strategies

Whether planners or opportunists, burglars make a series of rudimentary and strategic decisions about their choice of crime targets. Many target-selection decisions are based on simple common sense, whereas others tend to defy rational weighing of potential rewards and costs (Figgie 1988). Burglars vary dramatically in how they select their targets, but common considerations include (a) convenience and familiarity, (b) occupancy and guardianship, and (c) expected yield and attractiveness.

Convenience and Familiarity. Like legitimate activity, burglary is constrained by time, effort, resources, and ability. Like ordinary workers, typical burglars want to minimize the time and effort they expend to complete the task. Efficiency is improved through repetition. When pressed by time and other demands, burglars select targets that are convenient and resort to familiar tactical strategies for crime commission. Familiar patterns may involve standard methods of entering dwellings, standard search sequences for goods within homes, specialization in particular goods, using the same fences to sell stolen property, and the selection of houses with particular structural designs.

Several features of burglary and its distribution are explained by convenience and familiarity. For example, both factors may account for why typical burglars victimize someone within their own neighborhoods or within close proximity. Convenience and familiarity may also explain why burglars often select targets along their transportation routes to work or leisure activities. Most persons on their way to work, school, shop, or visit friends repeatedly follow the same routes. Burglars, in the process of these daily routine activities, may notice particular neighborhood patterns and emerging opportunities for crime. The importance of convenience and familiarity are echoed in these comments made by burglars (Cromwell et al. 1991:45):

> ... When I was younger I used to ride my bicycle over to the skating rink. If I saw a house I liked while I was coming to the rink, I'd do it [burglarize] on the way home.

> When I'm going to work or over to a friend's house or someplace, I keep my eyes out for a good place to hit. I've been watching this one house on my way to work for a couple of weeks.

Structures that are convenient, however, may not necessarily be the most attractive targets, depending on burglars' particular life situations. For example, novice and young burglars motivated by cheap thrills and excitement may select more remote targets because convenient ones dramatically increase the chances of being identified and caught. In contrast, burglars who are drug addicts or desperate for other reasons may be willing to leave caution behind and select the most convenient targets. Purely opportunistic burglars are somewhere between these extremes; largely by definition, opportunists pick their victims out of convenience, but a host of other factors also influence their selection decisions.

Familiarity with the routine habits of particular crime targets is obviously important in successful burglaries. However, a rudimentary awareness of daily routines in the wider neighborhood, especially work and school schedules, is also crucial information. Take, for example, these comments made by burglars about how they choose particular neighborhoods (Cromwell et al. 1991:45-46):

> ... These people out here [lower middle-class neighborhood] don't have much money. You know the wives got to work and there aren't hardly any of them home during the day. I come out here about 9:00 [a.m] and have the whole neighborhood to myself.

> ... This neighborhood is full of families with kids in elementary school. I don't do this part of town in the summer. Too many kids playing around. But now [February] the best time to do crime out here is between 8:00 and 9:00 [a.m.]. All the mothers are taking the kids to school. I wait until I see the car leave. By the time she gets back, I've come and gone.

Occupancy and Guardianship. Two important deterrents for most burglars are signs of occupancy and the level of protection or guardianship over structures. Buildings that are occupied and secure are less accessible to typical burglars.

Interviews with convicted burglars reveal that signs of occupancy are a critical factor in their target-selection decisions. The vast majority of burglars say they would never purposely enter occupied residences and that their greatest fear is encountering residents upon entry or while they were still in the house (Bennett and Wright 1984; Cromwell et al. 1991). Offenders go to various and sometimes elaborate lengths to determine occupancy within dwellings. Here are some basic approaches and staging strategies burglars use to figure out whether and when a structure is unoccupied (see Bennett and Wright 1984; Cromwell et al. 1991):

- Targeting houses by following obituary and funeral announcements and burglarizing them during services.

- Faking car trouble, knocking on front doors, and breaking in if no one answers.

- Scanning mailboxes and telephone directories for names and addresses of residents, then calling them (preferably on a car phone when parked nearby) to see whether the homes are vacant.

- Picking houses with "for sale" signs posted, posing as potential buyers and slipping in back doors when external searches reveal that the owners are out.

- Casing homes for occupancy patterns by using legitimate work channels. Delivery workers, landscapers, and door-to-door salespersons are legitimate occupations that are frequently used to gather information for criminal activities.

- Reading newspapers and watching television programs that reveal out-of-town travel patterns of local college and professional athletes, entertainers, politicians, and celebrities.

- Disguised as service or repair persons, knocking on residents' front doors. If someone answers, offenders make it obvious that they have accidentally arrived at the wrong address. If no one answers, they pry open doors

and fake a conversation with non-existent persons inside
to dupe potential onlookers. They continue the charade
by walking around outside houses with clip boards and
gazing at features like power outlets, telephone cables
or antennae, or water meters. They then return to the
front door and enter the home as if invited in.

Occupancy patterns are but one form of guardianship that protect structures from illegal entry. Various types of security equipment and target-hardening activities function in a similar manner.
Private security measures include locks and metal bars on windows
and doors, exterior flood lights, property-marking stickers, guard
dogs, fences, guarded entrances, and electronic alarms and motion
detectors. Neighborhood watch programs and security patrols are
examples of collective guardianship. As mentioned previously, the
effectiveness of security measures depends on their type and the
type of burglar. Locks and bars are easily overcome by even the most
incompetent burglars, whereas security alarms and guard dogs are
often sufficient to ward off offenders.

Ironically, there are also several situations or reasons why security activities may actually increase, rather than decrease, dwellings'
risks of burglary. First, visible signs of elaborate security may give
potential offenders the impression that a "big score" must be inside.
Second, more protected structures may provide a greater challenge
for those who burgle for thrills and excitement. Third, a six- to eight-
foot high board or masonry fence is often thought to deter burglary
because it limits offenders' access to the dwelling and increases their
public visibility and subsequent risks of detection. Once successfully navigated, however, a solid fence provides immediate cover
for offenders. Some burglars even state that a privacy fence is essential in their selection of targets. The value of fences is clearly
reflected in the succinct comments of one burglar:

> . . . Once I'm inside the fence, I can slow down and take my time.
> The place is mine (Cromwell et al. 1991: 37).

Expected Yield and Target Attractiveness. From the perspective of
reasoning offenders, it is axiomatic that particular structures are
selected as burglary targets because they are perceived as attractive.
"Attractiveness" is difficult to measure precisely, but means that the
expected yield or immediate gains outweigh the immediate risks of

detection. Unfortunately, knowledge of the actual yield and risks of detection for any particular burglary situation does not necessarily predict who will be victimized because burglars often operate from the perspective of "bounded" or "limited" rationality. Under this decision-making model, offenders only consider some factors or information at their disposal, employing shortcuts or rules of thumb based on past experiences to speed up the decision process (Cornish and Clarke 1986; Cromwell et al. 1991).

Although target attractiveness is highly subjective, burglars expect to net some minimal dollar amount for each offense. A working assumption of most burglars is that every house has something worth stealing and that most dwellings in a neighborhood contain essentially the same quality and quantity of "stealable" items—televisions, VCRs, stereo equipment, and expensive jewelry (Cromwell et al. 1991).

Beyond this minimal level of expected yield per burglary, physical features of dwellings and surrounding areas provide immediate cues about the value of internal property. Even novices can predict that homes with impeccably manicured lawns will have valuables inside. Burglars describe other specific visual cues of wealth (Cromwell et al. 1991:34):

. . . I look for those satellite TV dishes. If they got one of those, they got expensive electronic stuff inside.

. . . If you see a Jeep or a RV [recreational vehicle] or a boat, you can usually find some sporting equipment. A lot of the time you find guns.

. . . If they got an old wreck parked outside, they don't have nothing. It's not worth the time. I look for a new car. Something like an Oldsmobile.

Burglary Syndromes

Burglars come in all forms and their victims' characteristics are equally diverse. However, two important dimensions are burglars' criminal careers and the level of planning involved in target selection. We treat the difference between novices and professionals as the primary dimension for distinguishing burglary syndromes, and distinguish between planners and opportunists as a secondary dimension.

Novice Burglars

Novice burglars are the most common offenders. Novices are typically young, urban, lower- to middle-class males who prey on residential and commercial buildings with very little sophistication and often with other offenders. By definition, novices are not firmly entrenched in a burglar identity or criminal subcultures; their criminal histories are varied without discernable patterns of specialization or escalation. Offending is motivated primarily by financial needs for nonsubsistence pursuits and the search for cheap thrills, excitement, and peer validation. Drug and alcohol use often precipitates the crime. Novices are easily deterred by dogs, alarms, and other types of target hardening. They select targets because they are convenient and offer little resistance. Stolen goods often include small electronic equipment, drugs and alcohol, and jewelry. Novice or low-level burglars achieve minimal monetary gains for their efforts because they victimize poor targets and lack access to more sophisticated criminal peers, tipsters, and fences capable of handling diverse and large-quantity commodities. Cromwell et al. (1991: 49-50) identifies several additional characteristics of these offenders:

> ... The novice frequently learns from older, more experienced burglars in the same neighborhood. These older burglars are often relatives, frequently older siblings. The novice is usually initially allowed to go along with the older burglar, acting as the 'lookout' for the older youth. ... A major determinant of whether the novice stays with the older group or returns to his or her own age cohort is whether he or she can locate and develop a market for the property obtained from burglaries. ...

Novice burglars can also be subclassified according to the level of planning they devote to the target-selection process. Planners may search out the urban landscape for a variety of crime targets, accepting and rejecting them depending on the presence of particular cues. Once they select a target, novices may also develop rudimentary contingency plans and do a dry run to better coordinate and orchestrate the tactical elements of crime commission. Fortunately, novices simply lack the experience necessary to skillfully plan successful thefts and to accurately gauge the relative benefits and risks associated with a particular crime target.

The typical novice burglar, however, is more often an opportunist than a detailed planner (Reppetto 1974; Walsh 1980). Burglars are considered opportunistic when they discover a suitable target by chance and commit the offense then and there. Burglaries in which there is a major time lapse between target selection and the actual burglary are not considered opportunists (Bennett and Wright 1984). Young novice offenders do not usually set out to commit a crime, but rather act on impulse when opportunities presents themselves (Reppetto 1974). Some researchers claim that most burglars make opportunities by searching for suitable and available targets (Maguire 1982). Quick entry and exit through open doors and windows are the telling marks of opportunistic burglars.

Several experiences and conditions make novices more seasoned robbers. These factors often include the development of the technical and organizational skills necessary to pull off bigger jobs and the establishment of contacts with those who market stolen goods. By mastering these skills, novices may advance to what has been variously called "middle-range," "serious," or "journeyman" burglars (Cromwell et al. 1991; Maguire 1982; Shover 1991). These "up and coming" professional burglars often actively search for criminal opportunities over a wide area and select unoccupied structures with entry points that afford obstructed views to potential witnesses. They are less easily deterred by common security measures and more likely to work alone than novice offenders. Their superior technical and perceptual skills also increase their ability to select lucrative targets. As budding professionals, however, they have not yet developed major tipster networks and a reliable cadre of fences who can handle large quantities of goods (Shover 1991).

Professional Burglars

Although the frequency and style of professional burglaries are overdramatized, few burglaries appear to be professional jobs. Increasingly, however, there have been numerous rumors and several factual accounts of professional burglars entering neighborhoods in urban areas with moving vans and burglarizing several houses at a time. These and other professional thefts are characterized by high levels of skill and finesse. By definition, burglary is a lifestyle for these offenders. The length of their criminal careers depends in a large part on how successful they are in avoiding apprehension.

Professional burglars are distinguished from novices and journeyman by the level of their technical skill, their organizational abilities, and the status accorded them (Cromwell et al. 1991). The diverse and often complex tasks involved in large-scale professional burglaries make it a social enterprise (Shover 1973). These crimes usually involve extensive planning and a well-defined division of labor among co-offenders, in the style of military commando units. The special skills required for successful offending include reliable sources of information about the habits and routines of targets, the types and locations of expensive goods, and precise arrangements for disposing of and distributing stolen merchandise. Professional burglars often live in the fast lane even though gambling, drinking, and drug use may raise suspicion and increase their risks of apprehension. Contrary to popular images of bumbling drug addicts, drug addiction does not preclude a person from being a professional burglar. In fact, many professional burglars may rely on their crimes to support a drug habit.

Burglary Prevention and Intervention Strategies

Two general approaches have been used to control residential and commercial burglary. Similar to other crimes, the primary burglary prevention approaches include criminal sanctions and opportunity-reduction strategies.

The Criminal Justice Response

The ability of the criminal justice system to deter burglary depends on swift, certain, and severe sanctions. Some aspects of burglary and its motivations increase the deterrent value of punishments, whereas other aspects of burglary decrease the potential effectiveness of criminal sanctions in controlling it.

If certainty of punishment is measured by rates of crime detection and conviction, the likelihood of apprehension and legal punishment for burglary is relatively low compared to other major forms of crime. The uncertainty of punishment for burglars is revealed by the following patterns: First, victimization surveys indicate that only about one-half of residential burglaries are reported to the police (Perkins and Klaus 1996). Second, only about one out of every eight burglaries known to the police are cleared by the arrest of a suspect (UCR 1995). Third, a felony or misdemeanor conviction occurs in about two-thirds of the burglary cases filed in the largest 75

U.S. counties (Smith 1993). When these successive rates of detection, arrest, and conviction are combined, the overall probability of being caught and formally punished for burglary is less than five out of 100.

Court data on felony court processing reveal several trends about the severity of punishment for burglars. First, among those burglary defendants convicted in the 75 largest U.S. counties in 1992, felony convictions are about six times more likely than misdemeanor convictions (Smith 1993). Felony convictions are about four times more common than misdemeanor convictions for violent offenders. Second, about 80 percent of convicted burglars are given a jail or prison sentence, and the average prison sentence is about 5 years. Incarceration rates and the length of prison sentences for burglars are lower than most violent crimes but higher than most property offenses (Langan and Graziadei 1995).

Given that most burglars exercise some degree of rational calculation and planning, legal sanctions are more likely to deter these offenders than more expressive and spontaneous property or violent criminals. In fact, interviews with burglars suggest that the threat of apprehension and imprisonment plays a major role in their desistance in criminal behavior or selection of another form of criminal activity. Convicted burglars, for example, often mention the possibility of serving longer sentences or "harder time" as a deterrent for reoffending (Cromwell et al. 1991:85-86):

> . . . I can still do six months in county or even a year in the joint, but as I get older the time gets harder to do. Didn't used to be. I could do a nickel [five years] with no sweat. Can't no more. . . .

> . . . A year ain't no time. I can do that. I don't want to take no chances on having to serve five or six or seven years. That's more than I could do. . . .

> . . . Automatically, they would send me to a maximum security unit. The possibilities would be slim, because of my label [recidivist], that I would make parole. . . .

> . . . I've been down twice before and the next one could be the 'bitch' [life imprisonment as a habitual offender]. It's not worth it anymore. . . .

For those burglars who do not plan on desisting in criminal activity, the threat of severe punishment may serve as a partial deterrent, resulting in the commission of less serious forms of property offending. Of the many types of property crime, shoplifting (called "boostering") is a common adaptation. Shoplifting is an attractive alternative for many ex-burglars for several reasons. First, shoplifted merchandise is often more valuable than stolen items because the items are new and typically have price tags attached (Cromwell et al. 1991). For maximum financial return, it is not uncommon for boosters to return stolen property to the same store for cash refunds. Second, shoplifting is rarely treated as a felony, often resulting in a fine, restitution, probation, or at most a short jail sentence even among offenders with extensive prior records. Third, many shoplifted items are easily converted into cash without the need for fences and co-offenders who may "rat" on them. Fourth, boosters may get the same psychological benefits from shoplifting that they do from burglary. Both crimes may be a means for offenders to showcase their talent and involve some thrill and excitement. Fifth, shoplifters run lower risks of physical injury or death from irate workers than do burglars who unexpectedly confront residents in their homes. For all these reasons, shoplifting is often a parallel and attractive substitute for burglars.

Opportunity-Reduction Strategies

The primary prevention methods employed against burglary have been specific target-hardening activities and the general approach of "crime prevention through environmental design" (CPTED). Rather than addressing the root causes of criminal behavior, these prevention activities are designed to reduce physical opportunities for burglary. It is explicitly assumed that significant strides in burglary prevention can be achieved by designing or redesigning physical environments and adding security measures. The wide variety of possible opportunity-reduction measures includes increasing surveillability in the design of multi-unit dwellings, adding cul-de-sacs and limiting transportation routes in housing projects, improving locks, marking property, creating neighborhood or block watch programs, hiring private security patrols, and installing alarms and electronic security systems, gated entrances, exterior lighting, and closed circuit television.

Given that as many as 70 percent of burglars in some studies are classified as opportunists (Cromwell et al. 1991) and the vast majority of these offenders are young novices, these opportunity-reduction strategies should impact burglary levels. However, the collective benefits of these security measures are minimized by several observations. First, opportunities for residential and commercial burglaries are so widespread that added security precautions in most buildings would have little impact on reducing these opportunities. Second, most target-hardening efforts are easily overcome with sufficient motivation—doors and windows are often easily broken or pried open, locks and bars can be cut, electronic alarms can be disabled in many cases by simply turning off the external power supply, and barking dogs can be silenced by doggie biscuits. Third, private and collective security measures are often taken in areas that are at low risks of victimization in the first place. Residents in low-income areas cannot afford the most effective crime prevention devices and cannot easily coordinate collective crime-control programs such as Neighborhood Watch. Finally, rather than eliminate burglary opportunities, protective measures may simply displace crime to other, more vulnerable residents (Miethe 1991). Under these combined conditions, opportunity-reduction programs are likely to have minimal returns on reducing national burglary rates.

Summary

Residential and commercial burglary is a major form of property crime in America today. More than 2 million burglaries have occurred in the U.S. each year since 1970, and between 5 percent and 10 percent of American households are touched by this crime each year. Similar to violent criminals, arrested burglars are disproportionately male, young, ethnic and racial minorities, and urban residents. Victims of residential burglaries often share the same characteristics as their offenders. Typical burglars have extensive prior records, exhibit few signs of specialization or escalation, select targets that are convenient and unoccupied, use force to break in through doors or windows, work with other co-offenders, are often deterred by alarms and dogs, are under the influence of drugs or alcohol, and engage in some planning after searching for and finding potential targets. Novice and professional burglars have different methods of operation and are distinguished by their experiences, skills, and contact with reliable fences for disposing of stolen property. The risks of getting caught and the severity of punishment for burglars are relatively low when compared to violent crimes, but burglars often mention the threat of severe criminal sanctions as a reason for desistance in criminal activity or for their participation in less serious forms of property offending. Efforts to reduce opportunities for burglary through target-hardening strategies and environmental design are commonly advocated prevention programs. These protective actions may reduce an individual resident's risks of burglary, but are unlikely to reap major collective benefits in reducing national burglary rates.

Chapter Six

Motor Vehicle Theft

Motor vehicles are stolen for various reasons. Some teens steal cars to joyride and impress their friends, others use stolen vehicles as getaway transportation for other criminal offenses, some steal cars solely for immediate transportation, and experienced car thieves hawk or "chop" them for quick cash. The level of sophistication in these crimes differs widely. Elaborate schemes involve global markets and high-tech thefts, but novice car thieves' tools of the trade are typically household items like hammers, screwdrivers, and scissors. Physical violence is a major part of carjackings, but most vehicle thefts do not involve direct confrontations between offenders and owners.

This chapter describes the variation in the type and nature of motor vehicle theft. We examine the frequency of motor vehicle thefts and changes in theft rates over time, the characteristics of offenders and victims, situational elements and circumstances, target-selection strategies, and methods of crime prevention.

Definitions of Crime Types

Motor vehicle theft involves the completed or attempted theft of a self-propelled vehicle that travels on a surface (UCR 1995). The vast majority of stolen vehicles are automobiles. Police classification of this crime excludes many types of vehicles such as motorboats, construction equipment, airplanes, and farming equipment. Thefts of materials within or on a motor vehicle—stereos, tape decks, airbags, hub caps, etc.—are officially classified as larceny rather than as motor vehicle theft. However, the theft of these items is often used

147

as evidence of an attempted motor vehicle theft. City-wide rates of auto theft vary widely depending upon how related property thefts are classified by particular jurisdictions.

UCR estimates undercount the prevalence of motor vehicle theft in several respects. First, the UCR counting rule requires that only the most serious offense in a multiple-offense situation is recorded. Carjackings, for example, are counted only as robberies even though auto theft was the primary target. Second, some state criminal codes classify all vehicle thefts as "simple" or "grand" larcenies, but other states have separate statutes for motor vehicle theft. Stolen auto parts and accessories are also variously treated as either auto thefts or larcenies. While UCR documents clearly spell out how vehicle theft should be counted, reporting agencies may not comply with these rules because they are contrary to prevailing state laws. Under these conditions, UCR data provide conservative estimates of national trends in motor vehicle theft and related types of "auto crime."

Variation in state laws and charging practices also contributes to a distorted national view of the prosecution and adjudication of motor vehicle thieves. For example, a large minority, if not majority, of arrested auto thieves are juveniles who are prosecuted in juvenile or family courts. Confidentiality restricts access to juvenile records and specific courts may vary dramatically in their disclosure of juvenile dispositions to federal reporting agencies. Another problem with court data is that many auto thefts are prosecuted as "possession of stolen property." The preference for possession charges is understandable, given that the mere occupancy of a vehicle without the owner's consent is all that is required to establish criminal liability. Under these conditions, prosecution and adjudication data on motor vehicle theft may seriously mask what happens to typical auto thieves in the criminal justice system.

Trends over Time and Social Correlates

Rates of motor vehicle theft do not exhibit a stable pattern over the last thirty years (see Figure 6.1). Starting in the 1960s, the motor vehicle theft rate steadily increased every year until 1971, remained between 425 and 510 per 100,000 until 1986, increased again from 1986 to 1991, and has decreased each year since 1991. The national rate of 561 per 100,000 in 1995 is the lowest rate since 1988 (UCR 1995).

Nearly 1.5 million motor vehicle thefts were known to the police in 1995, translating into an average theft rate of one out of every 139

Figure 6.1
Motor Vehicle Theft Rates in the U.S. over Time

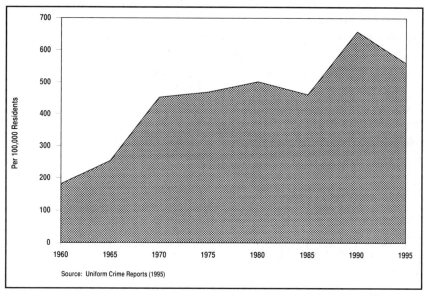

Source: Uniform Crime Reports (1995)

registered motor vehicles. Almost eight out of every 10 stolen vehicles are automobiles (UCR 1995). The annual monetary loss from auto theft is nearly $7.6 billion, for an average of $5,129 per vehicle (UCR 1995). National victimization data estimate that about 1.8 million attempted and completed motor vehicle thefts occurred in 1994 (Perkins and Klaus 1996). Over the last two decades, the proportion of American households victimized annually by auto theft ranged from 1 to 2 percent.

The type and rate of motor vehicle theft differs by region of the country, population size, and sociodemographic characteristics of the geographical area. About one out of every 100 registered motor vehicles in the Western States are stolen, followed by one per 132 vehicles in the Northeast, one per 148 in the South, and one per 190 vehicles in the Midwest. Washington, D.C., Arizona, and California, in that order, have the highest rates of motor vehicle theft. Automobiles are the stolen vehicle in over 90 percent of the thefts in the Northeast compared to less than 72 percent of those in the Western States (UCR 1995). Motor vehicle thefts in suburban counties and rural areas increased over time, but these crimes primarily occur in large metropolitan areas. Theft rates are about five times higher in large, central cities than in small cities and towns. Cities and geographical areas within them with higher levels of ethnic and racial diversity, higher population mobility, lower per capita income, higher unemployment, and higher proportions of single-parent families have the highest rates of motor vehicle theft (Miethe and Meier 1994). Internationally, the U.S. rate of motor vehicle theft is higher than most other countries. Based on Interpol data for 1987 and 1988 (Clarke and Harris 1992a), the top ten countries with the highest motor vehicle theft rates per 100,000 inhabitants are: Australia, England and Wales, Sweden, Denmark, Norway, the United States, Scotland, Northern Ireland, France, and Spain. Japan's rate of motor vehicle theft, in contrast, is more than 18 times lower than the U.S. rate.

Offender Profile

Compared to their distribution in the U.S. population, arrested motor vehicle thieves are disproportionately male, African American, and young (see Figure 6.2). Unfortunately, this profile, based on police data, represents only about 10 percent of all motor vehicle

Figure 6.2
The Offender Profile in Motor Vehicle Theft

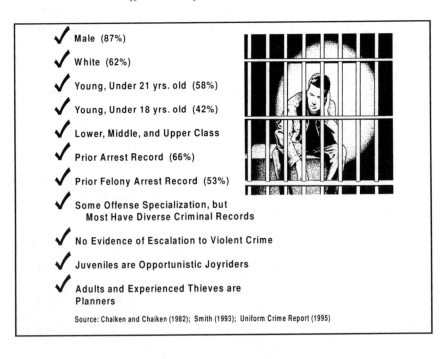

✓ Male (87%)

✓ White (62%)

✓ Young, Under 21 yrs. old (58%)

✓ Young, Under 18 yrs. old (42%)

✓ Lower, Middle, and Upper Class

✓ Prior Arrest Record (66%)

✓ Prior Felony Arrest Record (53%)

✓ Some Offense Specialization, but Most Have Diverse Criminal Records

✓ No Evidence of Escalation to Violent Crime

✓ Juveniles are Opportunistic Joyriders

✓ Adults and Experienced Thieves are Planners

Source: Chaiken and Chaiken (1982); Smith (1993); Uniform Crime Report (1995)

thieves because (1) only 80 percent of thefts are reported to the police and (2) only about 14 percent are cleared by an arrest. Given that reporting and arrest decisions vary by the offender's sociodemographic profile, inferences about the characteristics of motor vehicle thieves from arrest data should be viewed with caution.

Males are far more likely to be arrested for auto theft than females, and these gender differences have remained stable over time. About 95 percent of the arrestees for motor vehicle theft in 1970 were male and 87 percent in 1995 (UCR 1970, 1995). African Americans are overrepresented by a factor of three in arrests for motor vehicle theft, accounting for 38 percent of those arrested in 1995. Persons under 21 years old account for the majority of arrestees for motor vehicle theft, and almost half of them are under 18 years old (UCR 1995). Although motor vehicle theft peaks at age 16 (Gottfredson and Hirschi 1990), a larger percentage of motor vehicle thefts are now being committed by older offenders.

There are competing views about how individuals' social class influences the likelihood of motor vehicle theft. According to the "favored-group" perspective, white middle-class youths are thought to have high rates of car theft because of the early development of car consciousness and driving skills among suburban youth. Based on the "disadvantaged-group" perspective, lower-class minority youth are said to be the most likely offenders because they are blocked from legitimate access to success and use stolen cars as a source of transportation and status. Although some authors find that car thieves intent on joyriding are generally young, male, and middle class (Gibbons 1973), other research reveals no significant class differences in rates of auto theft by juveniles (Higgins and Albrecht (1982).

Car thieves often have extensive records of criminal activity. Nearly two-thirds of felony theft offenders (including both grand larceny and motor vehicle theft) had prior arrests and more than half of them had prior felony arrests (Smith 1993). More than 10 percent of felony theft offenders had 10 or more previous arrests. Studies of recidivism indicate that juvenile auto thieves and burglars are the most likely of any other group of offenders to be rearrested or have a second court referral (Gervais 1980; OJJDP 1988). A national study of criminal careers found that 80 percent of convicted auto thieves are rearrested within four years of their release (UCR 1970).

Offense Specialization and Escalation

Motor vehicle thieves, like other offenders, have assorted criminal histories. Some specialize and others do not. A pattern of escalation from minor status offenses to auto theft and other property offenses is evident in some criminal histories, whereas other offenders use property crimes as a stepping stone to violent crime.

Data on the criminal records of auto thieves indicate a wide range of behavioral patterns. Chaiken and Chaiken (1982) report that the most common pattern of repeat offending for auto thieves involves little specialization in this or other property offenses. Instead, the most common auto thieves are also robbers, assaulters, burglars, and drug dealers. Other researchers, however, find more support for offense specialization among auto thieves. Davis (1992) concludes that the strongest level of juvenile specialization is for auto offending, and this is also the case for chronic juvenile offenders. Blumstein et al. (1988) find that auto thieves, especially African American offenders, are among the offenders most likely to specialize. Cross-national studies provide some additional evidence of specialization in auto thefts. A study of 100 car thieves in Great Britain indicates that more than half of them report they specialized in car crimes, and nearly half confess to have stolen more than 100 cars (Nee 1993).

There is only limited evidence of escalation among motor vehicle thieves. Some car thieves have a developmental career from "status" offending—like truancy and vandalism—to auto theft (Smith, Smith, and Noma 1984), though there is no evidence that car thieves systematically become violent predators. Chronic violent offenders have extremely diverse histories of prior involvement in property, drug, and violent crimes (Chaiken and Chaiken 1982).

Planning and Spontaneity

There are two competing images of typical car thieves. Juvenile novices, on the one hand, are often portrayed as opportunists who steal cars for thrills in the presence of co-offenders. These acts are impulsive, spur-of-the-moment crimes precipitated by unlocked doors, keys left in the ignition, or other acts of carelessness by car owners. There are no elaborate searches for potential targets; rather, opportunities are presented to offenders and they take advantage of them. Alternatively, professional car thieves also may be opportunists, but they make their opportunities and exercise greater planning and sophistication in the search for attractive targets. Experienced offenders possess more elaborate equipment and skills to disengage car alarms, unlock doors, crack open ignition switches, and remove "clubs" and other crime prevention devices from steering wheels. For both novices and professionals, the mere possession of some equipment (like "slim jims," hammers, scissors, screwdrivers) is circumstantial evidence of some planning and calculation.

Although planning and calculation are important factors in the successful execution of many auto thefts, the majority are best characterized as spontaneous and opportunistic acts. The prevalence of joyriding as a criminal motivation and the fact that the peak age of auto theft is age 16 cast serious doubt on the image of the crime as a rational, calculated, planned offense (Gottfredson and Hirschi 1990). The following description supports the characterization of typical offenders as opportunists (Gottfredson and Hirschi 1990:35):

> . . . in the typical auto theft, a car left unlocked on a public street or in a public parking lot with the keys in the ignition or in plain view is entered by a 16-year-old male or group of males and is driven until it runs out of gas or until the offenders must attend to other obligations. . . .

Victim Profile

Victim characteristics in motor vehicle theft involve the sociodemographic profile of the cars' owners and the physical characteristics of the stolen property. The victim characteristics of owners are summarized in Figure 6.3.

Data from the National Crime Victimization Survey reveal that risks of auto theft are not uniform across different groups. Compared to their counterparts, those who are between 30 and 59 years old, ethnic and racial minorities, renters, and central- city residents are most at risk of auto theft (Miethe and Meier 1994; Perkins and Klaus 1996). When adjustments are made for which groups are most likely to own motor vehicles, risks of victimization are still higher for these groups, though some other differences do emerge. For example, those who are poor and/or live alone are more likely to be victims of auto theft than other persons after we take into account the low likelihood of members of these social groups' owning cars (Harlow 1988). Rates of motor-vehicle theft are also higher among residents of high-crime areas, those who spend more time away

Figure 6.3
The Victim Profile in Motor Vehicle Theft

Highest	Lowest	Size of Difference
Female Headed Household	Male Headed Household	1.0
30-59 yrs. old	> 60 yrs. old	2.5
African American	White	2.0
Latino	Non-Latino	2.0
Family Income <$7,500	> $7,500	1.9
Urban Resident	Rural Resident	4.8
Renter	Owner	1.7

Source: Bastian, 1995; Miethe and Meier, 1994; Perkins and Klaus, 1996

from their homes at night, and those who live within several blocks of commercial businesses (Miethe and Meier 1994).

Some cars are more likely to be stolen than others. Many foreign countries become attractive markets for particular types of stolen cars because these countries do not have vehicle identification (VIN) standards, markings of car parts, manufacturing and shipping records, and registration and title files to check on the status of suspected stolen vehicles (Blake 1995). Theft export rings operating in the U.S. provide particular types of luxury cars to different global markets. For example, Oldsmobiles, Mercedes-Benzes, and Jaguars are highly prized in Eastern Europe, BMWs and Cadillacs are favored in the Middle East, and Central and South American drivers prefer Ford Explorers and Nissan Pathfinders (Blake 1995).

The most commonly stolen vehicles in the U.S., as reported by the National Insurance Crime Bureau (see Blake 1995), are:

1. Honda Accord

2. Oldsmobile Cutlass Supreme

3. Ford Mustang

4. Toyota Camry

5. Oldsmobile Royale

6. Honda Civic

7. Chevrolet Camaro

8. Cadillac DeVille

9. Chevrolet Caprice

10. Toyota Corolla

Several factors account for the variations in rates of motor vehicle theft. Joyriders, for example, prefer to steal new, expensive sport cars to "look good," but they often resort to older passenger cars that have inferior anti-theft devices. The high incidence of theft of Fords made from 1969 to 1974 is attributed to their poor ignition locks which made them easier to steal (Clarke and Harris 1992a). The high theft rate per number of registered vehicles for Saturns and other cars with GMC ignition systems is explained by the same factor. New cars are typically stolen for their accessories (especially audio equipment and air bags), whereas older vehicles are stolen for the market in used body parts (Clarke and Harris 1992a).

As a way of explaining the vulnerability of particular car models to theft, Clarke and Harris (1992b) ranked new cars on three separate categories of theft: (1) stripping of parts, (2) theft for temporary use, and (3) theft for permanent retention, chopping, or resale. The researchers found major differences in each type of vehicle theft. German-made cars like Volkswagens, Saabs, and Mercedes often have the best accessories and are the most commonly stolen vehicles for stripping purposes. American-made performance vehicles like Monte Carlos, Firebirds, Camaros, and Corvettes have the highest theft rankings for temporary use. The permanent retention group, in contrast, include a mix of very expensive high-performance cars (like Mercedes and Porsches) and less-expensive foreign cars (like Nissans and Renaults). Based on comparisons across categories, Clarke and Harris (1992b) conclude that risks of auto theft tend to reflect variation in the attractiveness of cars for joyriding or for profit. From this perspective, semi-professionals and professionals steal expensive high-performance cars with expensive equipment and accessories, whereas joyriders want fast, American-made, sporty cars. These preferences reflect the needs of particular types of offenders rather than the accessibility of particular automobiles or their levels of security (Clarke and Harris 1992b).

Passenger cars account for over three-quarters of the stolen vehicles in the U.S., but their rate of theft per number of registered vehicles is actually lower than for other vehicles. According to the National Highway Traffic Safety Administration (see Clarke and Harris 1992a), light trucks have the lowest theft rate (564 per 100,00 registered light trucks), followed by passenger cars (628 per 100,000), motorcycles (1,414 per 100,000), and heavy trucks and buses (1,853 per 100,000). The high theft rate for motorcycles is probably due to their attractiveness for joyriders and low security, and large trucks and buses are especially attractive targets for more developed and sophisticated criminal organizations.

About 9 out of 10 car thefts are reported to the police, but vehicles are recovered in only about two-thirds of the cases (Harlow 1988). Nearly one-third of the recovered stolen vehicles are completely stripped at "chop shops" and another third are stripped of easy-to-sell accessories like radios, air bags, and seats (Blake 1995). Stripping was far less common in the 1970s, suggesting that car thieves have become more profit oriented over time.

Situational Elements and Circumstances

The circumstances surrounding motor vehicle theft involve motivations, victim-offender relationships, and situational dynamics. Data on the prevalence of these situational elements are summarized in Figure 6.4 and described below.

The Motivation for Motor Vehicle Theft

People steal cars for four basic reasons: (1) joyriding, (2) transportation, (3) commission of other crimes, and (4) commercial theft (Cole and Boyer 1989). These reasons encompass both expressive and instrumental motivations.

As a primarily impulsive and spontaneous act committed by teenage boys, joyriding is often characterized as an expressive act with little or no extrinsic value. However, this image of joyriding ignores its ability to fulfill the needs and values of juveniles (Miller 1958). Joyriding offers to offenders and their peers validation of their "toughness," skill, and personal autonomy. Committing a crime of any type can also bring momentary excitement and thrills in otherwise mundane lives. Under

Figure 6.4
Situational Elements in Motor Vehicle Theft

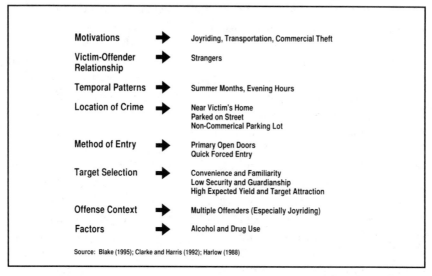

Source: Blake (1995); Clarke and Harris (1992); Harlow (1988)

these conditions, even largely expressive and spontaneous acts of joyriding have strong instrumental motivations.

The instrumental nature of car theft is clearly revealed in its other motives. The "why walk when you can drive?" mentality may be the primary motivation for opportunistic thieves who steal for short-term transportation purposes. The car thief who steals for getaway transportation or for profit is obviously motivated by instrumental goals.

Victim-Offender Relationships

The vast majority of motor vehicle thefts involve persons who are strangers to their victims. The major exceptions to this pattern are (1) "stolen" vehicles that are driven by children without parental approval (most of which are subsequently crashed), (2) vehicles that are liberated by ex-spouses or ex-lovers, and (3) juvenile groups who steal their rivals' cars. Some joyriders steal and trash the cars of people who have mistreated them, frequently their neighbors. However, thefts involving known parties are clearly the exception.

Situational Dynamics

A number of situational elements define the nature of motor vehicle theft and its social, spatial, and temporal distribution. Particular situational elements include temporal and spatial patterns, methods of entry and levels of sophistication, group contexts, and alcohol and drug use.

Temporal and Spatial Patterns. Motor vehicle thefts occur most often at night, near victims' homes, in noncommercial parking lots, or on the street. More than two-thirds of motor vehicle thefts (when the time of the crime was known) occur during evening hours. About one-third take place near the victim's home (Harlow 1988). Given the widespread use of commercial parking lots in large cities, it is somewhat surprising that less than 5 percent of all auto thefts occur in these locations. The low rate of auto theft in these locations, however, is explained by the higher security and guarded entrances often present at commercial lots. In the same vein, the low rate of car theft from garages is due to the lower visibility and accessibility of motor vehicles in these locations. Motor vehicles are more vulnerable to theft at night because (1) fewer people are around or awake at night to provide surveillance and guardianship over property and (2) higher consumption of alcohol at night may result in fewer safety precautions taken by victims and reductions in offenders' inhibitions.

Rates of motor vehicle theft are typically higher in summer months than winter months. August and July are the peak months for auto theft, and rates are lowest in February (UCR 1995). Two common explanations are provided for the high rate during summer months. First, Americans drive their cars more during the summer, increasing cars' exposure to a wide range of potential offenders. Second, hotter weather increases criminal opportunities because it is associated with increased rates of leaving doors unlocked, windows down, and convertible tops open (Blake 1995).

Method of Entry. Like burglars, most motor vehicle thieves enter structures through open entrances. Common opportunistic thefts occur when victims run into stores or residences for quick errands, leaving their car running. Locks and alarms deter most juvenile and novice car thieves, but more seasoned professional thieves can easily defeat most security systems (Clarke and Harris 1992a). Forced entries are often quick, involving shattered side windows or pried-open front doors. The common *modus operandi* for carjackers is to approach vehicles in parking lots, residential streets, service stations, or intersections and use the threat of force to take over the victims and the vehicles.

Co-Offending Patterns. Motor vehicle thefts are often committed in group contexts with multiple offenders. This is especially true of joyriding, when the desire to impress peers is a common motivation. Professional auto thieves also work in groups and take advantage of a division of labor. Similar to organized burglary teams, special-ized roles in auto theft rings include "lookouts" or "points" who search parking lots and streets for attractive targets, the "muscle" who commit the auto theft, and the "chop shops" or "fences" who quickly dispose of the vehicles and their accessories. Most of the sophisticated scams run by car thieves involve large-scale criminal organizations. More than half of carjackings are done by groups of two or more offenders (Rand 1994).

Co-offenders facilitate the completion of the practical demands of auto theft, and help satisfy several psychological needs necessary for crime commission. For example, co-offenders may bolster the confidence of novice offenders and increase their feelings of invin-cibility. The need to save face in the presence of peers may also prompt reluctant young offenders to go along with the crowd.

Alcohol and Drug Use. Alcohol and drug use play a major role in the commission of expressive acts of motor vehicle theft. Alcohol and drug use decrease inhibitions and impair judgment, leading people to do things that they would not do otherwise. A large num-ber of car thefts, theft of automobile accessories, and malicious de-struction of vehicles that occur at night are precipitated by the use of alcohol or drugs. About 60 percent of car thieves have positive drug tests (BJS 1992). Drug and alcohol use by groups of adolescent males increase the likelihood of taking another person's car on a joyride.

Target-Selection Strategies

Similar to other offenders, motor vehicle thieves make a series of rudimentary and strategic decisions about their choice of crime targets. Although joyriders and professional auto thieves vary greatly in the importance they place on these factors, common tar-get-selection considerations include (a) convenience and familiarity, (b) occupancy and guardianship, and (c) expected yield and attrac-tiveness.

Convenience and Familiarity. Some offenders seek distant and novel targets for greater anonymity and more of a challenge, but typical auto thieves rely on convenience and familiarity in the pur-suit of targets. Convenient vehicles, by definition, are readily avail-able with little or no effort. Motor vehicles parked on streets and open lots are more accessible and convenient than those parked in garages or secure commercial lots. Convenience may explain why streets and open lots are the most common locations for motor vehicle theft (Harlow 1988).

Familiarity is a major factor in the selection of particular types of crime targets and the method of crime commission. Once motor vehicle thieves experience success with a particular target-selection method, they are unlikely to change. Familiar patterns involve selecting particular types of motor vehicles, using standard entry methods, mapping the routine activities of the targets' owners, standard search and casing routines to identify potential victims, and using the same fences or chop shops to sell stolen property.

The factors of convenience and familiarity, however, are not equally important for different types of motor vehicle thieves. Novices and joyriders, for example, may be especially guided by convenience and familiarity. These offenders may select mid-priced American-made passenger cars because they have driven them before and know how to pry open locks and "hotwire" them. Nonetheless, offenders motivated by cheap thrills and excitement may select more remote targets because convenient ones dramatically increase the chances of being identified and apprehended. Auto thieves who are drug addicts and steal for quick cash returns are more willing to ignore caution and select any vehicles that are convenient. More advanced thieves and professionals, in contrast, place only secondary importance on these factors, preferring instead vehicles that have high resale value and expensive accessories. For these offenders, a wider array of situational factors determine the timing and choice of crime targets.

Occupancy and Guardianship. Two important deterrent factors for most motor vehicle thieves are signs of occupancy and the level of protection or guardianship over the vehicle. Occupied and secure vehicles are less accessible to opportunistic thieves and for most novice offenders present insurmountable obstacles. Vehicles are occupied in less than 10 percent of all motor vehicle thefts (Harlow 1988). Most stolen vehicles are unlocked and do not have added security measures.

Whether thieves select vehicles that are protected and occupied depends on the level of motivation for offending and the type of offender. Joyriders want to avoid confrontation with victims and often lack the expertise to defuse vehicle alarms. Drug addicts are motivated by similar factors, but may select occupied vehicles to increase the yield from stealing accessories and robbing drivers of their personal possessions. In contrast, carjackers prefer occupied vehicles because of the thrill of the crime and they do not have to disable security systems to steal them. Luxury autos like Mercedeses and BMWs are attractive targets for carjacking because they are difficult to steal any other way.

Expected Yield and Target Attractiveness. It makes intuitive sense that particular vehicles are selected for theft because they are perceived as attractive. Vehicles' attractiveness depends on their visibility, access, and convenience, but this term usually applies to the expected yield or return from their theft.

What makes a vehicle attractive for most financially motivated thieves is directly tied to the offenders' needs and contacts with stolen-property brokers. Some cars are stolen because the offender has the same vehicle and needs spare parts. Cars with good stereos, car seats, and air bags are attractive targets because their accessories are easily fenced at high prices. Air bags, for example, yield between $100 and $600 profit (Blake 1995). More elaborate planning and sophisticated criminal networks are needed to steal and distribute expensive luxury vehicles through theft export rings. The working assumption of most burglars that every house has something worth stealing does not appear to characterize motor vehicle thieves. Instead, vehicle thefts occur because particular targets offer some particular reward or benefit to offenders.

Motor Vehicle Theft Syndromes

Motor vehicle thefts come in various forms and can be classified in several ways. The two most basic features that distinguish types of motor vehicle thieves are the motivation for their crimes and the criminal careers of the offenders. Motive is classified as either joyriding or financial, and criminal careers are classified as either novices or professionals. However, because most joyriders are novice offenders, and professionals are motivated by financial concerns, the primary variation in vehicle thefts is reduced to differences between joyriders and financially motivated thieves.

The Joyrider

Joyriders are typically young urban males who steal cars for temporary use to impress co-offenders and peers. Peer pressure and the consumption of drugs and alcohol often provide the false courage to commit these thefts. Little sophistication or planning is involved in the selection of crime targets. Typical joyriders are unskilled in the techniques of theft and therefore must take advantage of clear opportunities. Unlocked cars with keys left in the ignition or cars left running while drivers perform quick errands elsewhere are prime situational targets for joyriders. Carjackings of occupied vehicles provide joyriders a high-risk means of compensating for their lack of technical skills.

Although it is difficult to estimate the proportion of motor vehicle thefts that are motivated by joyriding, several types of circumstantial evidence suggest that it is the most common reason for these crimes. First, auto thieves peak at age 16 and decline over the life course (Gottfredson and Hirschi 1990). Unless young juveniles are used by older professional to steal cars, it is hard to imagine that juveniles would be motivated by anything other than cheap thrills, excitement, and peer pressure or validation. Second, the majority of stolen vehicles are abandoned and recovered, suggesting that they are stolen primarily for purposes of temporary transportation. If financial gain was the primary motive for auto theft, fewer cars would be recovered and more of them stripped of all valuable accessories.

Changes in car design and security over the last three decades, however, have decreased the physical opportunities for joyriding and altered the method of crime commission. For example, front triangular windows, which were easily broken or forced open, began to disappear from new cars in the early 1960s, and manufacturers also stopped producing cars that allowed drivers to pocket their keys without locking the ignition (Tremblay, Clermont, and Cusson 1994). Steering column locks and front-hood locks were introduced in the early 1970s, and door-lock knobs were first replaced by buttons and later with latches recessed in front door panels to make unlawful entry more difficult. The number of cars with alarm systems has also increased substantially since the 1980s (Tremblay et al. 1994).

These changes in manufacturing activities have influenced the likelihood and nature of joyriding in several respects. First, these changes discourage a significant portion of joyriders because they are either in too much of a hurry to search for unprotected vehicles or uninterested in acquiring the latest knowledge on car theft technology (Tremblay et al. 1994). Second, greater protection for new cars may encourage joyriders to select older and unprotected models as their targets. American-made performance cars produced in the mid-1980s, like Chevrolet Camaros, are especially vulnerable to joyriding because they are perceived as "hot" cars by offenders and are more easily stolen than luxury cars. Third, security devices deter joyriders from stealing parked vehicles, but anti-theft equipment may inadvertently increase the likelihood of joyriders becoming carjackers. As a substitute for stealing unoccupied vehicles, carjacking provides the temporary transportation needed for joyriding, and the completion of this act may better fulfill some psychological needs for "kicks" and excitement.

Joyriding is often only a temporary phase for many auto thieves. Once the norms against stealing others' property are neutralized, these thieves may soon realize the financial benefits of their activity. This transition from a free-spirited, pleasure-seeking joyrider to a young entrepreneur requires the development of technical and organizational skills necessary to pull off bigger jobs and escape detection, and the establishment of contacts for marketing stolen goods. By mastering these skills, some novice joyriders advance to "middle-range," "serious," or "journeymen" auto thieves motivated primarily by financial gain.

Financially Motivated Vehicle Thieves

Financially motivated vehicle thieves come in a multitude of forms. Pure opportunists have no predisposition to theft, but steal unsecured cars or their contents because they translate into quick cash. Other offenders are financially motivated to steal parts to replace damaged ones in their own cars. Drug addicts convert stolen cars into instant cash to support their habits. Some car owners also engage in financial fraud by destroying their own cars or selling their accessories, reporting the items as stolen, and then collecting on insurance policies. In contrast, chronic or habitual thieves steal cars as their sole source of income. Among these offenders, some specialize in particular types of vehicles, others concentrate on stripping specific accessories. Financial motives are also evinced by offenders who steal cars as getaway transportation when committing more lucrative criminal acts. Ironically, a larger number of these car thieves are now turning to carjacking as their preferred crime. The advantages of carjacking over institutional robbery was clearly revealed by a former Los Angeles car thief (*U.S. News* 1992:42):

> . . . If you hold up a 7-Eleven, chances are you could get shot. You're on film. And the most you get is $40. . . . So with carjacking, the

risk is less and the payoff is bigger—you get the car plus whatever they have in their wallet. . . .

Regardless of the criminal careers of offenders or their degree of specialization, almost all financially motivated motor vehicle thieves require contact with criminal or legitimate organizations to convert stolen property into cash. Professional car thieves cultivate strong working relationships with organized fencing and theft rings that can move property quickly to local, national, and global markets. Less experienced thieves rely upon individual customers to sell their stolen vehicles and use local chop shops to break down vehicles into various parts. Conventional service stations, motor and body repair shops, and salvage yards are common markets for stolen parts. Cheaper parts and quicker delivery time are strong incentives for legitimate auto-repair businesses to deal with chop shops rather than manufacturers (*U.S. News* 1992). Crooked auto-body shops often recruit thieves to steal particular parts and accessories. Salvage yards and body shops across the country pay illegal suppliers about $5,000 for the front end, back clip, engine, radio, doors, and bumpers of a typical late-model car (Behar 1993).

As targets for victimization, there are several reasons why thieves prefer to steal parts and accessories rather than entire vehicles. First, car accessories and parts are worth much more sold separately than whole vehicles. Chop shops may pay up to $1,000 for a vintage vehicle, but even inexperienced thieves can pawn off basic parts like stereos, airbags, rims and wheels, and batteries for a good return. Second, novices and small-time auto thieves have a greater market for stolen parts than for stolen vehicles. It takes far greater organization and resources to develop networks for stolen vehicles than to shop around for buyers of parts. Third, it is more difficult for law enforcement personnel to determine whether auto parts are stolen than whole vehicles. Vehicle identification numbers (VIN), car registrations, and titles hamper the disposal of stolen vehicles, but parts do not have the same problem. The lack of identification numbers on most parts makes it easier for both buyers and thieves to claim ignorance when legally challenged for possession of stolen property. Under these conditions, it is not surprising that thefts from vehicles greatly exceed thefts of vehicles (Clarke and Harris 1992a), and that up to 40 percent of the stolen-car business is exclusively for parts (*U.S. News* 1992).

The fastest growth area in the U.S. auto-theft industry involves the use of professional thieves to steal and export vehicles. Experts estimate that as many as 200,000 U.S. vehicles are stolen each year and shipped overseas or driven across our borders by export rings (Blake 1995). The most common markets are Western and Eastern Europe, the Middle East, the Caribbean, and Central and South America. Foreign countries are attractive markets for stolen vehicles because many of them do not have VIN standards, component part markings, registration and title files, manufacturing and shipping records, or other documentation to check on the status of suspected stolen vehicles (Blake 1995). Liberal trade barriers, economic and social reforms, and the unavailability of luxury car models and their spare parts are some of the reasons why cars like Mercedes-Benzes, BMWs, Lincoln Town Cars, and Cadillacs are popular targets for professional export rings. Bad road conditions in many Central and South American countries create a high demand for stolen four-wheel-drive vehicles.

A number of strategies are used to steal vehicles and their accessories for financial gain. Here are some of the more common and resourceful approaches used by car thieves:

- The "Strip and Run," in which thieves steal cars, strip them for parts, then abandon them, leaving only the frames. The police eventually recover the vehicle and close the cases, leaving the thieves free to purchase frames at insurance or police auto auctions and then re-attach the parts. The end result is road-worthy cars that are no longer listed as stolen (Blake 1995:27).

- The "Salvage Switch" or "VIN Switching," in which cars that are extensively damaged, burned, stripped and deemed unworthy of repair are bought from salvage yards for their titles and VINs. Thieves then steal cars of the same make and model and switch VINs—removing the rectangular VIN plates from the salvaged cars and placing them in the stolen cars, allowing them to register the cars as rebuilt and sell them to unsuspecting purchasers (Blake 1995:27).

- The "Scissors Job" in which particular ignition locks on widely sold American-made passenger cars can be disabled and easily started by jamming a pair of scissors in them. According to police surveillance video tape, it takes car thieves using this approach only about 10 seconds to break outside windows, unlock the drivers' doors, disable the ignition locks, start the cars, and drive away.

- "Insurance Fraud," in which car owners report vehicles stolen and then hide them for 30 days—just long enough for insurance claims to be paid. Once the claim is paid, the vehicles are often "found" abandoned but in need of repair. The claimants use the insurance money to purchase better cars, and the insurance companies become the owner of the lemon car (Blake 1995: 28).

- "International Fraud," in which fraud artists buy or rent expensive vehicles, insure them to the full extent, then sell them through overseas conspirators. Owners report the cars stolen to the U.S authorities. Not only do owners collect on the insurance policies, they typically receive two or three times the vehicles' American value on the overseas market. Insurance companies are left to pick up the tab (Blake 1995:28).

- "Bump and Run" carjacking, in which thieves stage minor rear-end accidents. When unsuspecting motorists get out to inspect the damage, they are held up by one thug while the other drives off (*U.S. News* 1992:42).

- "Insurance Fraud," in which owners either contract with a middle person to steal their cars and sell the parts, abandon the vehicles on city streets in hopes it will be stolen or stripped, or simply run their cars into rivers (*U.S. News* 1992:43).

- "Valet Theft," in which offenders dressed like valet attendants open car doors for the drivers, get the keys and possibly tips, and then quickly drive away.

Motor Vehicle Theft Prevention and Intervention Strategies

The primary prevention and intervention strategies used to control motor vehicle theft include criminal sanctions and opportunity-reduction programs.

The Criminal Justice Response

The ability of the criminal justice system to deter motor vehicle theft depends on swift, certain, and severe sanctions. As true of other crimes, there is little evidence that formal legal sanctions serve as a deterrent for motor vehicle theft.

If the certainty of punishment is measured by rates of crime detection and conviction, the likelihood of getting caught and legally punished for motor vehicle theft is fairly low. Auto thefts are reported to the police more than almost any other major form of crime, but only about one in seven of these reported auto thefts are cleared by an arrest (Perkins and Klaus 1996; UCR 1995). About 18 percent of those arrested for auto theft receive a felony conviction, and a jail or prison sentence is given for 13 out of every 100 arrests for auto theft (Langan and Dawson 1993). When the successive rates of detection, arrest, conviction and imprisonment are combined, less than 1 percent of these offenders are caught and serve time for their crimes. Sting operations, in which the police set up shop as dealers in stolen autos and accessories, increase the risks of arrest, but these programs have not usually reduced the level of property crime in the community (Clarke and Harris 1992a).

Court data on felony case processing reveal several trends about the severity of punishment for auto thefts (see Langan and Graziadei 1995). A lower proportion of persons arrested for felonies involving auto theft are convicted than any other group except aggravated assault. First- or second-time car thieves rarely served any time at all. The following remarks by a police officer paint a gloomy picture for the deterrent effect of punishment on car thieves (*U.S. News* 1992:40):

> . . . A lot of times all the courts do is put them [car thieves] on probation. Word gets around. Nowadays, auto thieves don't even run. . . .

Given that most motor vehicle thieves exercise some degree of "rational" calculation and planning (no matter how elementary), the threat of legal sanction has some potential in deterring these offenders. Unfortunately, the low certainty and severity of legal punishments in actual practice undermine any potential deterrent value of legal sanctions.

Efforts to deter motor vehicle theft by increasing criminal sanctions are the basic justification for several current laws designed to reduce markets for auto theft. Recent federal legislation, for example, increases penalties for auto theft and carjacking, cracks down on auto-title fraud by linking state computer systems, mandates that some parts be marked with the VIN, and insists that repair shops certify the legitimacy of parts (*U.S. News* 1992). However, this legislation has not successfully reduced the markets for motor vehicle theft because profits far exceed the penalties for crime commission, and the laws are restricted to only particular types of vehicles and accessories.

Opportunity-Reduction Strategies

The primary method of theft prevention in the U.S. and other countries is specific target-hardening activities that decrease the physical opportunities for auto thefts. Rather than addressing the root causes of criminal behavior, these prevention activities are designed to reduce the accessibility and increase the guardianship over vehicles. This approach explicitly assumes that significant strides in the reduction of motor vehicle theft can be achieved by adding security measures to make theft more difficult and by increasing public awareness through crime-prevention education. Some basic theft-prevention tips for car owners are fundamental in decreasing the risk of victimization (see Table 6.1).

The wide variety of possible opportunity-reduction measures includes increasing surveillability in the design of streets and parking lots, improving anti-theft hardware and technology, and increasing technology for monitoring car ownership. Specific types of opportunity-reduction strategies involve the following activities and programs (see Clarke and Harris 1992a; *U.S. News* 1992):

- Sensors that set off alarms if glass is cracked or shattered.

- Motion and shock sensors that sound alarms if cars are jolted or bounced.

- Remote-triggering devices that shut off cars' electronics. After carjackings, owners can hit transmitters and stop cars dead within a block or so of the crime scenes.

- Electronic tracking systems, like "LoJack" and "Teletrac," that allow police to track stolen vehicles with electronic signals.

Table 6.1
Theft Prevention Tips

* Close your windows, lock your doors, and take the keys with you.

* Park with the front wheels turned sharply toward the curb and apply your emergency brake to discourage towing.

* Activate any anti-theft devices you may have. Better yet, install a device that is passive and automatically activates itself a short time after the key is removed.

* Put all packages and personal items out of sight. Items left in the open invite theft.

* Drive in the center lane when on highways. This reduces your chances of becoming a victim of "bump and run" theft.

* Use your garage at home; lock both your vehicle and the garage.

* Don't park on the outskirts of a shopping center, motel, or other parking lot. Park near the entrance, especially if you will be leaving your car unattended for an extended period.

Source: Blake 1995

- Fluorescent "Curfew Decals" on rear passenger windows that indicate that cars are not normally driven between 1:00 a.m. and 5:00 a.m. and authorizing the police to stop anyone driving cars during these hours to check registration.

- Toll-free hotlines funded by insurance companies that provide rewards leading to the arrest of car thieves.

Although anti-theft programs and measures reduce the opportunity for joyriding and opportunistic car thefts, there are several reasons why these crime-prevention measures may be of only lim-

ited effectiveness. First, even with greater security and public awareness, numerous physical opportunities remain. Older cars often lack
security systems, and many victims are still careless in their driving
habits. Second, most target-hardening activities are easily circum-
vented by skilled professional thieves. Even novice car thieves can
disable "the club" and other steering wheel blockers. Third, greater
vehicle security may create a more serious problem by turning
joyriders into carjackers. Displacement from newer to older cars and
changes from car theft to other forms of property offending are also
likely responses to increases in auto security (Mayhew et al. 1976).
Thus, while reducing the opportunity for theft by inexperienced
offenders, these crime-control efforts may have only a modest impact on reducing the overall level of motor vehicle theft.

Summary

Motor vehicle theft is a common occurrence in contemporary
American society. Nearly 1.5 million cars and trucks were stolen in
1995. The majority of these thefts involve automobiles that are stolen
for temporary transportation and joyriding. Typical offenders are
young urban males who steal cars with their friends for "kicks,"
excitement, and to impress peers. Many auto thieves have prior
criminal records, but there is little evidence of offense specialization
or escalation in their criminal careers. Alcohol and drug use is often
associated with joyriding. The type and model of stolen vehicles
depends on the particular needs of the offender. Youthful joyriders
prefer sporty American-made performance cars because they are
fast and "look good," whereas more skilled and professional thieves
seek out more expensive high-performance cars like Mercedes-
Benz, Porsche, BMW, or less expensive foreign cars.

Joyriding remains the most popular motive for this crime, but a
rising profit motive has changed the nature of auto theft over time.
A growing number of vehicles are now stolen and quickly delivered
to chop shops to meet the high demand for cheap auto parts and
accessories. Almost half of all cars stolen today are used exclusively
for their parts. Organized theft rings now provide vehicles and accessories to thriving national and international markets. Although
anti-theft equipment and other opportunity-reduction strategies are
widely endorsed and may reduce some physical opportunities for
joyriders, these efforts have little impact on more skilled and professional thieves. Through a process of displacement, increased vehicle security may inadvertently contribute to the rise in carjackings

and an increase in other types of property offending. Some auto thieves acknowledge the threat of legal sanctions, but the ability of the criminal justice system to deter the crime is limited because few car thieves are apprehended, and prison terms are rarely imposed in the small number of cases that do result in convictions.

Chapter Seven

Occupational and Organizational Crime

Much criminal activity occurs within legitimate occupational and organizational contexts. These crimes at work take several forms. Some offenses are called "occupational crimes" because they are carried out by individuals or groups in the normal course of their occupations. The victims of these offenses are organizations or the public at large. Employee theft, embezzlement, tax evasion, unnecessary surgery or drug prescriptions, and charity fraud are common examples of occupational crimes. "Organizational crimes," in contrast, are offenses committed by an organization as a whole or by individual members with the help, encouragement, and support of the organization. False advertising, commercial fraud, illegal mergers and acquisitions, price fixing and collusion, violations of civil liberties, and unsafe manufacturing or production activity are examples of corporate or organizational offenses. The term "white-collar" crimes is often used to describe both occupational and organizational offenses that occur in the course of otherwise respected and legitimate occupations or financial activities (Coleman 1994). Estimates of the prevalence of white-collar crime vary widely, but it is clearly the most costly economic crime in contemporary American society.

This chapter describes the variation in the type and nature of occupational and organizational crime. We examine the definitional issues surrounding white-collar crime, its frequency and how it has changed over time, offenders' and victims' characteristics, situational elements and circumstances, and methods of crime prevention.

Definitions of Crime Types

Criminologists have long recognized the prevalence of crime in work environments. For Sutherland (1940), who coined the term, a white-collar crime is any crime committed by persons of high respectability and high social status in the course of their occupations. The condition of respectability was important for Sutherland because it (1) meant that poor people are not the only ones who commit crime and (2) allowed support for his theory of "differential association" as a general theory of both lower-class and upper-class criminality (Green 1990).

Sutherland's definition of white-collar crime, however, has been criticized. Tappan (1947), for example, criticized the definition on the grounds that administrative law violations are included, rather than only criminal charges. The terms "respectability" and "social status" have also been criticized because they are relative concepts that lack concrete definitions. Other researchers (e.g., Clinard and Quinney 1973) abandon the term white-collar crime and instead distinguish between corporate and occupational crime. Horning (1970) uses the term blue-collar crime to signify employee crimes committed by persons in occupations that are not traditionally considered among the most respectable.

The concept of occupational crime is used by other researchers only to identify a general source of criminal opportunity and is restricted to nonviolent offenses (Edelhertz 1970). Green (1990), for example, defines an occupational crime as "any act punishable by law which is committed through opportunity created in the course of an occupation that is legal." Under this definition, occupational crime can be white- or blue-collar, involve self-serving offenders and corporately sponsored crime, and cover both criminal activity and administrative law violations.

An incredible number of different terms describe crimes that occur in organizational contexts. Some of these terms include economic crime, commercial crime, business crime, marketplace crime, consumer crime, respectable crime, crime at the top, suite crime, elite crime and deviance, official crime and deviance, political crime, governmental crime, state (or state-organized) crime, corporate crime, occupational crime, employee crime, avocational crime, technocrime, computer crime, and folk crime (Friedrichs 1996). The term occupational crime is often used to designate crimes committed by individuals for their own self interests, whereas organizational crime signifies those offenses committed for the benefit of an organization (Clinard and Quinney 1973).

There are various ways to classify occupational and organizational crimes. According to a typology developed by Edelhertz (1970), the following subcategories are used to classify white-collar offenses:

- *Crimes Against Government by Public Officials*: accepting bribes for political favors, travel per diem fraud.

- *Crimes Against Government by Private Citizens*: welfare fraud, social-security fraud, tax fraud, unemployment/worker's compensation fraud.

- *Crimes Against Businesses*: embezzlement, employee theft, insurance fraud, credit fraud, false financial statements for credit, computer fraud.

- *Crimes Against Investors*: selling worthless land, selling worthless stock.

- *Crimes Against Consumers*: selling worthless products, selling defective equipment, selling contaminated food, overcharging customers for home or auto repairs, overcharging via false weights and measures, false advertising, unnecessary drug prescriptions, performing unnecessary surgery, charity fraud.

- *Crimes Against Employees*: discriminatory hiring/promotion practices, violations against federal safety standards.

- *Crimes Affecting Public Health*: industrial pollution of rivers, emitting toxic materials in the air, disposing toxic waste material in the vicinity of housing projects.

A more succinct four-category classification system is used by Green (1990). His categories are: (a) crimes for the benefit of an employing organization (*organizational occupational crime*), (b) crimes by officials through the exercise of their state-based authority (*state authority occupational crime*), (c) crimes by professionals in their capacity as professionals (*professional occupational crime*), and (d) crimes by individuals as individuals (*individual occupational crime*).

Organizational occupational crimes are offenses in which employers, rather than offenders themselves, are the major beneficiaries (Green 1990). Examples of this form of white-collar crime include price fixing by managers, falsification of production tests by technicians, and theft of trade secrets by employees. Although offenders may receive organizational benefits from these activities (such as promotions and salary increases), individuals pursue and commit these crimes as employees and for the company.

The major characteristic of *state authority occupational crimes* is that offenders are legally vested with governmental powers to make or enforce laws or to command others. These offenses include acts of police misconduct (such as stealing confiscated property or illegally assaulting a suspect), bribery of political or regulatory officials in exchange for favors, abuse of military power, and falsification of documents by notary publics and auditors. *Professional occupational crimes* are also crimes associated with particular occupations, but focus more on professional oaths, trusts, and ethical commitments to do what is in the best interest of clients or patients. Examples include sexual assault of patients during examinations by physicians, unnecessary treatments and surgeries by physicians and veterinarians, illegal distribution of prescription drugs by doctors, and the use of confidential information for personal gain by lawyers (Green 1990).

Individual occupational crimes are crimes that are committed by individuals as individuals in the course of their daily work life. These crimes include personal income-tax evasion, employee theft of goods and services, false expense reports, and sales fraud against the public or organizations (Green 1990). They also include crimes committed by owners of organizations (such as major stockholders, CEOs, or law partners) because the benefits from their crimes accrue directly to them.

Although the classification schemes devised by Edelhertz and Green may be criticized for excluding other dimensions of white-collar crime, they are nonetheless useful because they help organize and simplify the enormous variability in the types of occupational and organizational crimes. Edelhertz's (1970) classification scheme places primary emphasis on the characteristics of the victim, whereas Green's (1990) typology focuses on the motivation for offending and the attributes of offenders. Both perspectives assume that these offenses occur within an otherwise legitimate organizational context and do not require that occupational crimes be restricted to persons of high respectability or high social status.

Trends Over Time and Social Correlates

With the exception of arrests for embezzlement and fraud, comprehensive UCR data on white-collar crime are not available. Official police reports often lump together corporate and occupational crimes, and federal and state agency reports divide white-collar crime statistics among criminal, civil, and administrative agencies (Friedrichs 1996; Simpson, Harris, and Mattson 1993). Lacking uniform and comprehensive data reports, researchers in white-collar crime often extract data from a wide range of sources, including government agency and annual financial reports, newspapers, and journals. Unfortunately, each data source has severe limitations as a basis for developing a statistical profile of white-collar crime. The major problem with these sources is that the vast majority of occupational and organizational crime is undetected and not reported. Even in the case of embezzlement and employee theft, companies are reluctant to take formal action because they fear the loss of public trust and confidence if it becomes known that their companies have been victimized.

The lack of reliable and uniform data limits our ability to access the level of change and stability in the amount of occupational and organizational crime over time. Over the last decade, however, self-report studies of offending behavior, victimization surveys, and agency reports have emerged to provide some data on specific forms of white-collar crime.

Police and court data provide gross estimates of the number of particular types of white-collar crime over time. The number of arrests for embezzlement, for example, has vacillated over time, ranging from 10,000 in 1970, dropping to 8,500 in 1980, and rising to 15,200 arrests in 1995 (UCR 1995, 1980, 1970). When the number of arrests for forgery, fraud, and embezzlement are combined, the arrest rate increased by 12 percent from 1981 to 1990 (Poveda 1994). Arrest rates for index crimes increased by roughly the same proportion during the same time period. The number of suspects in federal criminal cases investigated for fraudulent offenses (including embezzlement, fraud, forgery, and counterfeiting) and violations of regulatory laws increased by about 64 percent over the 1980s compared to a 74 percent increase for all federal criminal cases (Poveda 1994). These data provide some indication that, at least for particular offenses, the increase in the number of white-collar crimes is similar to trends for conventional crimes.

Of the various types of occupational crime, the most comprehensive data are available for employee theft. Employee thefts vary widely in their nature, sophistication, and acceptance within the organization. At the pettiest level, employee thefts include the use of office supplies and machinery for personal purposes, making personal phone calls on business phones, and using company cars or company time for personal business. Rather than criminal activity, employees often view these activities as "wages-in-kind" or extra compensation to a formal paycheck (Friedrichs 1996). A criminal label is more likely to be attached to these offenses when the acquisitions involve money or expensive equipment, an elaborate *modus operandi*, and high levels of complicity between employees. Forms of employee theft include *pilfering* (also called petty theft), *larceny* (the unauthorized taking of something of value), *chiseling* (cheating or swindling), *fraud* (theft through misappropriation), and *embezzlement* (the appropriation of money or merchandise which has been entrusted to one's care).

Self-report studies and business surveys indicate that employee theft is one of the most common crimes in American society. About one-third of the employees in a large-scale survey of workers in retail, manufacturing, and service industries admitted to having stolen company property in the previous year, and about two-thirds reported other forms of employee misconduct such as abusing sick-leave privileges and falsifying time sheets (Clark and Hollinger 1983). Other studies estimate that half of the U.S. workforce steals from its employers (Friedrichs 1996). The vast majority of workers in other self-report studies say they supplement their legitimate incomes in technically illegal ways such as theft from their employers (Mars 1982).

Based on rough estimates and extrapolations from diverse sources, estimated annual losses from employee theft in the U.S. may be as high as $75 billion and typically run between $5 to $10 billion (Friedrichs 1996). Employee theft inflates the price of consumer items by 10-15 percent, and is associated with business failures, lost employee benefits, defaulted loans, and intensified mistrust within business (Friedrichs 1996; Green 1990).

The economic costs of white-collar crime are even more massive when other types of occupational and organizational crimes are included. The annual cost of bribery and corruption, for example, ranges from $3 to $15 billion. However, most people agree that the major adverse consequence of this crime is the loss of public trust and confidence in institutions and the subversion of democratic government (Coleman 1995). Antitrust violations, like illegal mergers and acquisitions, price fixing and collusion, and unfair competition are often considered the most costly white-collar crimes, exceeding $350 billion per year. Crimes within professions are equally expensive. Medicare and Medicaid fraud costs the public more than $1 billion a year, and about $4 billion each year is attributed to unnecessary surgeries (Coleman 1995). The U.S. government loses about $7 billion per year from corporations' failure to report taxable income. Billions of dollars have been lost from criminal fraud in the savings and loan crisis (Friedrichs 1996). The average computer crime nets about $400,000, and estimates of total losses from computer crime range from $1 to $200 billion a year (Coleman 1994; Friedrichs 1996).

Although white-collar crimes are often treated as economic violations, the physical toll from many of these offenses is equally staggering. Estimates of death from unnecessary surgeries are placed at 12,000 per year, and corporate negligence and safety violations have been identified as the major causes in the massive chemical cloud that killed at least 5,000 people and injured 200,000 others in Bhopal, India. Air and water pollution, toxic-waste disposal, and more general violations of federal safety and health standards cost billions of dollars each year, and are often linked to physical injury to and death of workers. More than 100,000 deaths per year are attributed to unsafe products and unsafe production techniques. Deaths and injuries from dangerous gas tanks in Ford Pintos and Mercury Bobcats, defective Firestone 500 tires, the production of the arthritis drug Oraflex, and the Dalkon Shield are specific examples of white-collar crimes with physical consequences to public consumers (Coleman 1995).

Correlates of White-Collar Crime

Several organizational and economic factors have been identified as correlates of the level and type of occupational and organizational crime. Organizations that treat workers poorly and provide a hostile work environment are most prone to employee theft, business fraud (like falsification of timecards or padding business expenses), industrial sabotage, and other types of occupational crime directed at companies themselves (Clark and Hollinger 1983). Within these environments, employees may feel that criminal behavior against the company is an entitlement or fringe benefit for working in such oppressive settings. In fact, many managers view certain types of employee theft or fraud (such as taking home inexpensive company property, padding time or business expenses) as functional to the organization because they help make up for low wages and other occupational problems (Coleman 1994). The level of internal security and monitoring is another organizational correlate of white-collar crime. Because they simply provide less opportunity for crime or convey a "zero tolerance" toward illegal behavior against the company, organizations with greater internal security are expected to have lower rates of occupational crime.

One of the strongest correlates of corporate crime is the nature of the government regulations under which an industry operates. Industries whose products and manufacturing processes have high potential for physical harm to the public are both the most stringently regulated and have the most crime (Coleman 1995). Clinard and Yeager (1980) found that the pharmaceutical, automobile, and petroleum industries had the highest number of corporate violations, and each of these industries was highly regulated, manufactured dangerous products, or had environmentally hazardous production activities.

Several studies have examined the relationship between firm size and level of criminal behavior. Some researchers argue that the anonymity and impersonality of large corporations and the diffusion of responsibility in them provide environments conducive to illegal activity. In contrast, others argue that small firms are more likely to violate the law because they lack the professional expertise to monitor and manage the government regulations that control business activities (Coleman 1994). No clear relationship between firm size and criminal conduct, however, has been demonstrated in the literature. In one of the most comprehensive studies of corporate crime across a large number of industries, Clinard and Yeager (1980) found that larger firms had more total violations, but these differences disappeared after adjustments were made for the greater volume of business done by large firms.

Given the importance of the profit motive in white-collar crime, several studies have examined the relationship between economic conditions and criminal activity. The majority of studies reveal that firms with declining profitability are more likely to break the law

(Coleman 1994). Across a variety of industries and firms, declining profits and relatively poor economic performance are associated with higher levels of corporate crime. The type of violation is also linked to economic conditions. Firms in difficult economic environments commit more serious anti-trust violations, whereas firms operating in good economic conditions commit more minor violations (Simpson 1986). Other economic and firm characteristics, such as growth rate, diversification, and the economic concentration in particular industries, have been found in some studies to be related to rates of corporate crime.

Offender Profile

Profiling offenders in white-collar crime is a different task than studying those involved in other types of crime because offenders may be either individuals or organizations. Because data are limited, some sociodemographic attributes are more common among particular types of occupational criminals, and some organizational or firm characteristics are more common than others among corporate criminals (see Figures 7.1 and 7.2).

Police data are available on arrests for forgery, fraud, and embezzlement, but these offenses are usually low-level and less serious

Figure 7.1
The Profile of Corporate Offenders

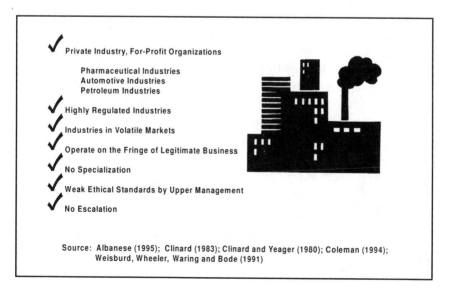

✓ Private Industry, For-Profit Organizations

    Pharmaceutical Industries
    Automotive Industries
    Petroleum Industries

✓ Highly Regulated Industries

✓ Industries in Volatile Markets

✓ Operate on the Fringe of Legitimate Business

✓ No Specialization

✓ Weak Ethical Standards by Upper Management

✓ No Escalation

Source: Albanese (1995); Clinard (1983); Clinard and Yeager (1980); Coleman (1994);
Weisburd, Wheeler, Waring and Bode (1991)

Figure 7.2
The Profile of Occupational Offenders

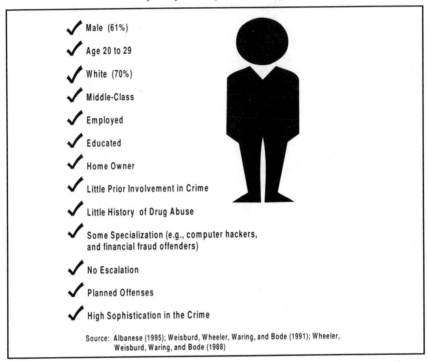

✓ Male (61%)

✓ Age 20 to 29

✓ White (70%)

✓ Middle-Class

✓ Employed

✓ Educated

✓ Home Owner

✓ Little Prior Involvement in Crime

✓ Little History of Drug Abuse

✓ Some Specialization (e.g., computer hackers, and financial fraud offenders)

✓ No Escalation

✓ Planned Offenses

✓ High Sophistication in the Crime

Source: Albanese (1995); Weisburd, Wheeler, Waring, and Bode (1991); Wheeler, Weisburd, Waring, and Bode (1988)

occupational crimes. The typical occupational offender derived from arrest data is male, white, and between 20 and 29 years old. Males comprised about two-thirds of the suspects in these white-collar crimes, and a similar proportion are white (Albanese 1995). Nearly half are in their 20s. When compared to suspects arrested for violent, property, and public-order offenses, occupational offenders are more likely to be older and female. The higher proportion of arrests for females and older persons is explained by the greater planning and access to business operations required for occupational crimes than conventional crimes (Albanese 1995). Increases in women's labor-force participation and greater access to financial opportunities and positions of trust also account for the rise in female embezzlers over time (Coleman 1995). Typical perpetrators of occupational fraud and abuse are college-educated white males (Association of Certified Fraud Examiners 1995).

Contrary to the image of rich, powerful criminals, most convicted white-collar offenders are middle-class—that is, they live significantly above the poverty line, but are not from the upper echelons of wealth and social status (Weisburd, Wheeler, Waring, and Bode 1991). When compared to other property offenders, white-collar offenders are more likely to be employed, better educated, own homes, and have less prior involvement in the criminal justice system (Wheeler, Weisburd, Waring, and Bode 1988). In a study of the characteristics of convicted white-collar offenders in federal criminal cases, persons who commit frauds are quite similar in their sociodemographic profile to offenders involved in regulatory violations (BJS 1995). However, both groups of white-collar offenders are older, more educated, and less likely to have criminal records or histories of drug abuse than other federal offenders.

Although rates of occupational offending vary by offenders' socio-demographic characteristics, the severity of wrongdoing also differs. Studies of embezzlers, for example, reveal that male offenders make far more from their white-collar crimes than do women. Male embezzlers are more likely to hold managerial jobs than female employees (who are more often tellers and clerks) and subsequently have greater access to financial resources (Daly 1989). Losses from frauds by managers and executives are 16 times greater than those caused by non-managerial employees, four times greater for male than female offenders, five times greater for suspects with post-graduate degrees than high school graduates, and 28 times greater for occupational thieves over 60 years old than those 25 or younger (Association of Certified Fraud Examiners 1995).

Another aspect of the offender profile is his or her occupational role. Offenders' occupations are important because each occupation provides its own special array of illegal opportunities (Coleman 1995). To be bribed, for example, offenders must have a particular job that offers something in return for illegal payment. Police officers who work in vice and narcotics are the most prone to police corruption because they are in constant contact with criminals willing to pay large sums of money to gain their cooperation (Knapp Commission 1972). Purchasing agents, government inspectors, and politicians are also in attractive positions for bribery opportunities. Similarly, there are clear economic advantages for commissioned salespersons and other "fee-for-service" employees to capitalize on criminal opportunities in their occupations, whereas salaried workers have less financial incentives for defrauding customers.

One major element of offenders' profiles in corporate crime is the difference between profit-seeking private organizations and nonprofit organizations. Private industry is far more frequently involved in organizational crimes such as price-fixing, consumer fraud, false advertising, stock manipulation, and deceptive sales practices because these activities are driven by profit motives (Coleman 1994). Nonprofit and government employees, in contrast, are rarely involved in these offenses because such corporate crime is not necessary for organizational survival. Among for-profit organizations, companies in the pharmaceutical, automobile, and petroleum industries often have the largest number of corporate violations (Clinard and Yeager 1980). Market volatility and the nature of government regulation explains the high rate of crime in these industries. Less solvent and more financially strapped organizations are also more prone to corporate crime.

A common image of white-collar offenders is that they are one-shot criminals who do not reoffend after their initial contact with the criminal justice system (Weisburd et al. 1993). Both the shame of getting caught and the loss of social status are viewed as inhibiting factors in the development of criminal careers for white-collar offenders. However, empirical findings challenge this assumption by showing that the criminal records of many white-collar offenders are similar to burglars, auto thieves, and other conventional property offenders. Weisburd et al. (1993), for example, report that nearly half of their sample of federal white-collar offenders are repeat offenders. One-shot offenders tend to be older and take advantage of a particular criminal opportunity. Many corporations have extensive histories of administrative and regulatory violations. The most profitable organizations and corporations are often those that operate continuously on the fringe of legitimate business practices.

Offense Specialization and Escalation

Corporations rarely specialize in a particular type of criminal activity, but instead undertake a variety of illegal and unethical practices to maintain profit margins and market position. Corporations involved in price-fixing conspiracies, for example, are also likely to be involved in other financial frauds and prohibited regulatory practices. The participation of upper management in particular types of organizational misconduct often sets the ethical tone or climate for the acceptance of other forms of corporate crime (Clinard 1983).

Contrary to corporate offending, repeat offenders of occupational crimes exhibit greater signs of specialization. Specialization is due, in part, to the fact that occupational offenders must take advantage of the particular opportunities available to them. Computer hackers, for example, use their skills to gain access to financial accounts and security systems. The choice of specific crime targets may vary over time, but computer hackers nonetheless specialize in using their computer expertise to engage in occupational crime. Likewise, telemarketers may employ a variety of scams to defraud consumers, but they tend to specialize by using "a modification of the basic theme" across financial fraud situations. For both occupational and organizational crime, there is little evidence of escalation in seriousness over criminal careers.

Planning and Spontaneity

Some white-collar crimes may be spontaneous acts precipitated solely by the availability of criminal opportunities, but the vast majority are calculated and planned. Regardless of the type of offense, white-collar offenders are often viewed as rational calculators who select particular targets and modes of offending that increase the payoffs and decrease the risks of detection.

The level of sophistication required to commit many white-collar crimes is further evidence of crime planning. Offenses such as price fixing, insider trading, collusion, stock fraud, defense- contract fraud, computer crime, telemarketing or "boiler room" scams, and pyramid schemes require a level of sophistication, expertise, and connections with co-conspirators far beyond that necessary for planning other criminal acts.

Victim Profile

White-collar crime victimization is especially diffuse across society, and victim attributes are extremely heterogenous (McShane and Williams 1992). Obvious victims are the individuals who are scammed by some financial fraud, organizations that are victimized internally by their employees, and small businesses placed at a competitive disadvantage by larger corporations' price-fixing and collusion. Government bodies, charitable organizations, and major corporations are also victims of these crimes. The ultimate victim of white-collar crime, however, is often the American public, which absorbs business losses by paying more for consumer goods and services.

The major problem with assessing victim characteristics in white-collar crime, however, is that most people are simply unaware of their victimization. Unless fully informed of the latest Occupational Safety and Health Administration (OSHA) standards, most employees do not know whether they are victimized by hazardous and illegal conditions in their work environment. Residents may only discover toxic dumping and hazardous materials in their neighborhood years later. Prohibited personnel practices such as discriminatory hiring or promotion standards are common in many organizations without employees' specific knowledge. Similarly, customers, clients, and patients may be totally oblivious to the fraudulent and unethical practices of their service providers. Retailers are often unaware that their inventory shrinkage is due to employee theft rather than to shoplifting (Green 1990). The complex nature of many white-collar crimes also makes business competitors, business partners, shareholders, large corporations, and government entities equally unaware of their victimization. Under these conditions, the use of victim-based surveys to measure white collar-crime is likely to severely underestimate the magnitude of the crime problem.

Most research on the characteristics of the victims of white-collar crime focuses on consumer fraud and other financial violations (see Figure 7.3). Ennis (1967) found that rates of consumer fraud are nearly twice as high in Western States than in other regions of the

Figure 7.3
The Victim Profile in Occupational and Organizational Crime

✓ Diffuse Victims (Individuals, Organizations,
   Government, Taxpayers, Consumers)

Consumer Fraud

✓ Western States

✓ Aged 20-39, Older Persons

✓ White Males and Females

✓ Relatively Affluent

✓ Victim Injury: Both Economic and Physical Harm in Larger
   Organizations

Employee Theft and Sabotage

✓ Most Common in Companies Where Employees Are Dissatisfied with
   the Organization's Supervisor

✓ Exploitive, Oppressive Work Environments

Source: Clark and Hollinger (1983); Ennis (1967); Ganzini, McFarland and Bloom (1990)

---

country. Urban residents are also at greater risk of victimization than rural residents, and persons between the ages of 20 and 39 are particularly prone to consumer fraud. Among combinations of race and gender, white males have the highest reported victimization rate for consumer fraud, and nonwhite females the lowest (Ennis 1967). More recent studies, however, reveal a somewhat different profile of fraud victims. For example, Ganzini, McFarland, and Bloom (1990) found that victims of financial fraud schemes tended to be older, female, and relatively affluent.

The controversial notion of victim proneness or provocation has been applied to explain why some individuals and businesses are more likely to be victims of white-collar crime than others. From this perspective, victims of white-collar crime play an active role in their victimization by acting careless, greedy, or not exercising sound judgment. Those who fall victim to "get-rich-quick" schemes or invest money in highly speculative ventures that turn out to be fraudulent are clear examples of contributory victims. Workers whose reckless actions lead to injury and struggling businesses that attempt to capitalize on the "something-for-nothing" or the proverbial "free-lunch" offers from other businesses or financial lenders also contribute to their own victimization. Although some authors are extremely critical of the very notion of victim provocation because of "victim blaming" (Friedrichs 1996), it is nonetheless undeniable that some white-collar victims directly contribute to their victimization.

Rates of white-collar victimization tend to be higher among large organizations than smaller businesses and individuals. Several factors account for these differences. First, the size and impersonality of large organizations often make it easier to commit crimes against them (Friedrichs 1996). Large, bureaucratic organizations have higher levels of task specialization, delegation of authority, and dependence on complex technology. These organizational factors increase the physical opportunities for crime and their subsequent vulnerability to victimization (Vaughan 1980). Second, people feel less guilty about stealing from large profit-oriented organizations than from small businesses and individuals (Smigel and Lawrence 1970). Victimization of corporations is often justified by denying injury (i.e., "they can afford it") or shifting blame to the corporation for its own corruption.

Self-report surveys and interviews with offenders reveal that characteristics of the work environment are also important determinants of victimization. Higher rates of employee theft and sabotage against a company, for example, are found where employees are dissatisfied with the organization or their supervisors (Clark and Hollinger 1983). Ironically, the quality of the workplace environment may affect both the risk of occupational crime and the level of public awareness of organizational crime within it. Work settings viewed as oppressive or exploitive often lead to employee theft and sabotage of work activities as "payback" for poor treatment, and disgruntled employees who observe organizational misconduct in these settings may be more willing to report abuses to external authorities. Under these conditions, both the amount of crime against the company and the public exposure of organizational abuses are tied to the quality of the work environment.

When applied to white-collar crime, the routine-activity approach assumes that particular targets for victimization are selected because they are visible, accessible, unprotected, and offer a higher yield than other potential victims (Miethe and Meier 1994). Consistent with this theory, offenders' particular occupational positions determine in large part their access to particular types of white-collar crime. Computer hacking, for example, requires access to a computer and the technical knowledge to use it. Given the opportunities to commit various occupational and organizational crimes, relatively unprotected and attractive targets are the most prone to victimization. From this perspective, organizations have higher victimization rates than small businesses and individuals because they provide more attractive opportunities. Elderly persons are more vulnerable to fraud schemes than other individuals because they offer a greater yield with less effort and resistance.

Situational Elements and Circumstances

The circumstances surrounding white-collar crime involve the motivations for its commission, the victim-offender relationship, and situational dynamics. Data on the prevalence of these situational elements are summarized in Figure 7.4 and described below.

The Motivation for Occupational and Organizational Crime

White-collar crime is motivated primarily by economic concerns and the desire to maintain or enhance resources or positions of power. Revenge and retaliation underlie industrial sabotage and

Figure 7.4
Situational Elements in Occupational and Organizational Crime

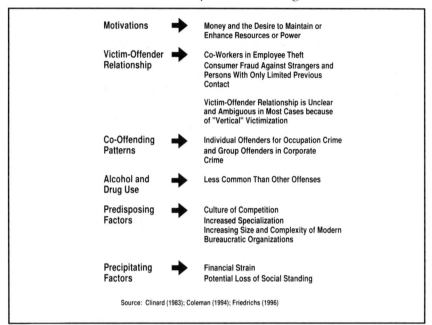

Motivations	➡	Money and the Desire to Maintain or Enhance Resources or Power
Victim-Offender Relationship	➡	Co-Workers in Employee Theft Consumer Fraud Against Strangers and Persons With Only Limited Previous Contact
		Victim-Offender Relationship is Unclear and Ambiguous in Most Cases because of "Vertical" Victimization
Co-Offending Patterns	➡	Individual Offenders for Occupation Crime and Group Offenders in Corporate Crime
Alcohol and Drug Use	➡	Less Common Than Other Offenses
Predisposing Factors	➡	Culture of Competition Increased Specialization Increasing Size and Complexity of Modern Bureaucratic Organizations
Precipitating Factors	➡	Financial Strain Potential Loss of Social Standing

Source: Clinard (1983); Coleman (1994); Friedrichs (1996)

some acts of employee theft, but these motives are clearly secondary to economic and power motivations in most white-collar offenses.

Financial motives are expressed in a variety of ways. Profit motives are clearly evident in cases of bid rigging, price fixing, insider trading, income-tax evasion, "Ponzi" and pyramid schemes, embezzlement, and the wide array of financial frauds committed by medical and legal professionals, telemarketers, service businesses, insurance companies, and banking institutions. However, organizational crimes that result from various cost-saving efforts are also motivated by financial considerations. These offenses include bribery of regulatory officials, manufacturing inferior or defective products, violations of product safety requirements, environmental pollution, and exposing workers to health and safety violations. Full compliance with federal regulations and industry standards cuts into profit margins, forcing marginal companies to circumvent these standards to remain competitive.

The importance of financial competition and greed are often echoed in the explanations offered for white-collar crime. The following comments made by middle-management executives illustrate the financial motives in unethical and illegal corporate behavior (Clinard 1983:57-60):

> ... All corporations are primarily interested in making a profit. Some are more aggressive and violate the law. After all, this is a capitalist system. . . .

> ... All corporations are profit-making companies; if things do not go right they do not stay in business. Very competitive areas are those in which there are more likely to be violations. . . .

> ... The corporation's desire to be No.1 makes for violations; there are some money-hungry corporations. . . .

> ... Much illegal behavior in a corporation is an act of financial desperation when losing money or position in the industry. . . .

State-organized crime is the best example of white-collar crime motivated by efforts to maintain power and resources. State-organized crime involves offenses committed by state officials in pursuit of their jobs as representatives of the state (Chambliss 1989). Forms of this criminal activity include state complicity in smuggling, assassinations, criminal conspiracies, spying on citizens, diverting funds illegally, selling arms to blacklisted countries, and supporting terrorists. The most celebrated crimes by state actors in the last three decades are Watergate (the Nixon White House's involvement in improper and illegal "political policing" endeavors) and the Iran-Contra Affair (the Reagan administration's involvement in the sale of weapons to Iran in exchange for funds to arm and support the Contras in Nicaragua) (Friedrichs 1996). Government and local agencies with enforcement and investigative powers such as the CIA, FBI, IRS, and police departments throughout history have engaged in various activities of dubious legality to maintain prevailing power relationships and harass or incapacitate dissents. Although criminal activity by state agents is often called "political" crime, it is classified here as organizational crime because it is carried out within the context of occupational roles.

The Victim-Offender Relationship

Rates of white-collar crimes committed against strangers, co-workers, and associates vary widely, depending on the type of occupational and organizational crime. Embezzlers, for example, steal from companies they work in because the crime requires access to specific positions of trust within organizations. Other types of employee theft, by definition, also involve a prior relationship between the perpetrator and the victim. White-collar offenses, such as engaging in prohibitive employment practices and exposing workers to hazardous work conditions, also occur within the context of ongoing victim-offender relationships. In contrast, consumer frauds committed by professionals and repair-service businesses often involve more tenuous victim-offender relationships. Consumers and clients may have several prior contacts with particular medical professionals or auto-repair shops before they are victimized by fraud schemes. In other cases, the victimization involves a one-shot attack against a previously unknown victim.

For the majority of corporate crimes, however, the victim-offender relationship is unclear. This is because the definition of victim in these offenses is problematic. For example, in "vertical" price-fixing schemes, some manufacturers attempt to dictate retail price levels and to lock out discounters (Friedrichs 1996). Are the victims in this case the retail stores who can't get discount prices for their goods, or the consumers who must pay more for these goods? In cases of insider trading, are institutional or individual investors the primary victims? Does it matter that individual investors have losses in the thousands of dollars, while institutional investors may lose millions of dollars? For each of these offenses, the "real" victims may be the general public, which loses confidence in the integrity of government and financial institutions.

Co-Offending Patterns

Most white-collar offenders are isolated offenders who work alone to commit their crimes. This is especially true for bribery, embezzlement, and other types of employee theft. Group offending is more common in cases of consumer fraud like telemarketing and business fraud and price fixing.

Alcohol and Drug Use

Alcohol and drug use is rarely mentioned in the context of situational factors for white-collar crime. The only possible exception is substance abuse as a triggering factor in employee theft. However, even for employee theft, alcohol and drug use appear to be of only secondary importance as explanatory factors.

Predisposing and Precipitating Factors

Occupational and organizational crime has been explained from a variety of perspectives. Common criminological theories like differential association, anomie, rational choice, social bond, neutralization, and conflict theory have been applied to explain the causes of white-collar crime and its distribution (Friedrichs 1996). Here, we summarize those social structural conditions that predispose particular individuals and organizations to white-collar crime (called predisposing factors) and the situational elements and contingencies that lead to crime commission (called precipitating factors).

Predisposing Factors. A number of structural elements in contemporary American society are viewed as predisposing factors for high rates of white-collar crime. The major factors include the culture of competition and changes in the structure and complexity of modern work activities.

According to Coleman (1994), the desire to expand and protect profits is only part of a larger motivational complex for white-collar crime. Along with financial self-interest is the desire for self-affirmation through "winning" competitive ventures. Within capitalistic economies, a culture of competition exists in which the accumulation of wealth and success in competitive struggles are major goals of individual economic activity. From this perspective, the strains of achieving or maintaining material and "social" success are the preconditions for occupational and organizational crime. Occupational crimes provide individuals the opportunity to maintain or enhance their status and economic position, and organizational crimes increase the opportunity for corporations to achieve similar goals.

Structural changes in the nature of work organizations over time have also increased the physical opportunities for white-collar crime. The most salient changes in work organizations are their increased complexity and the growth in specialized and expertise-based jobs over time.

Although specialization is a major structural feature of the division of labor in modern societies, task specialization in corporations is a predisposing factor for white-collar crime because it generates more opportunities for illegal behavior and obscures the operation of these practices within and outside the organization (Vaughan, Wheeler, Ruthman, Nagel, Hagan, Braithwaite, and Leigh 1982). The growth in expertise-based knowledge, essential for crimes such as computer hacking, decreases the ability of other workers to monitor and control organizational misconduct. The technical complexity of product development and manufacturing activities forces many government regulators to rely upon information from the producers themselves to evaluate compliance with industry standards (Miethe and Rothschild 1994). Coupled with the growth of task specialization, the size and complexity of modern bureaucratic organizations dramatically increase the likelihood that criminal activity will remain invisible to public scrutiny. Where complex accounting systems and regulatory guidelines are understood by only a few, there are greater opportunities for unlawful and unethical business practices. Growing expertise and specialization provide the technically competent offender a rich organizational environment for criminal activity.

Precipitating Factors. The decision to engage in white-collar crime is influenced by a wide assortment of situational and organizational factors. Traditional criminological theories explain the onset of white-collar crime by reference to such factors as strain, an excess of procrime definitions, the weakening of bonds to traditional society, and the learning of techniques to neutralize societal reaction. A routine activity theory identifies attractive targets and the absence of guardianship as precipitating factors for crime commission. Some white-collar offenders select targets that are familiar and convenient, unguarded, and attractive, whereas other offenders make rudimentary tactical decisions precipitated solely by an emerging opportunity.

Interviews with convicted white-collar offenders indicate that financial strain and the potential loss of social standing are major precipitating or triggering factors in their decision to engage in crime. Clinard's (1983) study of middle-management executives revealed that financial performance pressures and the need to maintain their positions strongly influenced their decisions to engage in corporate misconduct. In some cases, these pressures are so great on middle management that they will do essentially anything to maintain their positions. More than 90 percent of the middle managers said that work pressures led to unethical behavior within the corporation (Clinard 1983).

The thin line between legitimate and illegitimate business practices provides white-collar offenders with an immediate rationalization for their crimes. In fact, several studies have applied Sykes and Matza's (1957) work on techniques of neutralization to explain white-collar crime. These neutralizations or rationalizations include denial of injury, denial of victims, denial of responsibility, condemnation of the condemners, and pleas to a higher authority. Embezzlers, for example, often convince themselves that they are merely "borrowing" the money, presumably intending to return it as soon as they resolved momentary financial problems (Cressey 1953). Doctors who defraud Medicaid deny responsibility for their actions (calling the acts "mistakes"), minimize injury, and use a varied array of excuses and rationalizations (Jesilow, Pontell, and Geis 1993).

White-Collar Crime Syndromes

White-collar crime comes in a wide variety of forms and can be classified in several ways. The most basic distinction involves whether crimes are committed for individual purposes or to promote organizational goals. Within these categories of occupational and organizational crimes, secondary distinctions exist according to the type of victim injury (economic or physical) and primary characteristics of the victims (consumers, businesses, government). These variations in white-collar crime syndromes are described below.

Occupational Offenders

Occupational offenders are motivated by individual greed and self-interest. Their criminal activity often involves various forms of financial fraud, including embezzlement, employee theft, fraudulent business services, charity fraud, and illegal land and stock deals. These criminals vary, but they are generally more likely to be female, older, and less involved in prior criminal activity and drug use than traditional property and violent criminals. Although some offenses occur simply as a result of opportunities, typical occupational offenders engage in some degree of planning in the process of crime commission. Some of these offenses require little sophistication, but others require knowledge of complex technological systems. Financial pressures and the need to maintain social status are often the triggering factors in occupational crime. Here are several examples of particular types of occupational crimes that illustrate the nature of the offenses:

- "Data diddlers" engage in computer-assisted embezzlement by manipulating the information fed into computers for their advantage. Funds intended for deposit in one account are credited to different accounts controlled by the criminals (Coleman 1994).

- Through secret files or "Trojan horses," computer programmers can make electronic transfers, erase personal debts, or discover confidential information without detection (Coleman 1994).

- In "collective embezzlement," top management siphons off company funds for personal use.

- "Telemarketing" scams entice consumers to buy into worthless investments. Some recent telemarketing schemes include "cash loans," in which callers are charged $49 for a generic information package on how to apply for bank loans; "one-shot" credit cards in which callers pay a fee for a card that turns out to be usable only once; bogus health products such as water purifiers; and "blind pool" penny stock offerings based on misleading information about new small companies (Blake 1996).

- Some medical professionals "overutilize" billing for superfluous and unnecessary tests and other services. Specific forms of medical fraud include "ping-ponging" (referring patients to several different practitioners when their symptoms do not warrant such referrals), "family ganging" (extending several unnecessary services to all members of a patient's family), "fee-splitting" (sending patients to surgeons who will split the largest fee rather than to those who will do the best work), "steering" (directing patients to clinics' pharmacies to fill unneeded prescriptions), and "upgrading" (billing for services more extensive than those actually performed) (Friedrichs 1996; Pontell, Jesilow, and Geis 1982).

Economic and Physical Harm. The vast majority of occupational crimes involve primarily economic harm to victims. Physical injury is rare in these cases. In addition to economic costs, occupational crimes are often thought to decrease our confidence and trust in other people and organizations.

The economic losses from occupational crime are staggering. Multi-billion dollar losses are estimated annually for embezzlement and other types of employee theft, consumer fraud, health care fraud, phone and cellular fraud, insurance theft, and computer-related crimes (Coleman 1994; Friedrichs 1996).

Unnecessary treatment by medical doctors is the best example of occupational crimes involving physical injury to victims. Estimates are that up to one out of every four surgeries is not needed (Berger 1988). The rate of unnecessary surgery for particular body parts ranges from 29 percent of all prostrate surgeries, 31 percent of gall bladder removals, 32 percent of knee surgeries, 33 percent of hysterectomies, 43 percent of hemorrhoid operations, and 50 percent of all pacemaker implants. The practices of "fee-splitting" and referral "ping-ponging" of patients from one physician to another for treatment also increases the risks of physical injury. Doctor's participation in these types of medical fraud is attributed to the financial strain caused by the high operating costs of medical practice and the quest for higher income (Green 1990). Physical injury associated with medical fraud is usually unanticipated and unintentional.

Type of Victim. Occupational crimes and the societal reaction to them vary by the characteristics of the victim. Victims of these offenses are individuals and the public at large, businesses and corporations, and government agencies. Most occupational crimes, however, involve multiple sources of victimization. For example, employee theft directly victimizes the businesses in which the crimes take place, but the public is ultimately victimized by the increase in cost of retail products and goods to compensate for business losses.

The public response to occupational crime is often more severe for crimes against consumers than for crimes against businesses or the government. The increased sophistication of consumer fraud schemes makes all Americans susceptible to victimization, not just those wanting something for nothing, and decreases a "buyer-beware" mentality that blames the victim for crime. Occupational crimes against businesses and government agencies, in contrast, are often viewed as less serious and their victims receive less sympathy because they are thought to be culpable in the wrongdoing or are perceived as being able to more easily overcome the costs of victimization.

Organizational Offenders

Organizational crimes are offenses committed by employees on behalf of companies. False advertising, commercial fraud, illegal mergers and acquisitions, price fixing and collusion, violations of workers' civil liberties, and unsafe production activities are examples of corporate or organizational crimes. These crimes are designed to maintain and enhance organizations' economic positions and status in the market. As individual offenders or groups of offenders, various types of financial fraud and the circumvention of regulatory provisions increase companies' profit margins. When volatile market conditions threaten the financial stability and performance of corporations, middle management executives often go to extraordinary lengths to maintain their positions. Both legal and illegal cost-cutting measures help companies remain afloat. A climate for illegal activity is established in many companies by placing primary emphasis on performance standards, the removal of production and service activity from public scrutiny, and the reliance upon external agents to evaluate compliance with government standards.

The socio-demographic profile of the typical organizational offender is mixed. Companies with marginal financial performance are thought to be most suspectable to organizational crime to improve their market positions, but large corporate entities are also viewed as the most criminogenic organizations because illegal and unethical conduct provides the means of maintaining their economic advantage. Among individual offenders, senior staff with longer histories of employment within companies often commit corporate offenses to save the market position of their companies, whereas novice employees may take greater risks for companies to more quickly advance through organizational hierarchies.

Since access to key decision-making positions often involves seniority and specialized knowledge about company practices, middle-management executives and financial personnel are usually exposed to more criminal opportunities. The greater technical complexity of much organizational crime also gives those in technical positions a greater opportunity to conduct criminal activity on behalf of companies. CEOs play critical roles in establishing the ethical tone for entire organizations and the acceptance of organizational misconduct as "legitimate" practices.

The following examples of particular types of organizational crimes illustrate the diversity and magnitude of the offenses:

- Massive leaks of toxic chemicals from an old dumping ground in Love Canal, New York, forced 239 families to evacuate and demolish their homes. Another 311 homes have also been condemned. The disaster cost American taxpayers about $200 million. Lawsuits against the chemical company worth $15 billion are pending in the courts (Coleman 1994:80-81).

- Ford Pintos produced between 1971 and 1976 were recalled for repair of a defective gas tank that exploded upon low- to moderate-speed rear-end collisions. Ford denied allegations that it was aware of the defect in early crash tests but failed to make changes for financial reasons. Dozens of lawsuits have been filed, some resulting in multi-million-dollar judgments, and more than 50 people are believed to have died as a direct result of ruptured gas tanks (Coleman 1994:83-84).

- Executives of Richardson-Merrill ordered technicians to falsify data about the dangerousness of the drug MER/29, a cholesterol inhibitor intended for use by heart patients. By the time it was taken off the market, at least 5,000 users had suffered serious side effects—hair loss, severe skin problems, and cataracts. After pleading no contest to eight counts of misconduct, the company was given the maximum fine of $80,000. MER/29 brought in more than $7 million in gross revenues in its first year of production (Coleman 1994:85).

- A. H. Robbins was accused of knowingly misrepresenting the nature, quality, safety, and efficacy of the Dalkon Shield, an intrauterine birth-control device. At least 17 women have died and as many as 200,000 more have been injured by complications involving the Dalkon Shield. By 1995, Robbins paid out more than $378 million to settle 9,200 lawsuits from victims. Bankruptcy postponed compensation for another 40,000 to 50,000 victims. A federal court has accepted a plan to reorganize Robbins that includes the creation of a $2.5 billion fund to compensate the victims of the Dalkon Shield (Coleman 1994:86-87).

- The brokerage house of E.F. Hutton used a check-kiting scheme by writing checks for funds that had not yet been deposited and pocketing the interest that it saved. Hutton was essentially getting an interest-free loan by paying its bills with checks that were covered by other checks written on different banks, which were covered by checks written on still other banks. Hutton saved about $27 million in interest using this scheme. When discovered, the company agreed to plead guilty and pay several million dollars in fines and restitution (Coleman 1994:89).

- Dennis Levine, a highly placed merger and acquisitions specialist with the Wall Street firm of Drexel Burnham Lambert, was charged with using inside information to make $12 million in illegal profits and given a two-year prison term. Ivan Boesky, who made huge profits from tips he received from Levine and others, was fined $100 million and given a three-year prison sentence. Subsequent investigations by the Securities and Exchange Commission resulted in the indictment of more than 60 people in top Wall Street firms, including Michael Milken, the billionaire junk bond king (Coleman 1994:90-91).

- As part of its involvement in insider trading, Drexel Burnham Lambert pled guilty to six felony charges for "stock parking" (violating securities laws by illegally concealing ownership of stock) and illegal stock manipulations. Drexel agreed to pay $600 million in criminal fines and civil penalties. The huge fine and the loss of public confidence were major factors in Drexel's declaring bankruptcy after 55 years on Wall Street (Coleman 1994:89).

- The virtual collapse of the savings and loan industry in the late 1980s is often attributed to sharp increases in interest rates that made low-interest, fixed-rate loans by thrifts increasingly unprofitable. Most of the major losses and closures, however, were due to crimes and grossly unethical conduct by top savings and loan executives. From 1988 to 1990, a total of 21,147 written requests for investigations were filed with the Justice Department for fraudulent savings and loan activity. This crisis is expected to cost the government a total of $500 billion (Coleman 1994:91).

Although both individuals and corporations benefit from the criminal activities in the S & L and Wall Street scandals, they are considered organizational crimes because the ultimate gains are to the companies involved. Corporate gains are most evident in the cases of the Dalkon Shield, the Ford Pinto, the MER/29 drug, and E. F. Hutton's no-interest loans.

Economic and Physical Harm. As illustrated by the examples above, organizational crime involves both economic and physical harm. However, in contrast to most violent personal crimes in which physical injury is the specific intent of the crime, physical harm in most occupational offenses is a largely unexpected consequence of economic cost-saving efforts. A.H. Robbins' misrepresentation of the safety of the Dalkon Shield, for example, was motivated by financial considerations. Violations of OSHA standards by construction or manufacturing companies, industrial pollution, and the dumping of unsafe products by pharmaceutical companies in poor nations with lax drug-safety regulations are done for similar economic reasons even though death and illness are common consequences (Coleman 1994). Although economic motives are of primary importance in explaining organizational crime, both financial fraud and physical harm are common consequences of the desire to maintain and enhance organizations' status positions.

Type of Victim. Organizational crimes victimize individuals, businesses, and the government. In the insider trading and S & L scandals, individual stock holders and loan applicants are obvious victims, but so are other firms, the government, and the public at large, which ultimately pays for the crimes. As true of occupational crime, the public response to organizational crime is often more severe for crimes against individuals and employees than for crimes against businesses or the government. Business and government victims of organizational crimes are seen as less credible than individual victims because they are perceived as more culpable in the wrongdoing.

White-Collar Crime Prevention and Intervention Strategies

Two general approaches are used to control occupational and organizational crime. The primary prevention and intervention strategies include criminal sanctions and opportunity-reduction programs.

The Criminal Justice Response

The ability of the criminal justice system to deter occupational and organizational crime depends on swift, certain, and severe sanctions. The strong economic motivation underlying these crimes and the loss of social status from being caught for illegal behavior suggest that these rational offenders may be especially deterred by the threat of legal sanction. The evidence for deterrence in white-collar crimes, however, is largely inconclusive.

If the certainty of punishment is measured by rates of crime detection and conviction, the likelihood of getting caught and legally punished for white-collar crime is incredibly low. Few occupational and organizational crimes are known to the police because organizations don't report them because of fear of diminished consumer trust and confidence if crimes against them become public knowledge, and many individuals and consumers are simply unaware of their victimization.

Limited data exist on prosecution and conviction practices, but available information suggests that court practices are similar to other offenses. In a study of cases of forgery and counterfeiting, fraud, and embezzlement in eight U.S. states (Manson 1986), nearly 90 percent of the arrested offenders were prosecuted, a rate slightly higher than that for violent crimes, property crimes, and public-order offenses. A conviction resulted in about three-fourths of the prosecuted cases of white-collar crime. A prison sentence of more than one year, however, occurs in less than one out of every five prosecuted white-collar cases (Manson 1986). Conviction rates for white-collar crime are comparable to other felony offenses, but these offenders are slightly less likely to serve time for their crimes. Nearly 40 percent of the violent offenders and 26 percent of the property offenders receive a prison sentence compared to only 18 percent of white-collar offenders. When the successive rates of detection, arrest, conviction, and imprisonment are combined, a reasonable estimate is that less than 1 percent of white-collar offenders are caught and serve time for their crime.

Because UCR data contain a high concentration of low-level forgery, fraud, and embezzlement arrests, they do not represent the full array of white-collar offenders and tend to overestimate the effectiveness of the criminal justice system in prosecuting and convicting these offenders. More serious white-collar cases like insider trading and price fixing rarely result in arrests and escape criminal prosecution due to administrative or civil regulatory enforcement (Albanese 1995). Once an arrest is made for more serious white-collar crimes, however, the chances of conviction and imprisonment are quite high. Of the nearly 6,000 defendants charged with major financial institution frauds by U.S. attorneys from 1989 to 1994, about 86 percent are convicted and 77 percent received jail time (U.S. Department of Justice 1995). Conviction rates are similar for defendants who are employed in savings and loan institutions, banks, and credit unions.

Other data on prosecution practices further indicate that street crimes are punished more severely than white-collar offenses, both in terms of the proportion of convicted offenders given jail sentences and the length of incarceration (Clinard and Yeager 1980; Coleman 1994). Occupational crimes are also punished more severely than are organizational crimes. About 40 percent of convicted street criminals receive jail sentences compared to 18 percent of tax fraud offenders, 9 percent of embezzlers, and only one out of every 20 regulatory offenders (Coleman 1995).

The low rate of arrest for white-collar crime is clearly revealed in data for OSHA violations and anti-trust offenses. Over the 16 years of its existence, OSHA has issued only 18 health and 23 safety violations despite the fact that an estimated 128,000 people died on the job during that time period (Coleman 1995). Clinard and Yeager's (1980) study of America's 477 largest corporations also reveals only 56 cases in which corporate executives were charged with criminal offenses for their involvement in organizational crimes. Less than 700 criminal charges were filed against anti-trust violators in the 80-year period from 1890 to 1969 (McCormick 1977).

Among those rare organizational offenses that do result in an arrest, lower conviction and incarceration rates are attributed to corporate power. Specifically, corporate criminals have teams of the highest paid and most skilled attorneys in the nation, whereas the government must rely upon a smaller number of poorly paid, often young and inexperienced lawyers. Corporate attorneys have virtually unlimited time and ample funding to pursue endless appeals and delays, whereas prosecutorial resources are far more limited (Coleman 1995). Under these conditions, the lower conviction rate for corporate offenders and the lack of deterrent effect of criminal sanctions are understandable.

Given that most occupational and organizational offenders exercise some degree of rational calculation and planning, the threat of legal sanction has great potential in deterring these offenders.

Unfortunately, the low certainty and severity of legal punishments in actual practice undermines any potential deterrent value of legal sanctions. Nonetheless, both the threat of legal sanction and informal sanctions like shame, stigma, and the loss of social standing appear to play a major role as specific and general deterrents for white-collar crime (Braithwaite and Makkai 1991; Simpson and Koper 1992).

Opportunity-Reduction Strategies

Given that white-collar crime occurs in organizational contexts largely removed from public scrutiny, efforts to control it have often been based on increased security and internal and external monitoring of organizational practices. Within these organizational environments, fellow employees serving as whistleblowers have enormous potential to detect and expose occupational and organizational misconduct.

Increased security and surveillance are the most common responses to employee theft. Property marking, passwords limiting access to financial records, and security stations at building exits are some of the more basic methods of reducing opportunities for employee theft. Increasing public awareness of white-collar schemes, especially telemarketing fraud, is another way to reduce criminal opportunities. Other recommendations for strengthening surveillance include (1) increasing the skills, knowledge, and number of agency personnel, (2) creating laws that require disclosure of certain information on corporate activities, (3) public representation on boards of directors, and (4) mixing agency monitoring strategies to vary organizations' surveillance timing (Vaughan 1983).

Over the last decade, social scientists and government officials have become increasingly aware of the importance of whistleblowers in detecting, reporting, and controlling organizational misconduct. The greater complexity of modern work organizations and the technical expertise of workers has created a situation in which fellow employees have become major agents of social control. Federal and state laws have also increased the responsibility of workers to become whistleblowers and expose fraud, waste, and abuse. Under new federal provisions to decrease financial fraud, for example, auditors are now legally obligated to report cases of financial misconduct to external agents. Federal law and some state statutes prohibit retaliatory actions by employers against whistleblowers, and under the False Claims Act, whistleblowers are entitled to a substantial proportion (from 10 percent to 33 percent) of the damages collected in cases of fraud against the government (Miethe and Rothschild 1994). Along with the proliferation of regulatory agencies, these legal efforts are designed to increase whistleblowing by employees as a means of exposing occupational and organizational crime.

The final type of opportunity-reduction strategy involves changes in the ethical climate within corporations and the government (Coleman 1994). The work of Clinard (1983) and others suggests that CEOs and upper management strongly influence the level of crime in their organizations. Management's endorsement of a zero-tolerance policy toward unethical and illegal corporate practices, a position which is now largely antithetical to corporate America, sends a clear message throughout the entire organization. Other suggestions for improving ethics in modern work organizations include (1) mandatory ethics courses in business schools, (2) uniform ethical standards established by trade associations for each industry, and (3) methods of making ethical behavior more rewarding than criminal behavior (Coleman 1994).

Summary

White-collar crime is the most economically expensive crime in contemporary American society. Occupational crimes such as employee theft and consumer fraud result in multi-billion dollar losses each year, and the economic costs of organizational crimes such as price fixing and financial institution fraud are simply enormous. White-collar crime is strongly related to declining trust and confidence in corporations and government, and safety violations and the distribution of unsafe products result in the death and serious injury of more than 100,000 Americans each year. White-collar offenders are often viewed as persons of high social status who commit their offenses to maintain their status and economic positions. Depending upon the particular type of offense, victims of these crimes are individual consumers, businesses, and the government. Although threat of legal sanction has potential to deter these offenders, the risks of detection and arrest for occupational and organizational crimes are extremely low. Opportunity-reduction strategies to reduce the prevalence of white-collar crime include increased security, more internal and external regulators, improved business ethics, and the use of employees as whistleblowers to detect, expose, and control occupational and organizational crime.

Chapter Eight

Public Order Crimes

Many criminal offenses are universally considered wrong in and of themselves, but there is a wide class of behaviors in which criminal status depends on the jurisdiction and offenders' personal characteristics. These offenses are often called victimless crimes, vice crimes, or, more generally, public order crimes. Depending on the jurisdiction or age of offenders, behavior such as drug and alcohol use, gambling, panhandling, abortion, pornography, and consensual sexual relations may or may not be considered criminal. Other types of behavior in this general crime category include vandalism, loitering, trespassing, and disorderly conduct. Compared to other criminal offenses, public order violations are generally less serious and often rely upon informants and various sting operations to apprehend offenders. Aside from being criminal in itself, drug and alcohol use is often a major contributory factor in the onset of many violent and property crimes.

This chapter examines similarities and differences in types of public order crimes. We summarize definitions of these crimes, their frequency, and changes in them over time, offenders' characteristics, situational elements and circumstances, and the methods of crime prevention.

Definitions of Crime Types

Public order crimes are considered *mala prohibitum* offenses, meaning that they are wrong because they are prohibited by some legal body. The term "public order" is used to describe these crimes because they are thought to disrupt the serenity of community life and to pose a threat to social institutions like families.

Public standards regarding the criminality of public order offenses exhibit enormous variation across geographical areas. Prostitution, for example, is legal in some counties in Nevada but illegal in others, essentially legal in large urban areas across the country because prostitution laws are rarely enforced, and both illegal and strongly enforced in other jurisdictions. Similarly, the possession of marijuana has been legal for personal consumption in Alaska, treated as a civil violation in Oregon, and recent legislation in California and Arizona makes it legal to use marijuana for medical purposes. Marijuana possession is a felony in many states, punishable by a prison sentence upon conviction. Behaviors involving trespass, vagrancy, disorderly conduct, vandalism, gambling, and the production and distribution of pornography are included in criminal statutes in all states, but penalties and how vigorously the crimes are enforced vary widely within and across geographical areas.

Public order offenses fall under the general category of Part II offenses in the Uniform Crime Reports. This legal classification scheme uses the following definitions for particular types of public order violations (see UCR Reporting Handbook 1984: 79-82):

Drug-Abuse Violations: Includes all arrests for violations of state and local laws relating to the unlawful possession, sale, use, growing, manufacturing, and making of narcotic drugs. Specific drugs include opium or cocaine and their derivatives (morphine, heroin, codeine), marijuana, synthetic narcotics which can cause drug addiction (demerol, methadones), and dangerous nonnarcotic drugs (barbiturates, benzedrine). Possession is differentiated from sale and manufacturing.

Prostitution and Commercialized Vice: Includes sex offenses of a commercialized nature, such as prostitution; keeping bawdy houses, disorderly houses, or houses of ill fame; pandering, procuring, transporting, or detaining women for immoral purposes; and all attempts to commit any of the above.

Gambling: All charges which relate to promoting, permitting, or engaging in illegal gambling are included in this category. To provide a more refined collection of gambling arrests, distinctions are made between bookmaking (horse and sport book), numbers and lottery, and other types of gambling.

Liquor-Law Violations: With the exception of "drunkenness" and "driving under the influence," liquor-law violations, state or local, include: manufacture, sale, transporting, furnishing, possessing, etc., intoxicating liquor; maintaining unlawful drinking places; bootlegging; operating stills; furnishing liquor to minors or intemperate persons; using vehicles for illegal transportation of liquor; drinking on trains or public conveyances; and all attempts to commit any of the above.

Drunkenness: Includes charges of drunk and disorderly conduct being a common or habitual drunkard, and intoxication.

Disorderly Conduct: All charges of committing a breach of the peace, including: affray; unlawful assembly; disturbing the peace; disturbing meetings; disorderly conduct in state institutions, at court, at fairs, on trains or public conveyances, etc.; blasphemy, profanity, and obscene language; desecrating the flag; refusing to assist an officer; and all attempts to commit any of the above.

Vandalism: The willful or malicious destruction, injury, disfigurement, or defacement of any public or private property, real or personal, without consent of the owners or persons having custody or control by cutting, tearing, breaking, marking, painting, drawing, covering with filth, or any other such means as may be specified by local law. This offense covers a wide range of malicious behavior directed at property, such as: cutting auto tires, drawing obscene pictures on public restroom walls, smashing windows, destroying school records, tipping over gravestones, defacing library books, etc.

Vagrancy: Persons prosecuted on the charge of being a "suspicious character or person, etc.," including: vagrancy; begging; loitering (for persons 18 and over); and vagabondage.

Although the illegal behaviors underlying public order violations differ widely, they nonetheless share several basic characteristics. First, many of these offenses, especially prostitution, pornography, gambling, alcohol violations and drug use, are considered victimless crimes. Participants freely enter into "the willing exchange, among adults, of strongly demanded but legally proscribed goods or services" (Schur 1965: 169). Second, many of these crimes involve a basic exchange of goods and services. Products (like drugs, alcohol, and pornography) or services (like gambling and sex) are exchanged for money, sex, or other products and services (Lesieur and Welch 1995). Third, there is no consensus about the seriousness of public order offenses, how these laws should be enforced, and the punishment of violators. Homosexual activity and prostitution, for example, are viewed by some as simply private matters of sexual preference, whereas others consider these sexual acts abominations that require rigorous state intervention because they corrupt youth, undermine family values, and spread AIDS and venereal diseases. Societal reactions to drug and alcohol use, gambling, and pornography are equally diverse.

Drug use and prostitution are the most widely studied public order offenses and exhibit many similarities. As identified by Barlow (1990:362-363), these drug and sex offenses share the following characteristics:

- Participants in these crimes often do not view themselves as criminal, nor are they viewed as criminals by significant portions of the population.

- Illegal sex and drugs are sources of pleasure and tremendous profits. The profits, more than the pleasures, are a direct consequence of criminalization. The black market drives up both prices and profits, and entrepreneurs willing to take risks will not pay taxes on those profits.

- Illegal sex and drugs are prime targets of organized crime, with all three feeding off each other. For example, many prostitutes are drug addicts; most female drug addicts—at least in the ghetto—engage in prostitution; and organized crime controls large segments of both criminal drug use and criminal sex, and through the profits it makes is able to extend its control, protect itself from law enforcement, and increase the availability of illicit sex and drugs.

- Enforcement of laws dealing with drugs and sex requires a special type of policing: relying on informants and undercover detectives. It is also a major area of graft and corruption in the criminal justice system.

- Much of the behavior that is criminalized by drug and prostitution statutes is considered victimless, in that participants consider themselves willingly involved rather than being offended against.

- Both areas of crime are prime targets of "moral entrepreneurs" who see the involved behavior as evidence of declining morals and unreasonable permissiveness and who continually organize campaigns to broaden the laws and increase the penalties.

Are surveys honest?

Trends Over Time and Social Correlates

Differences in community standards and low public visibility of drug and alcohol use and consensual sexual acts severely question the reliability of national estimates of public order offenses and changes in them over time. Our knowledge of the prevalence of these crimes is based on arrest data and self-report studies of involvement in particular offenses. National estimates of arrests for various types of public order offenses are summarized in Figure 8.1. *I wasn't*

Arrest rates for public order violations vary over time and by type of offense. Arrest rates for drug abuse violations have skyrocketed in recent decades, from 25.5 per 100,000 residents in 1960 to 582.5 per 100,000 by 1995. The rates for liquor law violations and driving while intoxicated doubled from 1960 to 1980, increased through the 1980s and early 1990s, but dropped to a pre-1980 level by 1995. Prostitution arrest rates nearly doubled from 1960 to 1980 and have remained fairly stable over the last two decades. In sharp contrast, arrest rates for gambling violations, vagrancy, and public drunkenness have plummeted over the last three decades. Disorderly conduct arrests have also decreased over time, but the decline is less dramatic.

There were more than 5 million arrests for public order crimes in 1995. In order of their relative prevalence, UCR data for 1995 estimate that about 1.5 million persons were arrested for drug abuse violations, another 1.5 million for driving under the influence of alcohol, more than 700,000 arrested for disorderly conduct, another 700,000 for drunkenness, more than 400,000 for liquor law violations, about 200,000 for vandalism, nearly 100,000 for prostitution and commercialized vice, about 26,000 for vagrancy, and nearly

Figure 8.1
Trends in Arrest Rates for Selected Public Order Crimes over Time

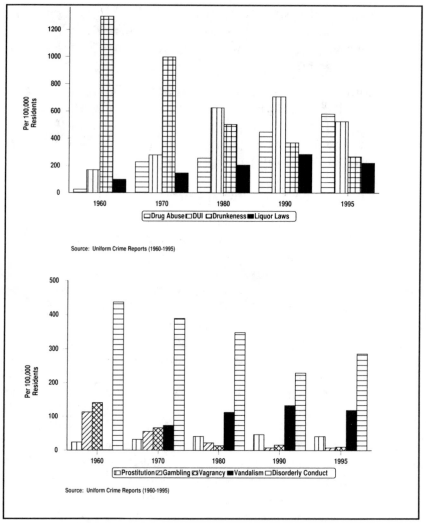

20,000 for gambling violations. The number of arrests for public order violations far exceed any other general crime type.

Arrest data dramatically underestimate the prevalence of public order violations. This is most apparent in alcohol and drug violations. Drug and alcohol surveys of juveniles reveal that more than one-third of tenth graders report using alcohol and more than one-third of high school seniors said they used marijuana in the last month (NIDA 1996). Nearly 5 percent of high school seniors report using marijuana daily. The level of alcohol use among juveniles has stayed relatively stable over the last two decades, and estimates of marijuana use are still below levels reported in the late 1970s. When alcohol use by other juveniles and drug use by any age group are considered, it is clear that arrest data only touch the surface on the prevalence of these public order violations.

Two of the strongest social correlates of public order violations are region of the country and size of geographical area (see Table 8.1). Arrest rates for prostitution, drug abuse violations, and vagrancy are highest in Northeastern and Western States and lowest in Midwestern and Southern States (UCR 1995). Arrest rates for drunkenness are far below national averages in Northeastern States, but rates of disorderly conduct and gambling are clearly above average in these states. Midwestern States greatly surpass others in arrest rates for liquor law violations, and Southern States arrest rates for drunkenness are far higher than those of the next highest region. National self-report studies indicate that marijuana and cocaine us-

Table 8.1
Social Correlates of Public Order Arrest Rates for 1995

	1995 Rate	Regional Differences				Population Size (Cities)		
		Northeast	Midwest	South	West	250,000	50-100,000	<10,000
Drug Abuse	582.5	766.9	413.0	501.4	695.1	1,024.9	552.7	454.7
DUI	526.0	303.8	589.0	537.0	614.4	328.5	400.5	832.3
Drunkenness	268.4	27.2	117.2	456.8	246.2	273.1	341.5	462.4
Liquor Law	221.6	239.0	381.1	152.4	208.4	241.7	205.6	454.4
Prostitution	41.3	47.9	41.1	33.7	48.5	137.0	28.6	1.6
Gambling	8.0	22.8	4.4	5.8	3.6	27.2	4.6	3.1
Vagrancy	10.4	18.8	5.6	5.1	16.2	29.1	8.8	8.5
Vandalism	118.5	142.4	146.4	85.8	133.4	143.3	126.1	171.9
Disorderly Conduct	285.9	431.7	452.8	239.4	144.3	411.4	338.5	481.2

Source: Uniform Crime Reports (1995)

age is highest in the Western States and lowest in the Northeast, whereas alcohol use is highest in the Northeast and lowest in the Southern States (NIDA 1991).

The relationship between population size and arrest rates varies among public order offenses. Arrest rates for prostitution, drug violations, gambling, and vagrancy are lowest in small cities and generally higher in large urban areas (UCR 1995). In contrast, small towns, rather than large cities, have the highest arrest rates for liquor law violations, drunkenness, driving while intoxicated, vandalism, and disorderly conduct. One possible explanation for these geographical differences is that law enforcement in small towns may have more time to devote to apprehending alcohol violators and to investigate cases of disorderly conduct because the overall crime rate in these areas is low.

Offender Profile

The offender profile in public order crimes is similar in many ways to violent crime and street-level property offenses. Gender, race, and age differences are found in arrest data for each type of public-order offense (see Table 8.2).

Table 8.2
Offender Arrest Characteristics for Public Order Crimes in 1995

	Gender		Race			Age		
	% Male	% Female	% White	% Blacks	Other	> 25	< 25	Peak Age
Drug Abuse	83.3	16.7	62.1	36.9	1.0	28.6	44.0	18
DUI	85.4	14.6	86.4	10.4	2.7	7.3	22.0	24
Drunkenness	88.2	11.8	80.8	16.4	2.8	10.5	23.3	21
Liquor Law	81.1	18.9	79.6	17.3	3.1	56.8	66.4	18
Prostitution	38.9	61.1	60.9	36.8	2.3	7.7	21.2	30
Gambling	84.8	15.2	53.3	41.3	5.4	19.7	31.4	20
Vagrancy	80.6	19.4	52.4	45.0	2.6	28.1	34.4	18
Vandalism	86.4	13.6	73.4	23.4	21.7	57.8	68.3	16
Disorderly Conduct	78.3	21.7	62.9	35.1	2.0	36.5	51.2	17

Source: Uniform Crime Reports (1995)

Males are about three times more likely than females to be arrested for any index crime, and this ratio holds for most public order offenses. Males comprise nearly 90 percent of those arrested for either drunkenness, vandalism, driving under the influence, or gambling violations (UCR 1995). More than three-fourths of those arrested for vagrancy, disorderly conduct, liquor-law violations, and drug abuse offenses are men. Only in the case of prostitution, where nearly two-thirds of the arrestees are women, are males underrepresented as offenders.

Minority overrepresentation in arrests for public order violations is not as great as it was for murder and robbery, but arrest trends still substantially differ by race. Nearly half of those arrested for vagrancy are African Americans, and so are about 40 percent of all those arrested for gambling, drug violations, disorderly conduct, and prostitution (UCR 1995). However, African Americans are only slightly overrepresented in arrests for alcohol-related crimes like liquor law violations and drunkenness. Only in the case of driving under the influence of alcohol is the proportion of arrestees who are African American (11 percent) less than their distribution in the entire U.S. population.

The age of public order offenders varies by type of crime. Given age restrictions on the use and possession of alcohol, it is not surprising that more than half of arrests for liquor law violations involve persons under 21 years old, and the most frequent violators are 18- and 19-year-olds (UCR 1995). Arrests for disorderly conduct peak at 17 years old, and decrease dramatically after the age of 30. The peak age for arrest for drug violations is 18, whereas persons in their mid-20s are most prone to arrest for driving while under the influence. Arrest for prostitution is most prevalent for persons in their early 30s. The peak age for gambling violators is between 18 and 20 years old. For each type of public order violation, arrest rates decrease dramatically from the mid-30s and each successive five-year age group (UCR 1995).

Self-report studies of drug and alcohol use provide less dramatic differences by gender, race, and age. Although men are more than four times more likely to be arrested for drug violations than women, national studies of drug use within the last year indicate that men are only about twice as likely as women to report using either marijuana or cocaine (NIDA 1991). African Americans are only slightly more likely than whites to report marijuana use in the last year, but about twice as likely to report using cocaine. Both marijuana and cocaine use is highest among persons between 18 and 25 years old, dropping off dramatically after the age of 35. More than half of high school seniors have used alcohol in the past month, with males slightly more likely than females to report using alcohol (Johnston, Bachman, and O'Malley 1995). These self-report studies illustrate some of the biases inherent in arrest data for drug and alcohol violations and suggest that an enormous amount of public order violations are undetected by the police.

Public order violators tend to have extensive histories of involvement in minor criminal offenses. Persons arrested for prostitution, public drunkenness, vagrancy, drug abuse, illegal alcohol use, and disorderly conduct often have prior arrests for similar offenses, trespass, petty theft, and various types of nuisance violations. More than half (53 percent) of those arrested for public order offenses have prior felony arrests, and this proportion increases to 70 percent when prior misdemeanor arrests are included (Smith 1993). Juveniles involved in public order violations are especially likely to have prior contact with the police for status offenses like running away and truancy. Compared to other types of criminals, public order offenders are more likely to have prior criminal histories.

Offense Specialization and Escalation

Although terms like drug addict and alcoholic imply a specific behavioral pattern, public order violators rarely exhibit signs of offense specialization. In other words, drug addicts often engage in an assortment of other deviant and criminal activities, and those involved in prostitution, vandalism, disorderly conduct, or vagrancy also participate in other forms of misconduct.

Within general types of public order violations, however, there may be some elements of offense specialization. Prostitutes who are "call girls," for example, may provide different services and cater to a different clientele than "street walkers." Gamblers may specialize in playing a particular type of game. Nonetheless, even those persons who specialize in a particular form of prostitution or gambling are often involved in drug and alcohol abuse, petty theft, and other types of criminal activity.

Although there is usually a short apprenticeship period for both prostitutes and drug users during which they learn the norms and techniques of their illegal activities, there is little evidence of escalation in the seriousness of public order offending over criminal careers. However, the strong association between serious felony offending and substance abuse suggests that some escalation may result from drug and alcohol abuse. Nearly two-thirds of state prison inmates claim to have used a major drug (such as heroin, cocaine, PCP, or LSD) on a regular basis before their arrests (Beck, Gilliard, Greenfeld, Harlow, Hester, Jankowski, Snell, Stephen, and Morton 1993). Alcohol use and abuse by victims or offenders is present in the majority of murders and physical assaults. As a precipitating condition in much street-level crime, drug and alcohol use may be considered a major source in the escalation of criminal behavior.

Planning and Spontaneity

Public order offenses vary widely in terms of whether they are planned or spontaneous acts. Some instances of prostitution, drug abuse, illegal drinking, vandalism, illegal gambling, and disorderly conduct may be spur-of-the-moment behaviors precipitated by peer pressure and the availability of opportunities, but perpetrators of these crimes in most cases clearly plan and create their criminal opportunities. Public order crimes that are profit motivated such as selling dope, manufacturing and distributing pornography, and operating illegal gambling establishments are planned activities that often require greater sophistication to reduce the risks of detection.

Little planning or sophistication, however, is required for participation in most public order violations. For example, vandals may decide to destroy property because they have a prior grievance with the owner, "skeezers" may select particular clients for prostitution because they know that these people will exchange sex for drugs, and gamblers and drug users rely upon prior contacts and experiences to lay down illegal wagers or score dope. As true of all crimes, greater sophistication and planning are required for successful participation in public order violations.

Situational Elements and Circumstances

The circumstances surrounding public order violations involve the motivations for their commission, the victim-offender relationship, and situational characteristics. Various motives explain the onset of and continued involvement in public order violations.

The Motivation for Public Order Violations

People engage in public order violations for a wide variety of expressive and instrumental reasons. Economic profit is the primary motivation for prostitution, gambling, drug trafficking, and the manufacturing and distribution of sexually explicit literature. However, additional motives like affection and peer acceptance are equally important in these offenses. Prostitutes, for example, often come from troubled homes, filled with chronic conflict, hostility, and extensive histories of sexual and emotional abuse (Weisberg 1985). These victims have learned early in life that sexual encounters can be used to obtain affection, power, and money. For many prostitutes, their working relations with repeat customers, fellow prostitutes, and pimps provide basic socioemotional needs like companionship, excitement, love, and affection.

When asked about their motivations for crime, street prostitutes give a variety of answers. The following quotes from female prostitutes give a fuller sense of these motives (Miller 1986: 162-163):

> . . . I like the excitement. It's dangerous, I guess, but you meet different people. I just relate, you know, I relate to people better who are in 'the life'. . . because . . . ah, like a square girl, what do they talk about? Nothin'! 'Oh, my boyfriend's this and that.' I think it's boring. I like to talk about somethin' excitin', about . . . like money and how she went about getting the money. Then I'll know the next time how to get it better. It's just a game. That's all it is. I realize it. It's not going to last forever. But I'm enjoyin' it while I'm doin' it.

> . . . For the money . . . because I needed it. . . . I did it 'cause I had to. I mean 'cause my mother couldn't do it, and my daddy was a dog, and that's all I can say. So when I look back, I say he was a dog because she [mom] couldn't make no money. She had too many babies. I just had to; I still do.

> . . . The reason most women does crimes is mens. I think it's more prostitutes, you know. Everybody's gettin' into the street life. Everybody's runnin' around. He's a pimp; she's a whore. . . . Whatever you do, don't keep on doin' this 'cause once it's in your blood, it stays there forever; you just get it in your bloodstream.

Most juvenile public order violators hope to enhance their image and gain status. Drug and alcohol use may provide cheap thrills and an alternative to an often mundane existence. Peer approval in some juvenile groups may be enhanced by being the troublemaker or the "loose cannon" who destroys property and creates turmoil with other criminal actions. Although vandalism and disorderly conduct by juveniles are often viewed as nonutilitarian or without reasonable purpose, these acts are motivated in many cases by a desire to enhance or maintain one's image within a peer group. Drug dealing by both juveniles and adults is functional for many users because it provides them their own private "stash" of drugs.

Victim-Offender Relationship

Public order violations are often called victimless crimes because the victims are willing participants in the illegal activity. Drug and alcohol use, prostitution, and gambling are the most common victimless crimes. However, we have become increasingly aware of the secondary victims of these crimes, such as family members and even society at large. From this perspective, family members are known victims of many of these crimes. Most victims of vandalism and drunk driving appear to be strangers, but vandals sometimes destroy property of people they know who have "dissed" them.

Situational Dynamics of Public Order Violations

Many public order violations involve elements of exchange between buyers and sellers of illegal goods and services. These transaction dynamics are important in understanding the occurrence of public order violations and the subsequent attempts to control them.

The exchange elements involved in public order violations are most evident in transactions involving prostitution, drug use, pornography, and gambling. Prostitutes must locate places for doing business and develop specific strategies for soliciting clients without being apprehended. Bellhops, cab drivers, bartenders, and other legitimate service workers are often used to arrange dates for call girls, whereas street walkers may simply conduct business in open, public areas. Whatever the type of prostitute, success at the business depends on the ability to identify safe customers, satisfy their demands, and avoid detection by police. The same general exchange occurs among drug users, distributors of pornographic materials, and gamblers; users must find suppliers, users and sellers must be able to satisfy their mutual demands, and the parties must be able to identify situational cues that reduce their risks of detection.

Interviews with drug dealers and prostitutes emphasize the importance of intuitive skills in being able to detect and avoid undercover police officers and informants. As revealed in the following quotes, the ability to detect situational cues is absolutely crucial to being a successful criminal (Faupel 1996:186):

> . . . I learned the ropes . . . how you spot cops . . . those undercover detectives with the bee stingers on their cars, little teeny antennae on top; and how you could pick those cars out; and how two detectives in a car, how there were certain characteristics about them that were always the same. You could smell them a mile away. . . .

> . . . Never take a [drug] deal that sounds too good to be true. . . . This guy came by and wanted to buy 15 bags for $10 apiece—no shorts. Now any kind of a hustler junkie coming off the street and he's got $150, he's not gonna come to you wanting 15 bags. He's gonna come to you wanting 25 or 30. You know what I'm saying? The deal was too good to be true.

Various criminological theories have been used to account for the onset of public order violations. Traditional criminological theories attribute causal importance to such factors as impersonal strain, an excess of pro-crime definitions, the weakening of bonds to traditional society, and the learning of techniques to engage in these crimes and to neutralize societal reaction. People blocked from legitimate opportunities may innovate by engaging in illegal profit-motivated offenses like gambling, drug selling, and manufacturing and distributing pornography, whereas others may freely choose to use drugs, alcohol, or engage in illegal sexual practices for cheap thrills or the immediate availability of criminal opportunities. Within each of these contexts, however, completion of the criminal act involves particular situational dynamics linking the buyer and seller of these goods and services. To minimize the risk of detection and being cheated, buyers and sellers of illegal goods and services understandably prefer to deal with familiar clients.

Public Order Crime Syndromes

There are various ways to classify public order violations. The most basic distinction involves differences in the type of illegal behavior. Major syndromes based on offense characteristics include (a) prostitution, (b) pornography, (c) substance abuse, and (d) gambling. Within each general category of public order crime, secondary distinctions include the offenders' roles (buyers or sellers) and degree of criminal involvement (professionals or novices, addicts or occasional or "recreational" users). These variations in public order crime syndromes are described below.

Prostitution

Prostitution, often considered the oldest profession, involves the exchange of sexual activity for economic returns. The social status and prestige associated with prostitution varies widely across cultures and time periods. Japanese geishas and some notorious bordello managers like Heidi Fleiss (the "Hollywood madam") and Sydney Biddle Barrows (the "Mayflower madam") are afforded relatively high status, whereas prostitutes such as street walkers and "b-girls" (who work in cooperation with bar or tavern managers) occupy the lower ranks of social status. In some countries, including the Netherlands, prostitution is legal and closely regulated to reduce the risks of disease, whereas in countries like Somalia, prostitution is punishable by death (Lesieur and Welch 1995). Aside from Nevada (where legal brothels are allowed in some counties), state laws in the U.S. define prostitution as a misdemeanor offense, though the laws are unevenly enforced in different jurisdictions.

Prostitution is widespread in contemporary American society. The estimated quarter of a million full-time prostitutes in this country are thought to be serving a total of 1.5 million customers a week (Lesieur and Welch 1995). Gross annual revenues from prostitution are estimated at $7 to $9 billion dollars (Pateman 1988). The major types of prostitutes in the U.S. include streetwalkers, brothel prostitutes, bar girls, "skeezers," and call girls.

Prostitutes who work the open streets to solicit customers are referred to as hustlers, hookers, or streetwalkers. Streetwalkers are the most visible and lowest paid prostitutes, found primarily in adult entertainment districts or "combat zones" in major cities. These prostitutes are most vulnerable to disease, arrest, and mistreatment by pimps and customers (Lesieur and Welch 1995). The financial rewards for streetwalkers are relatively low, and typical hookers must work long hours to make enough from "tricks" to meet monetary obligations. Even the best streetwalkers rarely gross more than $200 or $300 a day (Barlow 1990).

Many streetwalkers are poor, minority females with few legitimate avenues for making a living. Other streetwalkers are young runaways who have moved to the city streets to escape sexual and physical violence at home (Janus, Scanlon, and Price 1984). Some turn to prostitution to support drug habits (Inciardi et al. 1991).

Common settings for prostitution in the nineteenth and early twentieth centuries were called "houses of ill repute," bordellos, cathouses, and brothels. "Brothel prostitutes" work in large establishments usually owned and administered by a madam. Often a retired prostitute herself, the madam provides various services to the brothel, including the recruitment of women into prostitution and socializing them in the business, attracting customers, developing mutual working relations with law enforcement, and supervising activities within the establishment (Goldstein 1983). Although legal brothels in the United States now only exist in some counties in Nevada, the 1984 arrest of socialite Sydney Biddle Barrows (who operated a $1 million prostitution ring out of a bordello on West Seventy-Fourth Street in New York City) and the more recent arrest of Heidi Fleiss in Hollywood illustrate the persistence of commercial prostitution establishments. Most large cities have brothels that maintain themselves solely through a system of informal referrals (Barlow 1990).

Bar girls, also called b-girls, are prostitutes who work in cooperation with the management of drinking establishments. A prior arrangement is made so that prostitutes order diluted drinks for themselves, and clients are allowed to pick up the tab before the actual act of prostitution (Lesieur and Welch 1995). Drinking establishments near military bases have often been popular locations for bar girls (Winick and Kinsie 1971).

"Skeezers" are a relatively new form of prostitute that emerged with the introduction of crack cocaine to the street culture in the mid-1980s (Siegel 1995). The dominant characteristics of these prostitutes is that they barter sex to support their drug habits. Rather than feeling exploited, skeezers often report that they are treated fairly when bartering sex for drugs (Goldstein, Ouellet, and Fendrich 1992).

The most lucrative and professional type of prostitute is the call girl. Call girls have greater control over their selection of clients and reportedly charge as much as $500 per client, earning up to $100,000 per year (Siegel 1995). Call girls often have middle-class backgrounds, attempt to enhance the self-esteem of their clients, and, like other prostitutes, sexually satisfy their clients (Lesieur and Welch 1995). These prostitutes typically work in expensive hotels or their own apartments. As with other prostitutes, novice call girls must learn where to find clients, how to stay in business, and how to protect themselves from disease, police, competition, and customers (Barlow 1990).

Over the last decade, massage parlors and escort services have emerged as new fronts for prostitution. Massage parlors are good settings for prostitution because they provide a legal business for customer contacts, do not require employees to solicit business, and offer some protection against arrest and conviction because parlors are semi-private settings and entrapment is often a possible legal defense when customers actively solicit sex and then arrest the masseuses (Barlow 1990). Most localities have attempted to limit commercial sex in massage parlors by passing ordinances specifying that masseuses must keep certain parts of their bodies covered, and limiting the areas of the body that can be legally massaged (Siegel 1995). Escort services also often provide a legal front for commercial sex.

There are major differences in the status and treatment of the buyers and sellers of commercial sex through prostitution. First, the buyers or "johns" of prostitutes are typically men from all social strata, whereas the sellers are often young women with histories of school failure, drug abuse, disruptive family relations, emotional and physical abuse as children, and previous difficulties with keeping jobs (Jackman, O'Toole, and Geis 1967). Second, buyers of commercial sex are far less likely to be arrested and convicted than sellers. Police crackdowns on prostitution usually focus on the most visible streetwalker and rarely on her clients or pimps. Women, who are most often the sellers, are arrested nearly twice as often for prostitution as men (UCR 1995).

Prostitutes also vary widely in the nature of their criminal careers. Novice prostitutes, for example, often enter the trade believing that it is exciting and profitable to sell sex instead of "giving it away" (Davis 1978). A transitional period often follows, in which novices have not developed deviant identities and use prostitution as a part-time occupation. Many b-girls, exotic dancers and strippers, and escorts fall in this transitional phase and may subsequently desist before becoming involved in full-time prostitution. Professional prostitutes have the most extensive history of sexual services. As madams or high-class call girls, professionals have often risen from the ranks. The apprenticeship period between novice and professional is often quite short because the requisite skills necessary to solicit customers and avoid arrest, injury, and death must be learned quickly (Davis 1978). The prostitution lifestyle takes an incredible toll. The accelerated aging process associated with this lifestyle often puts an end to their criminal careers as prostitutes. Some financially successful prostitutes may establish their own business by employing others in either houses of prostitution or in a complex call-girl network or escort service. As true of other seasoned criminals, professional prostitutes are highly committed to their behavior as a way of life and are not easily deterred by the threat of legal sanction. In contrast, legal action may be sufficient to abate novices' desires for greater involvement in prostitution.

Pornography

Local community standards vary greatly in their definition and treatment of pornographic materials. Sexually explicit materials involving children are widely condemned, although it is estimated that more than $1 billion of a total of $2.5 billion spent annually on pornography can be classified as "kiddie porn" (Attorney General's Report 1986). The issue of censorship and First Amendment protections for printed material is rigorously debated across the country. Three major government-sponsored commissions in the U.S. and Canada have concluded that exposure to nonviolent pornography does not cause sexual violence against women, and some studies find a reduction in aggression by subjects exposed to nonviolent pornography (Lesieur and Welch 1995). Sexually explicit and violent pornography, however, is linked to sexual violence. Regardless of the impact of pornography on violent crime, there remain major differences in public attitudes about the social acceptance of pornography and what constitutes obscene material.

There are several unresolved issues about the buyers and sellers of pornographic materials. Manufacturers and sellers of sexually explicit materials are often criticized for exploiting women and children, vulgarizing culture, and eroding standards of common decency. More than a million children are believed to be used each year in pornography or prostitution, many of them runaways who are exploited by adults (Lederer 1980). Given a causal link between exposure to violent pornography and sexual violence, manufacturers and sellers of this material are thought to contribute to the victimization of specific groups. Although buying sexually explicit materials is often viewed as an issue of choice, controversy surrounds how best to protect young people from exposure to these materials.

Substance Abuse

Fundamental distinctions in substance abuse involve the type of drug, the extensiveness of users' histories, and differences in users and distributors. Illicit drug and alcohol use are often considered a matter of personal choice and generate less public condemnation than the acts of manufacturing or selling drugs to others. The legal penalties for possession and being under the influence of controlled substances are far less severe than they are for the manufacturing, selling, or trafficking of illegal drugs. The notion of a victimless crime is rarely applied to drug pushers and distributors. Instead, they are often viewed as preying on weak and vulnerable victims.

There is much debate about what are the most dangerous drugs in contemporary American society. Today, alcohol, tobacco, and marijuana are the drugs of choice among young people. However, drug use is wide and varied, with specific substances like crack (a smokable form of cocaine) and designer drugs (synthetic substances made to induce mood-altering effects) becoming popular at specific points in time. Much drug use by teenagers is best classified as sporadic and recreational, typically occurring in a group context. Marijuana use and "huffing" (inhaling vapors from substances like paint or oven cleaner) is also most common among young people. Crack is the preferred form of cocaine use among lower-class members, and powdered cocaine is more common among middle- and upper-class users.

According to Jones, Shainberg, and Byer (1979), general categories of illegal drugs include: *anesthetics* like PCP or "angel dust" that produce hallucinations and a spaced-out feeling; *volatile liquids* like lighter fluid, paint thinner, and model airplane glue whose vapors are inhaled; *barbiturates* or "downers," "goofballs," or "reds" that depress the central nervous system; *amphetamines* or "uppers" that stimulate the central nervous system; *cannabis (marijuana)* or "dope" that is smoked to distort auditory and visual perceptions; *hallucinogens* like Mescaline and LSD that result in vivid distortions of the senses and out-of-body sensations; *cocaine and its derivative forms* like freebase and crack that provide a powerful high and are highly addictive; *narcotics* like morphine, heroin, codeine, and methadone that are strong pain-killers; and *steroids* that are used to gain muscle bulk and strength for body builders and athletes. Whether prescription or illicit drugs, controlled substances are often used by addicts and persistent users to help cope with the struggles of everyday life.

Many adolescents begin their involvement in drug dealing with the use and distribution of small amounts of drugs (Chaiken and Johnson 1988). These petty dealers sell marijuana, crack, and PCP to their friends and personal acquaintances to support their own drug use. A smaller number of drug users who sell multiple drugs work with both adult drug distributors and adolescent users, and a more serious type of drug-involved youth sells drugs and also commits property and violent crimes. Adult drug dealers exhibit many of the same behavioral characteristics in the use and distribution of drugs. The most extreme form of drug dealing involves smuggling controlled substances that are imported from other countries. Although most street dealers are young lower-class males, smugglers are often middle-aged or older men who have strong organizational skills, established connections, capital to invest, and a willingness to take large business risks (Chaiken and Johnson 1988).

The individual and societal consequences of the habitual use of drugs and alcohol are far different than those of recreational or sporadic use of these substances. Both drug addicts and alcoholics have shorter life expectancies, more disruptive family relations, poorer work histories, and are more involved in other types of criminal activities, due to either diminished mental capacity or the need to support their habits. Most addicts finance their addiction through legitimate work and a variety of hustles, including begging, borrowing, stealing, drug pushing, and prostitution (Barlow 1990). Inciardi (1987) estimated that his sample of 356 Florida heroin addicts committed a total of 118,134 criminal offenses in one year alone. Estimates of the proportion of drunk drivers who are alcoholics range from 50 to 75 percent for first-time offenders and between 75 and 98 percent for second-time offenders (Forcier et al. 1986). Occasional abuse of drugs and alcohol is also tied to subsequent criminal behaviors like drunk driving and violent crime, but use of these substances in moderation typically has less serious individual and societal consequences.

Gambling

Illegal gambling is similar to prostitution, pornography, and illicit drugs in that there is often a thin line separating legal and illegal behavioral patterns. This distinction between legal and illegal gambling has become increasingly muddled because of the rapid growth in legalized gambling across the country. State-run lotteries and racetrack betting are now legal in most jurisdictions, with 48 states having legalized some form of gambling (LaFleur and Hevener 1992). The gross dollar volume from legal gambling has increased at least tenfold over the last two decades (Christiansen 1988). The growth in legalized gambling has also removed much of the moral stigma from gambling (Rosecrance 1988). Changes in the legal status of gambling are the major cause of the enormous reduction in gambling arrests from over 120,000 in 1960 to less than 20,000 by 1995 (UCR 1995).

Compulsive or pathological gamblers have many of the same personal, familial, and financial problems as drug addicts and alcoholics. These gamblers become outcasts as a result of neglecting their families, failing to repay loans, taking time out from work to gamble, and engaging in crimes to support an increasingly expensive addiction (Lesieur 1984). Check forgery, embezzlement, and other types of employee theft, larceny, and credit fraud are the most common offenses among pathological gamblers (Blaszczynski and McConaghy 1992). Compulsive gamblers differ from novices and occasional betters in the frequency, diversity, and amount of their wagering; they bet more frequently and heavily on a variety of gambling-related hustles and cons.

Public Order Crime Prevention and Intervention Strategies

Three general approaches have been used to control the number of public order violations. The primary prevention and intervention strategies include (1) efforts by criminal justice officials to increase the risks of getting caught and convicted, (2) treatment through counseling, education, and social services, and (3) opportunity-reduction programs that limit offenders' ability to commit these offenses and decrease the supply of prohibited substances.

The Criminal Justice Response

The ability of the criminal justice system to deter public order violations through swift, certain, and severe sanctions is limited at the onset by several structural characteristics of these crimes. First, many of these crimes, especially prostitution, substance abuse, and gambling, occur in private settings and often outside the plain view of police and citizens. Second, police awareness of these crimes is not only limited by their low public visibility, but equally by the absence of victims to serve as complaining witnesses. Third, most public order violations are misdemeanors that are not perceived as particularly serious by police or citizens. As a lower law enforcement priority, police departments in large cities may not have the time or resources necessary to rigorously monitor and apprehend these "morality" offenders. Fourth, even if law enforcement's response to these crimes was severe and consistent (which it is not), the mixed public attitudes toward public order violations undermine the possible deterrent effect of legal sanctions.

Compared to other types of criminal activity, the likelihood of getting caught and legally punished for public order violations is incredibly low. The low public visibility and the lack of a direct victim, as mentioned above, are major factors in reducing police awareness of these crimes. The nature of these offenses makes undercover officers and sting operations especially valuable law enforcement strategies. However, the success of these tactics in gaining convictions is somewhat limited because of the possibility of police entrapment as a defense.

National data on prosecution and conviction practices for public order crimes are not available. However, data on felony defendants processed in the 75 largest U.S. counties reveal several trends. First, about 69 percent of felony defendants charged with drug offenses are convicted, as are nearly 68 percent of those charged with other public order offenses (Smith 1993). The conviction rate is slightly lower for other types of felony charges. Second, the average prison sentence for felony drug offenders is about four years and about three years for other felony public order crimes. The severity of punishment is lower for public order crimes than for any other type of felony. Most public order offenses are misdemeanors, so data based on felony convictions grossly overestimate the magnitude of punishment for these offenses. The major exception to the low severity of punishment for public order violations is the stiff federal sentences for drug trafficking and being a drug "kingpin."

Given that most public order offenders exercise some degree of rational calculation and planning, the threat of legal sanction has some potential in deterring these offenders. Unfortunately, the low certainty and severity of legal punishments in actual practice undermine any potential deterrent value of legal sanctions for these crimes. The nebulous legal status of many public order violations and recent historical efforts to decriminalize various substances, prostitution, pornography, and gambling have also hampered the ability to reduce the prevalence of these behaviors through more informal mechanisms of social control like families, peer groups, schools, and religious organizations.

Treatment Approaches

Over the last three decades, many public order violations have become increasingly treated as medical problems rather than exclusively as criminal behavior. This approach is most evident in self-help organizations like Alcoholics Anonymous, Narcotics Anonymous, and Gamblers Anonymous. These organizations try to help people recognize their problems and resolve them through support from others. Programs such as Drug and Alcohol Resistance Education (DARE) in public schools are designed to increase the knowledge of the consequences of drug abuse and help children remain drug free. Drug Courts have been established in more than 200 jurisdictions to help convicted substance abusers deal with their problems.

The treatment of public order violations as medical problems has both benefits and costs. On the positive side, the medicalization of deviant behavior increases public tolerance and compassion for human problems. Under this perspective, alcoholics, drug addicts, compulsive gamblers, and habitual porn viewers are considered "sick," requiring treatment not punishment (Conrad and Schneider 1992). Problem drinkers who are drunk drivers are often required to attend education sessions that concentrate on the disease conception of alcoholism. The use of youth diversion programs that have strong counseling and education curricula is another way to treat wayward kids. The most successful "boot camp" programs have strong educational components to supplement the military training and regiment (MacKenzie, Brame, McDowall, and Souryal 1995).

There are two major shortcomings in medicalizing public order offenses and other social problems. First, the label of "treatment" may create some confusion about culpability and responsibility. If, for example, public order violators are sick, should we hold them liable for their actions? Second, this approach largely ignores wider social conditions because they are not individual deficiencies that are amenable to medical intervention. Therapists and "change" agents may provide all the counseling and interpersonal guidance in the world, but this approach typically fails to recognize and address structural sources of poverty and inequality in inner-city areas that are often the root causes of these social problems (Lesieur and Welch 1995). Counseling and drug or alcohol education may be the appropriate treatment for many young, first-time offenders. Unfortunately, participation in many types of public order violations provides for various social needs that are not met by counseling and psychotherapy. A large network of drug-treatment centers and residential programs has been established across the country, but little evidence has been found that these treatment programs can efficiently terminate substance abuse.

Opportunity-Reduction Strategies

Opportunity-reduction strategies for public order crimes involve a wide variety of efforts to control either the supply or demand for illegal goods and services. Police sweeps and periodic crackdowns on "hot spots" for prostitution, gambling, and drug dealing are designed to reduce the physical opportunity to do illegal business. In the case of drug suppression, major efforts have been undertaken to cut off drug supplies by destroying overseas crops and arresting members of drug cartels in Central and South America, Asia, and the Middle East (BJS 1992). Border patrols and military personnel are continuously involved in interdiction efforts to limit the supply of drugs entering the county. Breathalizers in legal drinking establishments offer patrons a way to monitor their alcohol consumption, whereas their installation in automobiles of convicted drunk drivers reduces the physical opportunity to repeat the offense. National educational programs such as "McGruff, the Crime Dog" and DARE are directed at teaching kids to refuse drugs, thereby reducing the demand for these substances. Anonymous hotlines in schools to report drug dealers attack the supply side. Opportunity-reduction efforts at the community level include neighborhood block watches, cooperative police-community ventures, and citizen patrols to take back their neighborhoods (Weingart 1993).

Although opportunity-reduction efforts remain a major response to public order violations, these efforts have been largely ineffective in controlling illegal behavior. Drug interdiction efforts, for example, have involved many multi-million dollar seizures, but the amount of narcotics produced each year is so vast that even dramatic reductions in the supply of drugs would have little impact on rates of consumption. Police sting operations and crackdowns in particular areas often merely result in the displacement of criminal activity to other areas of the city. Similarly, drug education is widely distributed across the country, but programs like DARE have been found to have no significant impact on drug use or on attitudes and beliefs about drugs (Rosenbaum, Flewelling, Bailey, Ringwalt, and Wilkinson 1994).

The public's demand for illegal goods and services is a major reason for the failure of opportunity-reduction strategies to control public order crimes. Our national appetite for illegal goods and services is also a key factor in the growing movement toward legalization of many of these activities.

Summary

Public order crime involves a wide array of behaviors that are not inherently or innately wrong but are considered criminal acts through legal pronouncement. Prostitution, drug and alcohol abuse, pornography, and illegal gambling are the major forms of public order crime. These behaviors are criminal in some jurisdictions but not in others. Arrest data and self-report studies indicate that there is widespread participation in these illegal activities across the country. With the exception of prostitution (where women are arrested more often than men), most known offenders of public order violations are young, urban males. Public order violations vary primarily in terms of (1) the type of illegal behavior, (2) the offender's role as a buyer or seller, and (3) the level of criminal involvement as novices or recreational users and habitual or addictive users. The primary strategies to control public order violations include the use of legal sanctions to deter criminal behavior, treatment approaches, and opportunity-reduction efforts. Although these control efforts have been widespread, there is little indication that they have been effective in reducing the prevalence of public order crimes. Public willingness to purchase these goods and services even if they are illegal is a major contributor to the failure of current control efforts and is a primary factor in the movement toward legalization of many of these prohibited activities.

Chapter Nine

Crime Control and the Anatomy of Dangerous Persons, Places, and Situations

A basic assumption underlying any crime typology is that offenses within one category differ from those in another. Burglaries, for example, may be committed against either commercial establishments or residences, but they are assumed to be different from other types of criminal behavior. Similarly, the victims and offenders involved in sexual assaults exhibit different characteristics, but sex offenses are thought to be unique from other violent crimes and property offenses. Phrased differently, each of the major crime categories is thought to have a distinct anatomy, varying by offender characteristics, motivations, victim characteristics, situational elements, and the most effective methods of crime control.

Previous chapters highlighted differences within crime categories, but this final chapter examines the similarities and differences found across crime types. Specifically, we summarize the commonality in the social profiles of the offenders, the temporal and spatial characteristics of different crimes, and the situational elements that underlie the major types of crime. We analyze these characteristics to define an anatomy of dangerous persons, places, and situations which are commonly involved in crime. The dominant characteristics of each crime type are then related to current crime-prevention strategies to develop suggestions for solving the crime problem in American society.

The Offender Profile

The offender profile includes the sociodemographic characteristics of offenders, their criminal histories, their degree of offense specialization, and the extent to which their criminal behavior is spontaneous or planned. The sociodemographic characteristics of offenders that are overrepresented in each major form of crime are summarized in Table 9.1.

The Offenders' Sociodemographic Characteristics

There are similarities and differences in the socio-demographic characteristics of offenders involved in different types of crime.

Table 9.1
Socio-Demographic Characteristics of Offenders
Overrepresented for Each Crime Type

Crime Type	Sex	Age	Race	Social Class	Prior Arrest?	Offense Specialization	Spontaneous Acts
Murder & Assault	Male	<25	African American	Lower Class	Yes	No	Yes
Sexual Assault	Male	<25	African American	Lower Class	Yes	Some	Mixed
Personal & Institutional Robbery	Male	<25	African American	Lower Class	Yes	No	No
Residential & Non-Residential Robbery	Male	<25	African American	Lower Class	Yes	No	Mixed
Motor Vehicle Theft	Male	<21	African American	Mixed	Yes	Some	Mixed
Occupational Crime	Male	<25	White	Lower, Middle Class	No	Some	No
Organizational Crime	Male	>25	White	Upper Class	No	Some	No
Public Order Crime	Both	<25	African American	Lower Class	Yes	Mixed	Mixed

White-collar offenders, especially those engaged in corporate crime, have the most divergent demographic characteristics.

Males as Criminals. Regardless of the particular crime type, males are clearly overrepresented as offenders. About nine of every 10 murderers and assaulters, sex offenders, robbers, burglars, and auto thieves are male. Males perpetrate a smaller proportion but still a substantial majority of white-collar crimes and public order offenses. Although the number of female offenders has increased over the last three decades (especially in cases of employee thefts and other larcenies), criminal offending remains primarily a male phenomenon. Male's greater participation in criminal acts is explained by their wider involvement with delinquent peers, less self-control, and greater exposure to criminal opportunities.

Young People as Criminals. Crime is committed disproportionately by the young. Juveniles are the most common auto thieves, although adults driven by profit have become increasingly involved in this offense. The vast majority of violent offenses (such as murders, assaults, rapes, and robberies), burglaries, and public order offenses are committed by persons under 25 years old. Occupational crime offenders tend to be in their 20s, but corporate offenders are often older. Corporate and other white-collar offenders are older than street offenders because opportunities for crime in the workplace are often age based. Peer pressure, cheap thrills, less self-control, and the impulsivity and unpredictability of youth are some explanations for the high offending rate for juveniles and young adults.

Minorities as Criminals. African Americans are clearly overrepresented in arrest statistics for the violent crimes of homicide, assault, robbery, and sexual assault. Arrest rates for these crimes are between four and five times higher for African Americans than their population distribution would predict. There is also minority overrepresentation in arrests for burglary, auto theft, and public order offenses, but racial differences are smaller in magnitude. White offenders, however, are disproportionately included in arrest data for occupational and organizational crime. Frustration caused by minority-group membership, the history of racial oppression, blocked economic opportunities, and selective enforcement and patrol in minority communities have all been offered as explanations for racial differences in offending.

Lower-Class Persons as Criminals. The social class of offenders varies by type of offense. The lower-class is disproportionately represented in arrest statistics for murder and assault, robbery, sexual assault, and burglary. Car theft for financial gain also appears to be more common among low-income persons, but joyriding by juveniles is equally prevalent across social classes. Occupational and especially organizational offenders are usually higher-income persons because these crimes are committed by employees within work contexts and require rank-specific opportunities for offending. The wide availability of criminal opportunities and the need to maintain or enhance one's economic status are common explanations for social class differences in occupational and organizational crime. Relative deprivation, thrill seeking to liven up otherwise mundane existences, and the lack of legitimate economic opportunities are widely used to account for high rates of criminal activity by lower-income persons.

The Criminal Career of Offenders

Depending on the type of crime, offenders have diverse histories of criminal activity. Auto thieves, burglars, and sex offenders have the most extensive criminal careers. The vast majority of these offenders have prior felony arrests. Murder and assault offenders are less likely to have long criminal careers. The low rate of prior arrests for occupational and organizational crime does not necessarily reflect lower levels of a criminal career for these offenders, but rather may simply reflect the lower rate of public disclosure of workplace crime.

Offense Specialization and Escalation

With the possible exception of white-collar crimes, there is little evidence of offense specialization among repeat offenders for any type of crime. Burglars and robbers may have some preferences for particular types of crime situations, but most offenders are fairly versatile in their selection of crime targets. Typical violent offenders have some experience with property crime and public order offenses, and typical property offenders have often committed a wide assortment of property thefts and public order offenses.

Although it makes intuitive sense that some offenders gravitate toward more serious crimes over their careers, a pattern of crime escalation is not evident for any major form of crime. Minor property offenses and public order violations are common in the histories of most offenders, but a steady progression from less to more serious crimes is not found in typical criminal careers.

Spontaneous or Planned Actions

There is much debate about whether typical offenders of various crimes engage in rational calculation of costs and benefits of criminal acts or whether criminal behavior is primarily a spontaneous act motivated by the immediate presence of criminal opportunities. Elements of planning and spontaneity are found in each of the major forms of crime.

A dominant image of homicide and, to a lesser extent, aggravated assault is that these criminal acts are spontaneous offenses that emerge out of particular circumstances in the heat of passion. Typical murders and assaults appear to follow this pattern. Some types of sexual assaults, especially those involving acquaintances, are also likely to be predominately expressive acts with little or no planning. Auto thefts involving joyriding by juvenile offenders are rarely premeditated and rational criminal events. However, the primary economic motive that underlies most robberies, burglaries, auto thefts by adults, and occupational and organizational crimes directly implies that these offenses are guided by some level of premeditation and planning. For the majority of offense types, offenders make their criminal opportunities or capitalize on readily available ones and then engage in some moderate degree of planning and calculation to commit their crimes.

Temporal and Spatial Distribution

Criminal opportunities and events are not equally distributed across time and place. Instead, some times of the day and particular locations are more prone to crime than others. As shown in Table 9.2, the temporal and spatial distribution of crime, however, is different for some types of criminal behavior.

Dangerous Times

Nighttime and weekends are the peak times for most violent crimes, property offenses, and public order violations. Occupational and organizational crimes do not exhibit a specific temporal pattern. Darkness is a criminogenic condition because (a) fewer people are around to provide protection for others during evening hours, (b)

Table 9.2
Time and Place Elements of Crime Profiles

	Night/Day	Season	Location	Type of Area
Murder	Night	Summer	Victim's Home	Low SES
Aggravated Assault	Night	Summer	Street	Low SES
Sexual Assault (rape)	Night	Summer	Victim's Home	Low SES
Personal Robbery	Night	Summer Early Fall	Near Victim's Home	Low SES
Institutional Robbery	Night	Summer Early Fall	Business	Central City
Residential Burglary	Day	Summer	Victim's Home	Low SES
Non-Residential Burglary	Night	Summer	Business	Low SES
Motor Vehicle Theft	Night	Summer	Near Victim's Home	Central City
Occupational Crime	Don't Know	Don't Know	Work	Don't Know
Organizational Crime	Don't Know	Don't Know	Work	Don't Know
Public Order Crime	Night	All	Don't Know	All types

nighttime provides greater anonymity and cover for crime commission, and (c) higher rates of drug and alcohol use during evenings and weekends lead to diminished criminal inhibitions and more victim carelessness.

Dangerous Places

The dangerousness of particular physical locations changes according to the crime. Victims' homes are the most common sites for homicides and assaults, sexual offenses, and, by definition, residential burglaries. Streets around victims' homes and deserted areas near parking lots and entertainment establishments are the major habitat for muggers and auto thieves. For most violent and property crimes, low-income areas in central cities have the highest rates of victimization. Isolated structures in industrial parks are especially prone to commercial burglary, whereas dwellings and businesses near major transportation arteries are often targets of robbery and auto theft. Bars and commercial gathering spots for groups of young adults are prime spots for public order violations. The notion of dangerous physical locations for white-collar crimes is less clear. Companies with lax internal security and histories of poor treatment of workers are most prone to employee theft, and corporations with decreasing profits and volatile market performance are the most susceptible to organizational crime.

Situational Elements and Circumstances

Crimes are motivated by different factors, involve victims and offenders with different interpersonal relationships, and vary in terms of the presence and absence of other situational factors. Table 9.3 summarizes these situational factors for different types of crime.

Motivations for Offending

Criminal acts fulfill a number of offenders' instrumental needs. The needs or goals of criminal activity, however, differ according to

Table 9.3
Situational Elements of Crime Profiles

Crime Type	Motivation	Victim-Offender Relationship	Percentage Co-Offenders	Alcohol / Drug Use	Victim Contribution
Murder & Aggravated Assault	Expressive	Non-Stranger	<50%	>50%	20-50%
Sexual Assault (rape)	Both Expressive & Instrumental	Non-Stranger	<10%	>50%	<10%
Personal & Institutional Robbery	Instrumental	Strangers	>50%	>50%	<10%
Residential & Non-Residential Burglary	Instrumental	Strangers	<50%	~50%	<40%
Motor Vehicle Theft	Both Expressive & Instrumental	Strangers	>50%	Don't Know	Don't Know
Occupational & Organizational Crime	Instrumental	Strangers & Non-Strangers	<10%	50%	<10%
Public Order Crime	Both Expressive & Instrumental	N/A	>50%	Mixed	N/A

the type of crime. Sexual assaults are often motivated by a desire for sexual conquest, dominance, power, and control. Robberies, burglaries, occupational and organizational crimes, and an increasing number of auto thefts are primarily motivated by economic rewards, but these crimes may also fulfill other desires such as revenge, cheap thrills, and status enhancement. Homicides and assaults, in contrast, are often expressive acts that occur in the heat of passion with little deliberation or concern about instrumental needs.

The Victim-Offender Relationships

A surprising number of criminal offenses involve victims and offenders who are acquaintances, friends, or family members. Although attacks by strangers have increased over time, the majority of homicides, assaults, and sex offenses are committed by known offenders. A sizeable minority of robberies and various types of occupational and organizational crimes also involve nonstrangers. Individuals with tangential relationships to victims, such as repair people or home-service providers, may provide tips to other offenders or commit household thefts themselves, but the vast majority of burglaries are committed by strangers. Crimes committed by strangers are more likely to be reported to the police because they are viewed as more serious and are associated with less public blame and criticism of the victim for the occurrence of the crime.

Co-Offender Patterns

The group nature of offending varies enormously within and across crime categories. Co-offenders are most evident in auto theft and public order crimes, and least common in violent offenses like murders, assaults, and rapes. Nearly all incidents of joyriding and auto theft for economic rewards occur in group contexts. Peers entice others to steal cars for cheap thrills. Economically motivated auto thieves rely upon co-offenders to perform specific tasks during crime commission and to distribute stolen property. Recreational drug and alcohol offenses typically occur in the presence of other users. Habitual drug users must have connections with drug suppliers. Prostitutes work closely with pimps and others like hotel operators and strip-club owners who financially benefit from this criminal activity.

Other types of crime also involve multiple offenders. Most commercial robbers, for example, use co-offenders to either immobilize or restrain customers, serve as look-outs, or drive getaway cars. Many residential burglars work in teams to scope out particular houses, defuse alarms, and remove stolen property. Typical consumer scams committed by occupational offenders involve task specialization and the use of multiple conspirators to reassure "marks" and pull off frauds. Organizational offenders engaging in price-fixing and collusion require support from other corporations or individuals for successful participation in criminal activities. Collective acts of interpersonal violence include lethal and nonlethal drive-by shootings by juvenile gang members and sexual assaults by groups of teenagers and young adults.

Within most general categories of crime, however, there is substantial variation in the likelihood of sole offenders. The vast majority of assaults and sex offenses, for example, involve one offender and one victim. Most muggers and purse snatchers work alone, and so do most home burglars, embezzlers, computer hackers, and business repair fraud operators. Auto thefts and public order offenses are most widely committed in group contexts and exhibit the least variation within crime types.

Alcohol and Drug Use

Drugs and alcohol are major precipitating factors in the onset of many crime incidents. The use of drugs and alcohol are common correlates of public order disturbances, violent offenses, and property crimes. As substances that impair judgment and reduce inhibitions, the majority of homicides and assaults involve alcohol and drug use by either victims, offenders, or both. Alcohol and drug use may provide youthful offenders the false courage to perform auto thefts, burglaries, and street robberies. Drug addicts and alcoholics may engage in a variety of predatory acts to support their habits. Alcohol and drug use is a less salient factor in cases of occupational crimes and, especially, organizational crimes.

Victim Precipitation

Victims play a variety of roles in increasing their risks of victimization and enhancing criminal opportunities. The routine activities and lifestyles of individuals may increase victimization risks if they increase their exposure to motivated offenders, enhance their attractiveness as crime targets, or decrease the level of protection or guardianship against illegal activity. Victims contribute more directly to their victimization by provoking others or by being careless and not exhibiting sound judgment while engaged in public activity.

A large minority, if not a majority, of homicides and assaults are victim-provoked by physical violence. In these cases of victim precipitation, the victim is the first in the assault situation to resort to the physical force that leads to their ultimate victimization. The level of victim precipitation for these violent crimes is more substantial if verbal threats and insinuating language are also included under the definition. Lower rates of victim precipitation are found for robbery and sexual assault. Carelessness on the part of victims is often noted in home burglaries, car thefts, and in cases of occupational and organizational crime. Public consumers and businesses that want "something for nothing," have lax security, and do not thoroughly check out business offers are most prone to victimization.

Target-Selection Processes

A major assumption underlying most criminological theories is that offenders make a series of rational choices when deciding whether or not to commit crimes and the subsequent selection of particular crime targets. From this perspective, victims are selected because they are convenient and familiar, lack protection or guardianship, have high expected yield, and are viewed as attractive to offenders.

The accuracy of the image of rational offenders and the importance of particular factors in the selection of crime targets varies within and across crime types. Homicides and assaults are usually spontaneous and largely impulsive acts, but victims of these acts are often family members, neighbors, or others convenient and familiar to offenders. Among violent offenders, however, serial murderers often prey on particular types of strangers such as prostitutes, young women, or children, suggesting that the perceived attractiveness of the victim, rather than convenience and familiarity, is the most important factor for these offenders. Joyriders select automobiles that are unlocked and unprotected, convenient, and familiar in terms of make and model, whereas economically motivated car thieves focus on the expected yield and attractiveness of the vehicles and their accessories. The combination of convenience and familiarity, low guardianship, and perceived attractiveness underlie the target-selection calculus for sexual assaults, robbery, and occupational and organizational crimes.

Crime Control Strategies

Efforts to control crime in American society have taken three general forms. First, the criminal justice system is designed to deter criminal behavior by the threat of legal sanction, apprehending suspects, and punishing offenders. Second, social welfare measures are intended to address the root causes of criminal offending by increasing legitimate opportunities, promoting anti-crime values, and integrating disparate groups into mainstream society. Third, opportunity-reduction strategies involve private and public efforts to reduce the occurrence of crime by increasing safety precautions and reducing the visibility and accessibility of crime targets. The effectiveness of these crime control efforts differs for different types of crime.

The Criminal Justice Response

Although the threat of legal sanction for crime commission is widely entrenched in American society and our punishments are often more severe than those in other countries, the ability of the criminal justice system to control crime has been limited in several respects. First, with the exception of murder and auto theft, only a small minority of many types of crimes are reported to the police. Occupational and organizational crimes are especially prone to underreporting because they often occur within organizational contexts far from public scrutiny, and company executives may fear loss of consumer confidence and business if illegal activity becomes public knowledge. Public order offenses like prostitution, drug, and alcohol offenses also rarely come to the attention of the criminal justice system. Second, among those offenses known to the police, arrest is an unlikely outcome. Arrests are made in less than two-thirds of murder cases and in only about one out of every seven known cases of burglary and car theft. Third, conviction and imprisonment are the exception rather than the rule for most arrested offenders. Charge dismissal and probation often characterize criminal processing. Fourth, for most chronic or habitual offenders, the risks of arrest and punishment are simply considered one of the inherent costs of criminal activity.

The potential deterrent value of punishment, however, is greater for some crime types than others. By definition, offenders who commit spontaneous or impulsive acts of violence are not thinking of the consequences of their acts, limiting the deterrent value of criminal sanctions for these offenses. However, criminal sanctions may deter economically motivated offenses and those precipitated by cheap thrills. Accordingly, most organizational and occupational crimes, auto thefts, robberies, burglaries, sex offenses, and public-order crimes are amenable to deterrence through the threat and application of certain and severe punishment. By increasing the certainty and severity of punishment, novice offenders are thought to refrain from criminal activity.

Although deterrence is a widely held justification for punishment, its value as a crime control strategy is mediated by the availability of legitimate opportunities for offenders. Specifically, if criminal offending provides for basic subsistence living and auxiliary needs such as peer approval, thrills and excitement, and dominance and control that are unfulfilled and unavailable through legitimate means, the threat of legal sanctions will not diminish the likelihood and level of criminal behavior. Compared to socially and economically disadvantaged persons, middle- and upper-class individuals should be more readily deterred by legal sanctions because they have greater opportunities to fulfill their desires through legitimate avenues and often have more to lose from engaging in criminal activity.

Social Betterment Measures

Traditional criminological theories have identified a variety of individual and structural correlates of criminal motivation. According to strain theory, lower-class individuals are blocked from achieving success goals through legitimate opportunities and thus resort to crime to fulfill those goals. Cultural deviance theories emphasize cultural diversity in heterogeneous societies, attributing higher rates of offending by young, urban, minority males to their greater acceptance of and exposure to pro-crime values. Social bond theory places importance on the weakening of attachments, commitment, and involvement in family and mainstream institutions that frees individuals to follow their natural criminal desires. These theories propose that criminal motivations can be reduced or controlled by increasing economic opportunities and individuals' attachments to conventional activities and institutions.

Social programs to reduce the economic motivations for crime focus on education, job training, and skill development among disadvantaged groups. Head Start, the Job Corps, and school busing are the most widely known programs, but reform efforts also include special education programs, youth-employment services, vocational training, "English as a Second Language" programs, and a variety of other public assistance programs.

Other forms of economically based crime control involve neighborhood restoration and revitalization programs to strengthen community bonds in socially disorganized areas. Neighborhood beautification projects and the infusion of financial support for community service are thought to reduce crime by promoting a sense of community and monitoring youths' activities. Unfortunately, although providing essential services to low-income residents, these efforts are often insufficient to overcome the cumulative disadvantage of lower-class life. Increasing community supervision and control may reduce criminal opportunities in low-income areas, but greater economic opportunities will have no impact on crimes motivated by interpersonal disputes, cheap thrills, and other non-economic concerns.

Social interventions in crime control also include various forms of individual and family counseling, drug and alcohol therapy, peer mediation, and alternative conflict resolution strategies. These approaches are directed at changing particular deficiencies of individuals and family units. Individual drug therapy and collective programs like DARE have been widely used across the country. Parental education programs such as PET (Parental Effectiveness Training) and the YMCA's Family Y'se program promote healthy interpersonal relations, family communication, and pro-social values. Peer mediation and alternative dispute resolution strategies focus on the development and utilization of more constructive means of anger control. Although these approaches make theoretical sense as crime control strategies, it is unclear whether they are effective once potential offenders are outside the programs' immediate control.

Reductions of Criminal Opportunities

The most common strategies for crime control focus on reducing criminal opportunities through environmental design, increasing public awareness of risky and dangerous situations, and target hardening. Employers can reduce the likelihood of employee theft by developing internal security and accounting systems within their companies. Auto thefts can be reduced by anti-lock equipment systems, whereas tighter business controls and greater internal and external monitoring by financial agents may diminish the opportunities for corporate offending. Gun ownership, alarms, exterior lighting, security fencing, and dog ownership are some of the private security measures that decrease the accessibility of crime targets for predatory violent crimes and property theft. Crime prevention tips for reducing the risks of violent crime often mention avoiding particular places at night, the strong association between victimization and drug or alcohol use, and limiting patterns of solitary public activities at night. Across all types of crime, criminal opportunities are reduced by decreasing physical proximity to motivated offenders, decreasing exposure to risky and dangerous situations, reducing one's attractiveness as crime target, and by increasing the level of protection against physical attacks or property thefts.

It is important to note that the effectiveness of opportunity-reduction strategies depends on characteristics of the offenders. Purely opportunistic offenders may be thwarted by opportunity-reduction efforts, whereas chronic and professional offenders can easily circumvent most crime prevention measures with their particular skills or by selecting a more available and accessible target. Spatial displacement of crime to other locations or the substitution of one type of criminal behavior for another is a likely consequence of most opportunity-reduction strategies because typical offenders do not specialize in a specific type of crime. Furthermore, effective target-hardening activities may have inadvertently created more serious forms of crime. The rise in carjackings, for example, may be due to the overall effectiveness of anti-theft devices in deterring thefts of unoccupied vehicles. Similarly, an increase in bombings of public buildings and abductions of citizens in public settings by terrorist groups may stem from the effectiveness of airport security in reducing air hijacking. Under these conditions, opportunity-reduction strategies may reduce risks of victimization, but this approach is unlikely to decrease the overall amount of crime in contemporary American society.

Summary

There are fundamental differences in offenders, victims, and situational elements within and across different types of crime. Some crimes are committed by lower-income people who prey on others that are similarly situated, whereas crimes committed in the course of legal occupations often involve people of high social status and respect. The designation of dangerous persons, places, and situations also varies within and across crime types. An understanding of this diversity is essential for developing realistic programs of crime control. Current efforts at crime control include the use of the criminal justice system to deter criminal motivations by apprehending and punishing offenders, the establishment of social welfare programs to provide legitimate opportunities and increase pro-social values, and crime reduction programs focusing on environmental design, public awareness campaigns, and increased personal and public safety precautions. Although these crime prevention measures have met with some success, the continued prevalence of crime in contemporary American society questions the overall effectiveness of these approaches to crime control.

References
and
Indexes

References

Albanese, Jay S. 1995. *White-Collar Crime in America.* Englewood Cliffs, NJ: Prentice Hall.

Amir, Menachem. 1971. *Patterns in Forcible Rape.* Chicago: University of Chicago Press.

Archer, Dane and Rosemary Gartner. 1984. *Violence and Crime in Cross-National Perspective.* New Haven, CT: Yale University Press.

Association of Certified Fraud Examiners. 1995. *Report to the Nation: Occupational Fraud and Abuse.* Association of Certified Fraud Examiners.

Athens, Lonnie H. 1989. *The Creation of Dangerous Violent Criminals.* New York: Routledge.

Attorney General's Commission Report on Pornography (Final Report). 1986. Washington, D.C.: U.S. Government Printing Office.

Bachman, Ronet. 1994. *Violence Against Women: A National Crime Victimization Survey Report.* Washington, D.C.: Bureau of Justice Statistics.

Bandura, Albert. 1973. *Aggression: A Social Learning Analysis.* Englewood Cliffs, NJ: Prentice-Hall.

Barlow, Hugh. 1990. *Introduction to Criminology.* 5th Edition. Glenview, IL: Scott, Foresman, and Company.

Bastian, Lisa. 1992. *Crime and the Nation's Households, 1991.* Washington, D.C.: Bureau of Justice Statistics.

—— 1995. *Criminal Victimization, 1993.* Washington, D.C.: Bureau of Justice Statistics.

Bavolek, S.J. 1985. "Etiology of Sexual Assault." In *Social Work Treatment With Abused and Neglected Children,* edited by Chris M. Mouzakitis and Raju Varghese.

Beck, Allen J. and Bernard E. Shipley. 1989. *Recidivism of Prisoners Released in 1983.* Washington, D.C.: Bureau of Justice Statistics.

Beck, Allen, Darrell Gilliard, Lawrence Greenfeld, Caroline Harlow, Thomas Hester, Lewis Jankowski, Tracy Snell, James Stephen, and Danielle Morton. 1993. *Survey of State Prison Inmates, 1991.* Washington, D.C.: Bureau of Justice Statistics.

Behar, Richard. 1993. "Car Thief at Large." *Time,* August 16, 1993: 47-48.

Beirne, P. and J. Messerschmidt. 1991. *Criminology*. San Diego, CA: Harcourt Brace Jovanovich.

Bennett, Trevor and Richard Wright. 1984. *Burglars on Burglary: Prevention and the Offender*. Hampshire, England: Bower.

Berger, Stuart M. 1988. *What Your Doctor Didn't Learn in Medical School*. New York: William Morrow and Company.

Black, Donald. 1984. *Toward a General Theory of Social Control: Selected Problems* (Vol. II). Orlando: Academic Press.

Blake, Kevin. 1995. "What You Should Know About Car Theft." *Consumer's Research* October 1995: 26-28.

Blake, Kevin. 1996. "Phone Scam Update: Seniors Beware." *Consumer's Research* February 1996: 23-27.

Blaszczynski, A. and N. McConaghy. 1992. *Pathological Gambling and Criminal Behaviour: Report to the Criminology Research Council*. Canberra, Australia.

Block, Carolyn Rebecca. 1995. *Major Trends in Chicago Homicide: 1965-1994*. Chicago, IL: Criminal Justice Information Authority.

Block, Richard L. 1977. *Violent Crime: Environment, Interaction, and Death*. Lexington, MA: Lexington Books.

Blumstein, Alfred, Jacqueline Cohen, Jeffrey A. Roth, and Christy Visher. 1986. *Criminal Careers and Career Criminals*. Vols. 1 and 2. Washington, D.C.: National Academy Press.

Blumstein, Alfred, Jacqueline Cohen, S. Das, and S.D. Moitra. 1988. "Specialization and Seriousness During Adult Criminal Careers." *Journal of Quantitative Criminology* 4(4): 303-345.

Bopp, W.J. 1986. "Profile of Household Burglary in America." *Police Journal* 46(2): 168-173.

Bowers, L., D. Jefferson, J. Strand, and J. Grohmann. 1991. *Sexual Assaults in Wisconsin, 1990*. Madison, WI.: Wisconsin Statistical Analysis Center.

Braithwaite, John and T. Makkai. 1991. "Testing an Expected Utility Model of Corporate Deterrence." *Law and Society Review* 25:7-39.

Brown, Stephen E., Finn-Aage Esbensen, and Gilbert Geis. 1995. *Criminology: Explaining Crime and Its Context*. 2nd Edition. Cincinnati, OH: Anderson.

Brownmiller, Susan. 1975. *Against Our Will: Men, Women and Rape*. New York: Simon and Schuster.

Bucknell University. n.d. *Some Tips on Acquaintance Rape Prevention: Avoidance Strategies for Women*. Bucknell University's Women's Resource Center and Susquehanna Valley Women in Transition.

Bureau of Justice Statistics. 1989. *Recidivism of Prisoners Released in 1983*. Washington, D.C.: National Institute of Justice.

———. 1992. *Drugs, Crime and the Justice System: A National Report.* Washington, D.C.: National Institute of Justice.

———. 1993. *Survey of State Prison Inmates, 1991.* Washington, D.C.: National Institute of Justice.

———. 1994. *Fact Sheet: Drug-Related Crime.* Washington, D.C.: National Institute of Justice.

———. 1995. *Compendium of Federal Justice Statistics, 1992.* Washington, D.C.: National Institute of Justice.

Burt, M. 1980. "Cultural Myths and Supports for Rape." *Journal of Personality and Social Psychology* 38 (February): 217-230.

Castillo, Dawn N. and E. Lynn Jenkins. 1994. "Industries and Occupations at High-Risk for Work-Related Homicide." *Journal of Occupational Medicine* 36(2): 128-129.

Chaiken, Jan M. and Marcia R. Chaiken. 1982. *Varieties of Criminal Behavior.* Santa Monica, CA: Rand.

Chaiken, Marcia and Bruce Johnson. 1988. *Characteristics of Different Types of Drug-Involved Offenders.* Washington, D.C.: National Institute of Justice.

Chambliss, William J. 1967. "Types of Deviance and the Effectiveness of Legal Sanctions." *Wisconsin Law Review,* Summer:703-719.

———. 1989. "State-Organized Crime." *Criminology* 27:183-208.

Christiansen, E.M. 1988. "1987 U.S. Gross Annual Wager." *Gaming and Wagering Business* 9(July 15):7-20, 37.

Clark, John P. and Richard Hollinger. 1983. *Theft by Employees in Work Organizations.* Washington, D.C.: National Institute of Justice.

Clarke, Ronald V. 1980. "Situational Crime Prevention: Theory and Practice." *British Journal of Criminology* 20: 136-147.

———. 1983. "Situational Crime Prevention: Its Theoretical Basis and Practical Scope." In *Crime and Justice: An Annual Review of Research,* Vol. 4 , edited by Michael Tonry and Norval Morris (pp. 225-256). Chicago: University of Chicago Press.

Clarke, Ronald V. and P.M. Harris. 1992a. "Auto Theft and Its Prevention." In *Crime and Justice: A Review of Research,* edited by Michael Tonry (pp. 1-54). Volume 16. Chicago, IL: University of Chicago Press.

———. 1992b. "A Rational Choice Perspective on the Targets of Automobile Theft." *Criminal Behavior and Mental Health* 2(1):25-42.

Clinard, Marshall. 1983. *Corporate Ethics and Crime: The Role of Middle Management.* Beverly Hills, CA: Sage.

Clinard, Marshall and Richard Quinney. 1973. *Criminal Behavior Systems: A Typology.* New York: Holt, Rinehart and Winston.

Clinard, Marshall, Richard Quinney, and John Wildeman. 1994. *Criminal Behavior Systems: A Typology.* 3rd Edition. Cincinnati, OH: Anderson Publishing Co.

Clinard, Marshall and Peter Yeager. 1980. *Corporate Crime.* New York: Free Press.

Cloward, Richard A. and Lloyd E. Ohlin. 1960. *Delinquency and Opportunity.* New York: Free Press.

Cohen, Lawrence E. and Marcus Felson. 1979. "Social Change and Crime Rate Trends: A Routine Activity Approach." *American Sociological Review* 44:588-608.

Cole, L.S. and G.D. Boyer. 1989. *Investigation of Vehicle Thefts.* Novato, CA.: Lee Books.

Coleman, James W. 1994. *The Criminal Elite.* 3rd Edition. New York: St. Martin's Press.

——. 1995. "Respectable Crimes." In *Criminology,* edited by Joseph F. Sheley (pp. 249-269). Belmont, CA.: Wadsworth.

Conklin, John. 1972. *Robbery and the Criminal Justice System.* Philadelphia: J.B. Lippincott.

Conrad, P. and J.W. Schneider. 1992. *Deviance and Medicalization: From Badness to Sickness.* 3rd Edition. Columbus, OH: Merrill.

Cornish, Derek, B. and Ronald V. Clarke. 1986. *The Reasoning Criminal: Rational Choice Perspectives on Offending.* New York: Springer-Verlag.

Cressey, Donald R. 1953. *Other People's Money: A Study in the Social Psychology of Embezzlement.* New York: Free Press.

Cromwell, Paul, James Olson, and D'Aunn Wester Avery. 1991. *Breaking and Entering: An Ethnographic Analysis of Burglary.* Newbury Park, CA: Sage.

Curtis, Lynn. 1974. "Victim-Precipitation and Violent Crimes." *Social Problems* 21: 594-605.

Daly, Kathleen. 1989. "Gender and Varieties of White-Collar Crime." *Criminology* 27:769-794.

Davis, K. F. 1992. *Patterns of Specialization and Escalation in Crime: A Longitudinal Analysis of Juvenile and Adult Arrest Transitions in the Gleuck Data.* Dissertation. Rockville, MD: National Criminal Justice Resource Service.

Davis, K.F. and H. Leitenberg. 1989. "Adolescent Sex Offenders." *Psychological Bulletin* 101(3): 417-427.

Davis, Nanette. 1978. "Prostitution: Identity, Career, and Legal Economic Enterprise." In *The Sociology of Sex,* edited by J.Henslin and E. Sagarin (pp. 195-222). New York: Schocken Books.

Dobrin, Adam, Brian Wiersema, Colin Loftin, and David McDowall. 1996. *Statistical Handbook on Violence in America.* Phoenix, AZ: The Oryx Press.

Donnerstein, E., D. Linz, and S. Penrod. 1987. *Question of Pornography: Research Findings and Policy Implications.* New York: Free Press.

Edelhertz, Herbert. 1970. *The Nature, Impact, and Prosecution of White-Collar Crime.* Washington, D.C.: U.S. Government Printing Office.

Ellis, Lee. 1989. *Theories of Rape: Inquiries into the Causes of Sexual Aggression.* New York: Hemisphere.

Ennis, Phillip H. 1967. *Criminal Victimization in the United States: A Report of a National Survey.* Washington, D.C.: U.S. Government Printing Office.

Erlanger, Howard. 1974. "The Empirical Status of the Subculture of Violence Thesis." *Social Problems* 22 (December): 280-292.

Farrington, David, H. Snyder, and T. Finnegan. 1988. "Specialization in Juvenile Court Careers." *Criminology* 26: 461-488.

Fattah, Ezzat A. 1991. *Understanding Criminal Victimization.* Scarborough, Ontario: Prentice-Hall Canada.

Faupel, Charles E. 1996. "The Drugs-Crime Connection Among Stable Addicts." In *In Their Own Words: Criminals on Crime,* edited by Paul Cromwell (pp. 180-188). Los Angeles, CA: Roxbury Press.

Federal Bureau of Investigation. 1960. *Crime in the United States—1960.* Washington, D.C: U.S. Government Printing Office.

———. 1961. *Crime in the United States—1961.* Washington, D.C: U.S. Government Printing Office.

———. 1970. *Crime in the United States—1970.* Washington, D.C: U.S. Government Printing Office.

———. 1992. *Crime in the United States—1992.* Washington, D.C: U.S. Government Printing Office.

———. 1994. *Crime in the United States—1994.* Washington, D.C: U.S. Government Printing Office.

———. 1995. *Crime in the United States—1995.* Washington, D.C: U.S. Government Printing Office.

Federal Bureau of Investigation. 1993. *Terrorism in the United States.* Washington, D.C.: U.S. Department of Justice.

Federal Bureau of Investigation. 1984. *UCR Reporting Handbook.* Washington, D.C.: U.S. Government Printing Office.

Feeney, Floyd. 1986. "Robbers as Decision-Makers." In *The Reasoning Criminal: Rational Choice Perspectives on Offending,* edited by Derek B. Cornish and Ronald V. Clarke (pp. 53-71). New York: Springer-Verlag.

Fehrenbach, P.A., W. Smith, C. Monastersky, and R.W. Deisher. 1986. "Adolescent Sexual Offenders: Offender and Offense Characteristics." *American Journal of Orthopsychiatry* 56(2): 225-233.

Felson, Richard and Marvin Krohn. 1990. "Motives for Rape." *Journal of Research in Crime and Delinquency* 27:222-242.

Ferri, Enrico. 1917. *Criminal Sociology*. Boston: Little, Brown.

Figgie International. 1988. *The Figgie Report Part VI—The Business of Crime: The Criminal Perspective*. Richmond, VA: Figgie International.

Finkelhor, David. 1986. "How Widespread Is Child Sexual Assault?" In *Out of Harm's Way: Readings on Child Sexual Assault, Its Prevention and Treatment*, edited by Dawn C. Haden (pp. 4-8). Phoenix, AZ: Oryx Press.

Finkelhor, David and K. Yllo. 1985. *License to Rape: Sexual Abuse of Wives*. New York: Holt, Rinehart, and Winston.

Forcier, M.W., N.R. Kurtz, D.G. Parent, and M.D. Corrigan. 1986. "Deterrence of Drunk Driving in Massachusetts: Criminal Justice System Impacts." *The International Journal of Addictions* 21: 1197-1220.

Fox, James Alan. 1996. *Trends in Juvenile Violence: A Report to the United States Attorney General on Current and Future Rates of Juvenile Offending*. Washington, D.C.: Bureau of Justice Statistics.

Friedrichs, David O. 1996. *Trusted Criminals: White-Collar Crime in Contemporary Society*. Belmont, CA: Wadsworth.

Gabor, Thomas, Micheline Baril, Maurice Cusson, Daniel Elie, Marc Leblanc, and Andre Normandeau. 1987. *Armed Robbery: Cops, Robbers, and Victims*. Springfield, IL: Charles C. Thomas.

Ganzini, L., B. McFarland, and J. Bloom. 1990. "Victims of Fraud: Comparing Victims of White Collar and Violent Crime." *Bulletin of the American Academy of Psychiatry and Law* 18:55-63.

Garofalo, B.R. 1914. *Criminology*. Boston: Little, Brown.

Gebhard, Paul, John Gagnon, Wardell Pomeroy, and Cornelia Christenson. 1965. *Sex Offenders: An Analysis of Types*. New York: Harper and Row.

Gervais, Pamela Erickson. 1980. *Recidivism of Adult Offenders: A Pilot Recidivism Study in Eleven Oregon Counties*. Rockville, MD: National Institute of Justice and National Criminal Justice Reference Service Microfiche Program.

Gibbons, Donald C. 1973. *Society, Crime, and Criminal Careers*. 2nd Edition. Englewood Cliffs, NJ: Prentice-Hall.

———. 1992. *Society, Crime, and Criminal Behavior*. Englewood Cliffs, NJ: Prentice-Hall.

Goldstein, Paul. 1983. "Occupational Mobility in the World of Prostitution: Becoming a Madam." *Deviant Behavior* 4:267-279.

Goldstein, Paul, Lawrence Ouellet, and Michael Fendrich. 1992. "From Bag Brides to Skeezers: A Historical Perspective on Sex-for-Drugs Behavior." *Journal of Psychoactive Drugs* 24:349-61.

Gottfredson, Michael R. and Travis Hirschi. 1990. *A General Theory of Crime*. Stanford, CA: Stanford University Press.

Gove, Walter R., Michael Hughes, and Michael R. Geerken. 1985. "Are Uniform Crime Reports a Valid Indicator of the Index Crimes? An

Affirmative Answer with Minor Qualifications." *Criminology* 23:451-410.

Green, Gary S. 1990. *Occupational Crime*. Chicago: Nelson Hall.

Greenberg, David F. 1881. "Methodological Issues in Survey Research on the Inhibition of Crime." *Journal of Criminal Law and Criminology* 72: 1094-1108.

Greenwood, Peter W. 1982. *Selective Incapacitation*. Santa Monica, CA: Rand.

Groth, A. Nicholas. 1977. "Adolescent Sexual Offender and His Prey." *International Journal of Offender Therapy and Comparative Criminology.* 21(3): 249-254.

———. 1978. "Patterns of Sexual Assault Against Children and Adolescents." In *Sexual Assault of Children and Adolescents,* edited by L.J. Burgess, N. Groth, L.L. Holmstrom, and S.M. Sgroi. Lexington, MA.: Heath.

Groth, A. Nicholas and Jean Birnbaum. 1979. *Men Who Rape: The Psychology of the Offender.* New York: Plenum.

Groth, A. Nicholas and C.M. Loredo. 1981. "Juvenile Sexual Offenders: Guidelines for Assessment." *International Journal of Offender Therapy and Comparative Criminology* 25(1):31-39.

Hakim, S. and A.J. Buck. 1991. *Deterrence of Suburban Burglaries: The Hakim-Buck Study.* Philadelphia, PA: Temple University.

Harlow, Carol Wolf. 1987. *Robbery Victims*. Washington, D.C.: Bureau of Justice Statistics.

———. 1988. *Motor Vehicle Theft*. Washington, D.C.: Bureau of Justice Statistics.

Henry, Andrew and James F. Short, Jr. 1954. *Suicide and Homicide*. New York: Free Press.

Hickey, Eric W. 1991. *Serial Murderers and Their Victims*. Belmont, CA.: Wadsworth

Higgins, Paul C. and Gary L. Albrecht. 1982. "Cars and Kids: A Self-Report Study of Juvenile Auto Theft and Traffic Violations." *Sociology and Social Research* 66(1): 29-41.

Hindelang, Michael, Michael Gottfredson, and James Garofalo. 1978. *Victims of Personal Crime.* Cambridge, MA.: Ballinger.

Holmes, Ronald and James DeBurger. 1988. *Serial Murder.* Newbury Park, CA: Sage.

Horning, Donald N. M. 1970. "Blue Collar Theft: Conceptions of Property Attitudes toward Pilfering and Work Group Norms in a Modern Industrial Plant." In *Crime against Bureaucracy,* edited by E.O. Smigel and H.L. Ross. New York: Van Nostrand Reinhold.

Howell, S. 1982. "Twisted Love: Pedophilia." In *Victimization of the Weak Contemporary Social Reactions,* edited by Jacqueline Scherer and Gary Shepherd (pp. 98-113). Springfield, IL.: Thomas.

Hsu, L.K.G. and J. Starzynski. 1990. "Adolescent Rapists and Adolescent Child Sexual Assaulters." *International Journal of Offender Therapy and Comparative Criminology* 34(1):23-30.

Inciardi, James A. 1987. *Criminal Justice.* 2nd Edition. San Diego, CA.: Harcourt.

Inciardi, J.A., A.F. Potteiger, M.A. Forney, D.D. Chitwood, and D.C. McBride. 1991. "Prostitution, IV Drug Use, and Sex-For-Crack Exchanges Among Serious Delinquents: Risks for HIV Infection." *Criminology* 29(2): 221-236.

Jackman, N., Richard O'Toole, and Gilbert Geis. 1967. "The Self-Image of the Prostitute." In *Sexual Deviance,* edited by J. Gagnon and W. Simon. New York: Harper and Row.

Janus, M., B. Scanlon, and V. Price. 1984. "Youth Prostitution." In *Child Pornography and Sex Rings,* edited by Ann W. Burgess and Marieanne L. Clark (pp. 127-146). Lexington, MA.: D.C. Heath.

Jesilow, Paul, Henry N. Pontell, and Gilbert Geis. 1993. *Prescription for Profit—How Doctors Defraud Medicaid.* Berkeley, CA: University of California Press.

Johnston, Lloyd, Jerald Bachman, and Patrick O'Malley. 1995. *Monitoring the Future.* Ann Arbor, MI: Institute for Social Research.

Jones, Kenneth, Louis Shainberg, and Curtin Byer. 1979. *Drugs and Alcohol.* New York: Harper and Row.

Kalish, Carol B. 1988. *International Crime Rates.* Washington, D.C.: Bureau of Justice Statistics.

Karmen, Andrew. 1990. *Crime Victims.* Pacific Grove, CA: Brooks/Cole.

Katz, Jack. 1988. *Seductions of Crime: Moral and Sensual Attractions for Doing Evil.* New York: Basic Books.

Kleck, Gary. 1991. *Point Blank: Guns and Violence in America.* New York: DeGruyter Press.

Knapp Commission Report on Police Corruption. 1972. New York: George Braziller.

Knight, Raymond A. and Robert A. Prentky. 1993. "Exploring Characteristics for Classifying Juvenile Sex Offenders." In *The Juvenile Sex Offender,* edited by H. E. Barbaree, W. L. Marshall, and S.M. Hudson (pp. 45-93). New York:The Gulliford Press.

Koss, M.P. 1981. *Hidden Rape on a University Campus.* Rockville, MD: National Institute of Mental Health.

Koss, M.P. 1992. "Underdetection of Rape: Methodological Choices Influence Incidence Estimates." *Journal of Social Issues* 48: 61-75.

LaFleur, T. and P. Hevener. 1992. "U.S. Gambling at a Glance." *Gaming and Wagering Business* 13: September 15- October 14: 34.

LaFree, Gary D. 1989. *Rape and Criminal Justice: The Social Construction of Sexual Assault.* Belmont, CA.: Wadsworth.

Langan, Patrick A. and John M. Dawson. 1993. *Felony Sentences in State Courts, 1990.* Washington, D.C.: Bureau of Justice Statistics.

Langan, Patrick A. and Helen A. Graziadei. 1995. *Felony Sentences in State Courts, 1992.* Washington, D.C.: Bureau of Justice Statistics.

Lanning, Kenneth V. 1987. "Child Molesters: A Behavioral Analysis for Law Enforcement." In *Practical Aspects of Rape Investigation,* edited by Robert R. Hazelwood and Ann Wolbert Burgess (pp. 201-256). New York: Elsevier Science Publishing.

LeBeau, James. 1987. "Patterns of Stranger and Serial Rape Offending: Factors Distinguishing Apprehended and At-Large Offenders." *Journal of Criminal Law and Criminology* 78: 309-326.

Lederer, L. 1980. *Take Back the Night.* New York: Morrow.

Lesieur, Henry R. 1984. *The Chase: Career of the Compulsive Gambler.* Cambridge, England: Schenkman.

Lesieur, Henry R. and Michael Welch. 1991. "Vice, Public Disorder, and Social Control." In *Criminology: A Contemporary Handbook,* edited by Joseph Sheley (pp. 175-198). Belmont, CA.: Wadsworth.

———. 1995. "Vice Crimes: Individual Choices and Social Controls." In *Criminology: A Contemporary Handbook,* 2nd Edition, edited by Joseph Sheley (pp. 201-229). Belmont, CA.: Wadsworth.

Life Skills Education. 1991. *Incest: A Family's Secret.* Northfield, MN: Life Skills Education.

Lofland, John. 1969. *Deviance and Identity.* Englewood Cliffs, NJ: Prentice-Hall.

Lombroso, Cesare. 1889. *The Criminal Man.* 4th Edition. Bocca: Torino.

Longo, R.E. and A. N. Groth. 1983. "Juvenile Sexual Offenses in the Histories of Adult Rapists and Child Molesters." *International Journal of Offender Therapy and Comparative Criminology* 27(2):150-155.

Luckenbill, David. 1977. "Criminal Homicide as a Situated Transaction." *Social Problems* 25: 176-186.

———. 1984. "Murder and Assault." In *Major Forms of Crime,* edited by Robert F. Meier (pp. 19-45). Beverly Hills, CA: Sage.

Lundberg-Love, P. and R. Geffner. 1989. "Date Rape: Prevalence, Risk Factors, and a Proposed Model." In *Violence in Dating Relationships,* edited by Maureen A. Pirog-Good and Jan E. Stets (pp. 169-184). New York: Praeger.

MacDonald, John M. 1975. *Armed Robbery: Offenders and Their Victims.* Springfield, IL.: Thomas.

MacKenzie, Doris Layton, Robert Brame, David McDowall, and Claire Souryal. 1995. "Boot Camp Prisons and Recidivism in Eight States." *Criminology* 33(3): 327-357.

Maguire, Mike. 1982. *Burglary in a Dwelling: The Offence, the Offender and the Victim.* London: Heinemann.

Maletzky, B.M. 1991. *Treating the Sexual Offender.* Newbury Park, CA.: Sage.

Manson, Don A. 1986. *Tracking Offenders: White-Collar Crime.* Washington, D.C.: Bureau of Justice Statistics.

Mars, Gerald. 1982. *Cheats at Work: An Anthropology of Workplace Crime.* London: Unwin Paperbacks.

Mayhew, Pat, Ronald V. Clarke, and Mike Hough. 1976. "Steering Column Locks and Car Theft." London: Home Office Research Unit.

McClintock, H.H. and Evelyn Gibson. 1961. *Robbery in London.* London: Macmillan.

McCormick, Albert E. 1977. "Rule Enforcement and Moral Indignation: Some Observations on the Effects of Criminal Antitrust Convictions upon Societal Reaction Processes." *Social Problems* 25: 30-39.

McDowall, David, Alan Lizotte, and Brian Wiersema. 1991. "General Deterrence Through Civilian Gun Ownership: An Evaluation of the Quasi-Experimental Evidence." *Criminology* 69(4): 1085-1101.

McShane, M.D. and F.P. Williams III. 1992. "Radical Victimology: A Critique of the Concept of Victim in Traditional Victimology." *Crime and Delinquency* 38:258-271.

Meese, Edwin. 1986. *Final Report of the Attorney General's Commission on Pornography.* Washington, D.C.: U.S. Department of Justice.

Meier, Robert F. 1984. *Major Forms of Crime.* Beverly Hills, CA.: Sage.

Mendelsohn, B. 1956. *The Victimology.* Cited in S. Schafer, *The Victim and His Criminal: A Study of Functional Responsibility.* New York: Random House.

Merton, Robert K. 1938. "Social Structure and Anomie." *American Sociological Review* 3: 672-682.

Messner, Steven F. and Kenneth Tardiff. 1985. "The Social Ecology of Urban Homicide: An Application of the 'Routine Activities' Approach." *Criminology* 23:241-67.

Miethe, Terance D. 1985. "The Myth or Reality of Victim Involvement in Crime: A Review and Comment on Victim-Precipitation Research." *Sociological Focus* 18(3):209-220.

——. 1987. "Stereotypical Conceptions and Criminal Processing: The Case of the Victim-Offender Relationship." *Justice Quarterly* 4(4): 571-593.

——. 1991. "Citizen-Based Crime Control Activity and Victimization Risks: An Examination of Displacement and Free-Rider Effects." *Criminology* 29(3):419-431.

Miethe, Terance D., Michael Hughes, and David McDowall. 1991. "Social Change and Crime Rates: An Evaluation of Alternative Theoretical Approaches." *Social Forces* 70(1):165-185.

Miethe, Terance D. and Robert F. Meier. 1994. *Crime and Its Social Context: Toward and Integrated Theory of Offenders, Victims, and Situations.* Albany, NY: State Univeristy of New York Press.

Miethe, Terance D. and Joyce Rothschild. 1994. "Whistleblowing and the Control of Organizational Misconduct." *Sociological Inquiry* 64:322-347.

Miller, Eleanor. 1986. *Street Women.* Philadelphia, PA: Temple University Press.

Miller, Walter. 1958. "Lower-class Culture as a Generating Milieu of Gang Delinquency." *Journal of Social Issues* 14:5-19.

Mosher, Donald and Ronald Anderson. 1987. "Macho Personality, Sexual Aggression, and Reactions to Guided Imagery of Realistic Rape." *Journal of Research in Personality* 20: 77-94.

Muehlenhard, C.L. and M.A. Linton. 1987. "Date Rape and Sexual Aggression in Dating Situations: Incidence and Risk Factors." *Journal of Counseling Psychology* 34(2): 186-196.

Mulvihill, Donald J., Melvin Tumin, and Lynn Curtis. 1969. *Crimes of Violence.* Washington, D.C.: U.S. Government Printing Office.

National Center for Health Statistics. 1993. *Mortality Detail, 1991 Data.* Hyattsville, MD: Public Health Service. Cited in Dobrin, Wiersema, Loftin, and McDowall (1996:12), Statistical Handbook of Violence in America. Phoenix: The Oryx Press.

National Institute of Justice. 1993. *Drug Use Forecasting, 1991 Annual Report.* Washington, D.C.: Bureau of Justice Statistics.

National Institute on Drug Abuse (NIDA). 1991. *National Household Survey on Drug Abuse.* Rockville, MD: Department of Health and Human Services.

National Institute on Drug Abuse (NIDA). 1996. *National Trends in Drug Use among American High School Students and Young Adults.* Rockville, MD: Department of Health and Human Services.

Nee, C. 1993. "Careers in Car Crime." *Home Office Research and Statistics Department Research Bulletin,* N 33: 1-4.

Nkpa, N.K.U. 1976. "Armed Robbery in Post-Civil War Nigeria: The Role of the Victim." *Victimology—An International Journal* 1(1):71-83.

Normandeau, Andre. 1968. *Trends and Patterns in Crimes of Robbery.* Ph.D. dissertation. Philadelphia: University of Pennsylvania.

O'Brien, M.J. 1989. *Characteristics of Male Adolescent Sibling Incest Offenders: Preliminary Findings.* Orwell, VT: Safer Society Press.

Office of Juvenile Justice and Delinquency Prevention (OJJDP). 1988. *Study Sheds New Light on Court Careers of Juvenile Offenders.* Rockville, MD:

National Institute of Justice and National Criminal Justice Reference Service Microfiche Program.

Oliver, William. 1994. *The Violent Social World of Black Men*. New York: Lexington Books.

Parker, Robert Nash with Linda-Anne Rebhun. 1995. *Alcohol and Homicide: A Deadly Combination of Two American Traditions*. Albany, NY: State University of New York Press.

Pateman, C. 1988. *The Sexual Contract*. Stanford, CA: Stanford University Press.

Paveza, G. J. 1988. "Risk Factors in Father-Daughter Child Sexual Abuse: A Case-Control Study." *Journal of Interpersonal Violence* 3(3): 290-306.

Perkins, Craig and Patsy Klaus. 1996. *Criminal Victimization, 1994*. Washington, D.C.: Bureau of Justice Statistics.

Peterson, Mark A. and Harriet B. Braiker. 1980. *Doing Crime: A Survey of California Prison Inmates*. Santa Monica, CA: Rand.

Pittman, David J. and William Hardy. 1964. "Patterns in Criminal Aggravated Assault." *Journal of Criminal Law, Criminology, and Police Science* 53(December):462-470.

Polk, Kenneth. 1994. *When Men Kill: Scenarios in Masculine Violence*. Cambridge, U.K.: Cambridge University Press.

Pontell, Henry N., Paul D. Jesilow, and Gilbert Geis. 1982. "Policing Physicans: Practioner Fraud and Abuse in a Government Medical Program." *Social Problems* 30:117-125.

Pope, Carl E. 1977. *Crime-Specific Analysis: The Characteristics of Burglary Incidents*. Washington, D.C.: U.S. Government Printing Office.

Poveda, T.G. 1994. *Rethinking White-Collar Crime*. Westport, CT: Prager Publishing.

Poyner, B. 1988. "Video Cameras and Bus Vandalism." *Journal of Security Administration* 11(2):44-51.

Prentky, Robert A. and Raymond Knight. 1986. "Impulsivity in the Lifestyles and Criminal Behavior of Sexual Offenders." *Criminal Justice and Behavior* 13: 141-164.

Prentky, Robert A. and V.L. Quinsey. 1988. *Human Sexual Aggression: Current Perspectives*. New York: New York Academy of Science.

Prescott, S. and C. Letko. 1977. "Battered Women: A Social Psychological Perspective." In *Battered Women: A Psychosociological Study of Domestic Violence*, edited by Maria Roy. New York: Van Nostrand Reinhold.

Rand, Michael. 1993. *Crime and the Nation's Households, 1992*. Washington, D.C.: Bureau of Justice Statistics.

———. 1994. *Carjacking*. Washington, D.C.: Bureau of Justice Statistics.

Reiss, Albert and Jeffrey Roth. 1993. *Understanding and Preventing Violence*. Washington, D.C.: National Academy Press.

Rengert, George and John Wasilchick. 1985. *Suburban Burglary: A Time and Place for Everything*. Springfield, IL: Thomas.

Reppetto, Thomas A. 1974. *Residential Crime*. Cambridge, MA: Ballinger.

Ressler, R.K., A.W. Burgess, and J.E. Douglas. 1988. *Sexual Homicide*. Lexington, MA.: Lexington Books.

Rogers, R. and R.M. Wettstein. 1988. "Incest." *Behavioral Sciences and the Law* 6(2).

Rosecrance, J. 1988. *Gambling Without Guilt: The Legitimation of an American Pastime*. Pacific Grove, CA.: Brooks/Cole.

Rosenbaum, Dennis, Robert Flewelling, Susan Bailey, Chris Ringwalt, and Deanna Wilkinson. 1994. "Cops in the Classroom: A Longitudinal Evaluation of Drug Abuse Resistance Education (DARE)." *Journal of Research in Crime and Delinquency* 31:3-31.

Rosenberg, Ruth and Raymond A. Knight. 1988. "Determining Male Sexual Offender Subtypes Using Cluster Analysis." *Journal of Quantitative Criminology* 4(4): 383-410.

Rossman, P. 1980. "The Pederasts." In *The Sexual Victimization of Youth*, edited by L.J. Schultz. Springfield, IL.: Thomas.

Russell, Diana. 1975. *The Politics of Rape*. New York: Stein and Day.

——. 1984. *Sexual Exploitation: Rape, Child Abuse, and Workplace Harrassment*. Beverly Hills, CA: Sage.

——. 1990. *Rape in Marriage*. Bloomington, IN: Indiana University Press.

Samaha, Joel. 1987. *Criminal Law*. 2nd Edition. St. Paul, MN.: West.

Sampson, Robert J. and W. Bryon Groves. 1989. "Community Structure and Crime: Testing Social-Disorganization Theory." *American Journal of Sociology* 94:774-802.

Sanders, William B. 1983. *Criminology*. Reading, MA.: Addison-Wesley.

Scarr, Harry A. 1973. *Patterns of Burglary*. Washington, D.C.: Government Printing Office.

Schur, Edwin. 1965. *Crimes without Victims*. Englewood Cliffs, NJ: Prentice-Hall.

Schwendinger, Herman and Julia Schwendinger. 1983. *Rape and Inequality*. Beverly Hills, CA.: Sage.

Serial Killer Hit List. 1996. World Wide Web.

Sheldon, William H. 1949. *Variety of Delinquent Youth*. New York: Harper.

Sheley, Joseph F. 1979. *Understanding Crime: Concepts, Issues, Decisions*. Belmont, CA: Wadsworth.

Sherman, Lawrence, Leslie Steele, Deborah Laufersweiler, Nancy Hoffer, and Sherry Julian. 1989. "'Stray Bullets and Mushrooms: Random Shootings of Bystanders in Four Cities, 1977-1988." *Journal of Quantitative Criminology* 5(4):297-316.

Shook, L.L. 1988. "Investigation of Pedophilia." In *Critical Issues in Criminal Investigation,* 2nd Edition, edited by Michael J. Palmiotto (pp. 197-214). Cincinnati, OH: Anderson.

Shotland, R.L. 1992. "The Theory of the Causes of Courtship Rape: Part 2." *Journal of Social Issues* 48(1): 127-143.

Shover, Neal. 1973. "The Social Organization of Burglary." *Social Problems* 20:499-514.

——. 1991. "Burglary." In *Crime and Justice,* edited by Michael J. Tonry, 14:73-113. Chicago, IL: University of Chicago Press.

Siegel, Larry J. 1995. *Criminology.* 5th Edition. St. Paul, MN: West.

Simpson, Sally S. 1986. "The Decomposition of Antitrust: Testing a Multi-Level Longitudinal Model of Profit Squeeze." *American Sociological Review* 51:859-875.

Simpson, Sally S., A.R. Harris, and B.A. Mattson. 1993. "Measuring Corporate Crime." In *Understanding Corporate Criminality,* edited by M.B. Blankenship (pp. 115-140). New York: Garland.

Simpson, Sally S. and Christopher S. Koper. 1992. "Deterring Corporate Crime." *Criminology* 30(3): 347-375.

Singer, Simon. 1981. "Homogeneous Victim-Offender Populations: A Review and Some Research Implications." *Journal of Criminal Law and Criminology* 72(2): 779-788.

Smigel, Erwin O. and Ross H. Lawrence. 1970. *Crimes Against Bureaucracy.* New York: Van Nostrand.

Smith, D.R., W.R Smith, and E. Noma. 1984. "Delinquent Career-Lines: A Conceptual Link Between Theory and Juvenile Offenses." *Sociological Quarterly* 25(2):155-172.

Smith, Pheny Z. 1993. *Felony Defendants in Large Urban Counties, 1990.* Washington, D.C.: Bureau of Justice Statistics.

Sutherland, Edwin. 1940. "White-Collar Criminality." *American Sociological Review* 5: 2-10.

Sykes, Gresham, and David Matza. 1957. "Techniques of Neutralization: A Theory of Delinquency." *American Journal of Sociology* 22:664-70.

Tamura, M. 1992. "Analysis of Traits of Child Molesters." *Reports of the National Research Institute of Police Science* 33(1): 30-41.

Tappan, Paul W. 1947. "Who is the Criminal?" *American Sociological Review* 12:96-102.

Tracy, Paul and Kimberly Kempf-Leonard. 1996. *Continuity and Discontinuity in Criminal Careers.* New York: Plenum Press.

Tremblay, P, Y. Clermont, and M. Cusson. 1994. "Jockeys and Joyriders: Changing Patterns in Car Theft Opportunity Structures." *British Journal of Criminology* 34(3): 307-321.

Tunnell, Kenneth D. 1992. *Choosing Crime: The Criminal Calculus of Property Offenders.* Chicago, IL: Nelson-Hall.

Uniform Crime Reports. 1988-92, 1994, 1995. Supplemental Homicide Reports. Ann Arbor, MI.: ICPSR.

United Nations. 1990. *Fourth World Crime Survey.* New York.

U.S. Department of Justice. 1995. *Attacking Financial Institution Fraud, Year-End Report, Fiscal Year 1994.* Office of the Deputy Attorney General. Washington, D.C.: U.S. Department of Justice.

U.S. News and World Report. 1992. "Willing to Kill For a Car: Auto Theft is Booming, and Carjacking Makes it a Deadly Menace All Over." September 21, 1992: 40-48.

U.S. State Department. 1995. *Patterns of Global Terrorism, 1995.* Washington, D.C.: U.S. Department of State.

Vaughan, Diane. 1980. "Crimes Between Organizations: Implications for Victimology." In *White Collar Crime: Theory and Research,* edited by G. Geis and E. Stotland (pp. 77-97). Beverly Hills, CA: Sage.

———. 1983. *Controlling Unlawful Corporate Behavior.* Chicago: University of Chicago Press.

Vaughan, Diane, Stanton Wheeler, M.L. Ruthman, Ilene H. Nagel, John L. Hagan, John Braithwaite, and L.H. Leigh. 1982. "Corporate and Organizational Crime." *Michigan Law Review* 80(7):1377-1528.

Walsh, Dermot. 1980. *Break-in: Burglary from Private Houses.* London: Constable.

Warr, Mark. 1988. "Rape, Burglary, and Opportunity." *Journal of Quantitative Criminology* 4:275-288.

Warren, J.I., R.R. Hazelwood, and R. Reboussin. 1991. "Serial Rape: The Offender and His Rape Career." In *Rape and Sexual Assault,* edited by Wolbert Burgess (pp. 275-310). New York: Garland.

Weingart, Saul. 1993. "A Typology of Community Responses to Drugs." In *Drugs and the Commmunity,* edited by Robert Davis, Arthur Lurigio, and Dennis Rosenbaum. Springfield, IL: Charles Thomas.

Weisberg, D. Kelly. 1985. *Children of the Night: A Study of Adolescent Prostitution.* Lexington, MA: Lexington Books.

Weisburd, David, Stanton Wheeler, Elin Waring, and Nancy Bode. 1991. *Crimes of the Middle Class: White Collar Offenders in Federal Courts.* New Haven, CT: Yale University Press.

Weisburd, David, Elin Waring, Ellen Chayet, D. Dickman, D. Fischer, and R.M. Plant. 1993. *White Collar Crime and Criminal Careers.* Washington, D.C.: National Institute of Justice.

Wheeler, Stanton, David Weisberg, Elin Waring, and N. Bode. 1988. "White Collar Crimes and Criminals." *American Criminal Law Review* 25(3):331-357.

Williams, Kristen M. 1976. "The Effects of Victim Characteristics on the Disposition of Violent Crimes." In *Criminal Justice and the Victim,* edited by William McDonald. Beverly Hills, CA.: Sage.

Williams, Linda S. 1984. "The Classic Rape: When do Victims Report?" *Social Problems* 31:459-467.

Winick, Charles and Paul Kinsie. 1971. *The Lively Commerce.* Chicago: Quandrangle Books.

Wolfgang, Marvin. 1958. *Patterns of Criminal Homicide.* Philadelphia: University of Pennsylvania Press.

Wolfgang, Marvin and Franco Ferracuti. 1967. *The Subculture of Violence: Toward an Integrated Theory in Criminology.* London: Tavistock.

Wolfgang, Marvin, Robert Figlio, and Thorsen Sellin. 1972. *Delinquency in a Birth Cohort.* Chicago: University of Chicago Press.

Wright, James D., Peter H. Rossi, and Kathleen Daly. 1983. *Under the Gun: Weapons, Crime, and Violence in America.* Hawthorne, NY: Aldine.

Wright, Richard A. 1994. *In Defense of Prisons.* Westport, CT: Greenwood Press.

Wright, Richard and Scott Decker. 1994. *Burglars on the Job: Streetlife and Residential Break-ins.* Boston: Northeastern University Press.

Wright, Richard A., Robert H. Logie, and Scott Decker. 1995. "Criminal Expertise and Offender Decision-Making: An Experimental Study of the Target Selection Process in Residential Burglary." *Journal of Research in Crime and Delinquency* 32(1): 39-53.

Zawitz, Marianne W., Patsy A. Klaus, Ronet Bachman, Lisa D. Bastian, Marshall M. DeBerry, Jr., Michael R. Rand, and Bruce M. Taylor. 1993. *Highlights from 20 Years of Surveying Crime Victims: The National Crime Victimization Survey, 1973-92.* Washington, D.C.: Bureau of Justice Statistics.

Author Index

Subject Index